MICHAEL HELLER

CREATIVE
TENSION

ESSAYS ON SCIENCE AND RELIGION

TEMPLETON FOUNDATION PRESS
PHILADELPHIA AND LONDON

Templeton Foundation Press
Five Radnor Corporate Center, Suite 120
100 Matsonford Road
Radnor, Pennsylvania 19087
www.templetonpress.org

Designed and typeset by Kachergis Book Design
Printed in the United States by Versa Press

Library of Congress Cataloging-in-Publication Data

Heller, Michael.
    Creative tension : essays on science and religion / Michael Heller.
        p. cm.
    Includes bibliographical references and index.
        ISBN 1-932031-34-0 (pbk. : alk. paper)
        1. Religion and science.   I. Title.
        BL240.3 .H45 2003
        261.5'5—dc21
                                        2003012637

03 04 05 06 07   10 9 8 7 6 5 4 3 2 1

CONTENTS

FOREWORD

Among those scholars who foster interdisciplinary dialogue between religion and science, two basically different styles of research have been practiced by scientists and by philosophers. The members of the first group feel at home with the mathematical formalism of new scientific theories but when they try to determine the philosophical significance of these theories their comments very often become naive and arbitrary. The representatives of the second group frequently focus their attention on methodological principles and logical distinctions but they know the essence of scientific procedures mainly from popular reports on new discoveries in physics or biology.

There are a few contemporary authors who are skillful enough to use the sophisticated language of modern mathematics and to assess competently the differences between, for instance, Augustine and Aquinas in their understanding of evil. According to historians, Leibniz was the last intellectual authority who comprehended the entire knowledge of his epoch. It was he who dreamt of a *mathesis universalis*—a universal mathematized language in which all philosophical problems could be formulated and solved. Professor Michael Heller does not share old Leibnizian dreams because he knows well the consequences of Kurt Gödel's incompleteness theorem that rules out finding a nontrivial logical system in which all questions could be answered. Nonetheless Heller's original contributions are appreciated both in physics and in ontology. His papers can be found not only in such scientific periodicals as the *Journal of Mathematical Physics* or *General Relativity and Gravitation* but also in philosophical *Festschrifts* dedicated to Wittgenstein or Teilhard de Chardin.

In his contributions to physics, the author of *Creative Tension* organized in Cracow a group of talented and young collaborators who originated their joint research by discussing the problem of initial singularity in cosmological models.[1] This very problem inspired long-lasting philosophical debates about whether the initial cosmological

1. In long-distance cooperation this group was transformed into the Cracow Group of Cosmology.

singularity could be regarded as the absolute zero of time. In continuing this research, Professor Heller tries to use the so-called noncommutative geometries as a new language in which one could describe both quantum and cosmological phenomena providing a new paradigm for unity in physics. In philosophy, he develops novel ideas to present a new version of Plato's ontology; the rational structure of reality that could be described in the language of mathematics seems for him much more important than the physical substratum. Consequently, in his ontological version of the so-called formal field theory, he argues that the world of observable physical parameters belongs to the domain of Platonic shadows, while the essence of reality is constituted of abstract relations and formal structures that can be described only in the language of sophisticated mathematics.

Michael Heller's fascination with religion originated in Siberia where, as a child, he was in exile with his family during World War II. Immediately before the war, his family lived in the eastern part of Poland, which was occupied in September 1939 not by the Nazis, but by the Soviet Army. Born in 1936, he returned to his native Poland after the end of the war, when he was nine years old. The struggle for survival in the severe conditions of Siberian life, as well as his personal experience of the important role of religion in such conditions, directed the attention of the young boy to religious issues. He knew that many people survived the extreme Siberian situation because they found in prayer both their spiritual force and their will to survive. His main dream after coming back to Poland was to become a priest and to help people in finding solutions to the most basic problems of life.

Science turned out to be his second intellectual fascination. When after his priestly ordination he undertook philosophical studies at the Catholic University of Lublin, he subsequently developed his own style of doing philosophy in interdisciplinary dialogue with modern science. His attention focused upon such issues as the very beginning of the universe, cosmic evolution, the nature of time, the existence of mathematical objects, and the preconditions of using mathematics in the description of physical processes. His close cooperation with prominent scientists, as well as his own creative efforts, resulted in his quickly becoming well known as one of the best European cosmologists and an outstanding philosopher who consistently tries to develop philosophy in the context of new scientific discoveries.

Heller's attempt to foster dialogue between science and religion grew up in the specific situation of the totalitarian system in which Marxism was officially recognized as the only "scientific philosophy." Ideological protection for philosophical systems very often results in skeptical distrust toward the protégé; scientists in Poland also displayed total distrust toward Marxism. When genetics and cybernetics were criticized by the Communist Party functionaries as pseudoscience and Niels Bohr's interpretation of quantum mechanics was rejected by Soviet academics as reactionary, there was among the Polish scientists a natural openness to the philosophical implications of scientific theories that could be defined without ideological bias. At that time the Church created a sphere of freedom where alternatives to the Marxist interpretations of scientific discoveries were freely discussed.

Already in the 1960s the then Archbishop of Cracow, Karol Wojtyla, expressed his support for this kind of research. From time to time, he used to invite to his episcopal residence scientists, philosophers, and theologians to discuss with them such topics as the ethical issues generated by new scientific technologies or the role of physical theories in reinterpreting the classical Thomistic arguments for the existence of God. In October 1978, when Cardinal Wojtyla was elected the Pope and had to remain in Rome, Michael Heller took care of this interdisciplinary group and continued its meetings, organizing them systematically once a month. When social transformations, inspired by the rise of "Solidarity," facilitated international contacts, many prominent scholars from the West were invited to take part in the Cracow interdisciplinary seminars. Among those who at that time visited Copernicus's city to discuss the philosophical and theological importance of modern science were Arthur Peacocke (Oxford), John Polkinghorne (Cambridge), Charles Misner (Maryland), Ernan McMullin (Notre Dame, Indiana), William Wallace (Washington, D.C.), Jean Ladrière (Louvain) and Carl Friedrich von Weizsäcker (Germany).

In records kept by those who systematically attended the interdisciplinary meetings that were still held in the residence of the Archbishop of Cracow, the most interesting stories deal with the period of martial law (1981–82). There was a day when special militia troops, similar to the antiterrorist groups in the West, attacked the Solidarity demonstration in Cracow's Old City. Tear gas was used and military vans blocked the entrance to the Main Square—the area where the residence of Cracow's bishops is situated. Despite this warlike landscape, many people decided to pass through the military checkpoint to enter the forbidden area, where on that day the philosophical consequences of Bell inequalities in quantum mechanics were discussed. The historic transformations of 1989 show that creative independent thought cannot be silenced, even by antiterrorist troops. The power of logic demonstrated its superiority in relation to the political power that used terror and violence.

Regardless of the exotic social context of the growth of Heller's ideas, in his philosophy one finds the most important classical issues discussed in the context of new scientific debates. In this philosophical fraternity one finds new forms of the old ideas that were developed by Plato and Leibniz, Popper, Penrose, and many contemporary searchers for unity in physics. Heller's ontological views seem close to the ideas shared by J. D. Barrow when he claims: "The ultimate laws of Nature may be akin to software running upon the hardware provided by elementary particles and energy. The laws of physics might then be derived from some more basic principles governing computation and logic."[2] This rational constituent of nature, expressed in the unreasonable effectiveness of the universal language of mathematics in describing physical phenomena, inspired many authors to ask philosophical questions. Their echo can be found in Albert Einstein's comments on the universal laws of physics and in the neo-Platonic concept of cosmic Logos. Both these traditions are combined in Heller's *Creative Tension* resulting in an intellectual adventure where science, philosophy, and theology are united in an attempt to answer the basic questions of our existence.

Joseph M. Życiński
Catholic University of Lublin

Joseph M. Życiński, Ph.D., is the archbishop of Lublin, professor of philosophy at the Catholic University of Lublin, and Poland-chair of the relationship between science and religion. He is the author of numerous books in the area of philosophy of science, relativistic cosmology, history of the relationship between natural sciences, and Christian faith.

2. J. D. Barrow, "Theories of Everything," in *Nature's Imagination: The Frontiers of Scientific Vision*, ed. J. Cornwell, Oxford: Oxford University Press, 1995, 62.

PREFACE

There are two human activities that require no more and no less than the total life commitment if one wants to pursue them adequately, namely, religion and science. This is so not because each of these activities leaves no time for doing something else, but because neither of them tolerates any rivals. To be truly religious and faithfully scientific requires total commitment.

Nevertheless, it happens, from time to time, that both of these activities meet in a single person. In such a case, the question imposes itself: Is it possible to be a religious person and, at the same time, a good scientist? How does one totally dedicate a single life to two such different and such demanding activities? It seems that there is only one solution to this apparently unsolvable situation—to attempt a synthesis so that these two activities coalesce into one coherent way of life.

The scientific cognition and the religious cognition (in every religious faith there are cognitive elements) are radically different from the methodological point of view. They speak different languages and think with the help of different conceptual tools—so different that they are hardly reducible to each other. If one tries to "synthesize" them too hastily, they usually form a logically explosive mixture. Any authentic and methodologically valuable synthesis must not ignore these differences but rather build on them, and any such synthesis should be done in the personality of the religious scientist rather than in the form of ordering propositions and classifying standpoints concerning religion and science. It is obvious, however, that such a synthesis must be prepared and constantly accompanied by logically organized reflection, thorough analyses, and even systematic studies.

The fact that this synthesis is never accomplished but is always becoming implies that sometimes it is more like a symbiosis than like a synthesis. As in the process of life itself, creative tensions are unavoidable.

The book I am now committing to the reader can be regarded as a collection of "notes" documenting some stages of the road traveled by the author toward this kind of synthesis—a collection of notes rather than systematic reports, because the chapters of this book were written on different occasions as a response to current needs and demands. In spite of this fact, the book forms a consistent whole displaying a sequence of steps that are to be followed if one seriously wants to reach the state of the peaceful coexistence of science and religion.

The book is divided into four parts:

Part One deals with methodological topics. It shows abuses, in this respect, of both science and theology, discusses theological interpretation of scientific theories, and proposes a program for a "theology of science."

Part Two looks at the science-religion interactions from the historical perspective. Among other topics, the evolution of ideas connected with the "place of man in the Universe" and the evolution of the matter concept are discussed.

Part Three concentrates on the problem of "creation and science." In this context, the questions of the initial singularity (Big Bang), quantum cosmology, and the role of probability and chance in science are subjected to a thorough analysis.

Part Four looks for vestiges of Transcendence in some key issues of contemporary science and methods it employs in investigating the word.

CREATIVE TENSION

PART ONE

FROM THE METHODOLOGICAL PERSPECTIVE

It is not true that all conflicts between science and religion can be resolved by obeying methodological rules and distinctions, but it is almost true that in all such conflicts some methodological anarchy is always involved. Moreover, both sides of the dispute are guilty of heavy trespasses in this respect. Religious people are often too quick to fill in lacunae in our understanding of the world with the idea of God's finger moving or correcting the world's machinery. This leads to the deplorable "God-of-the-gaps" theology. In the beginning of the modern science epoch, this was considered to be a "natural theology," but even now it operates implicitly in subcontexts of some interpretations of scientific theories. Antireligious people, on the other hand, who do not see such gaps or who believe that sooner or later they will be filled in with sound scientific constructions, claim that the scientific method has eliminated the idea of God from the modern image of the world. In this way, a methodological rule changes into an ontological presupposition and produces "no gaps, no God" antitheology.

These methodological intricacies are best visible in what is the biggest (in the literal sense) challenge to the human quest for understanding—the Universe itself. Is the Universe a contingent instant of existence or a self-explaining entity? Are recent cosmological models and theories able to throw some light on this question? The debate around this issue supplies a handful of examples illustrating the above-mentioned methodological pitfalls. We consider them in Chapter 1.

Facing such a complex situation, we should make an effort to straighten it out. This is the goal of Chapter 2. We try in it to distill from the current practice some indications of what does it mean to interpret cosmological theories theologically or philosophically.

First, we focus on a rather complex notion of physical theory, and then we analyze various ways of their interpretations. Finally, we apply the results of this analysis to the creation interpretations in cosmology. A zealous believer could be disappointed with our conclusions of rather minimalistic character. The point is, however, that we should by no means put God into the loopholes of our theories or, even worse, create such loopholes in order to justify God and God's action in the world.

How should the theologian react with respect to the above analyses? Should he or she abandon any contact with the sciences? Seemingly, this happens very often; in fact, however, it is impossible to do so. The scientific world image (whatever this means) is present in the cultural climate and intellectual atmosphere of any epoch, and no theology can avoid experiencing this climate and breathing this atmosphere. Even if a theology makes an effort to distance itself from the scientific image of the world, it implicitly makes use of at least some of its elements. Inertia of concepts and language involved in these processes could be enormous. If these processes do not remain under control, the image of the world, adopted implicitly, will almost for sure be outdated and no longer scientific. This set of problems is the subject matter of Chapter 3.

To keep under control elements of the world image coming from the sciences and interfering with the theological discourse is a minimum program for any theology aspiring to be of some service for contemporary people. To go beyond it would mean to undertake the effort of an authentic theological reflection on science, its method, and its results; that is, to create what could be termed a *theology of science*. The program for such a discipline is outlined in Chapter 4.

I THE ABUSE OF COSMOLOGY

INTRODUCTION

Cosmology gives us a global perspective of the Universe,[1] or at least what people at a given epoch consider to be a global perspective. The price that cosmology pays for this breadth is that, more than other sciences, it must base its theories on unverified, and perhaps unverifiable, assumptions. This peculiarity opens the door to philosophical and theological abuse.

As a natural science, cosmology is neutral with respect to philosophical or theological doctrines. Unfortunately, this does not prevent scientists, philosophers, and theologians from abusing it. It is usually the so-called God-of-the-gaps theology that snares too hasty a thinker. The trap consists not only in constructing "proofs" of God's existence from weak points of our knowledge, but also in rejecting God on the grounds that there are no gaps in our science in which God could safely dwell.

Is there some principle, some kind of methodological rigor, that would defend cosmology from dangers of this kind? My proposal is that the intrinsic "problem situation" in science, rather than metaphysical prejudices, should guide responsible research in science, especially in those regions that are remote from experiment.

NEVER SAY NEVER

In the once widely read book *God and the Astronomers*,[2] Robert Jastrow tells the story of the most remarkable discovery of modern cosmology: The Universe had a beginning. He says that for science alone it is "impossible—not just now, but ever—to find out what force or forces brought the world into being at the moment." At the end, Jastrow dots his *i*:

1. In this book, we spell the word "Universe" with the capital *U* when it denotes "our Universe" (then it is the same as, e.g., "our Galaxy"); otherwise we use lower case *u* (as when we speak of galaxies in general).

2. R. Jastrow, *God and the Astronomers,* New York: Warner Books, 1980 (first published by Reader's Library in 1978).

It is not a matter of another year, another decade of work, another measurement, or another theory; at this moment it seems as though science will never be able to raise the curtain on the mystery of creation. For the scientist who has lived by his faith in the power of reason, the story ends like a bad dream. He has scaled the mountains of ignorance; he is about to conquer the highest peak; as he pulls himself over the final rock, he is greeted by a band of theologians who have been sitting there for centuries.[3]

In spite of his professed skepticism, he says he is forced to take seriously the theological ramifications of the Big Bang:

When an astronomer writes about God, his colleagues assume he is either over the hill or going bonkers. In my case it should be understood from the start that I am an agnostic in religious matters. However, I am fascinated by some strange developments going on in astronomy—partly because of their religious implications and partly because of the peculiar reactions of my colleagues.[4]

Jastrow's book first appeared in 1978, and within half a decade cosmologists began to explore the questions Jastrow thought forbidden. Inflationary cosmology, at least in some of its interpretations, is precisely a theory of the forces that brought the world into being.

Another best-seller tells this story, Stephen Hawking's *Brief History of Time*.[5] The Big Bang theory, so admired by Jastrow, is a purely classical—that is, non-quantum—theory. But now we know that in the extreme densities of matter at the Big Bang, quantum effects must enter into play. So far, nobody has created a satisfactory quantum cosmology. Hawking's book tells about his search for such a theory.

When one tries to combine quantum mechanics with the general theory of relativity, new possibilities arise. The superdense Universe can come into existence via the quantum "tunneling" process, whereby particles can leap seemingly impossible barriers—including that between nonexistence and existence. This process turns out to be atemporal. In the extreme conditions of the Big Bang, there is no time in any meaningful sense of this term. Time acquires spatial properties; it gradually becomes distinct as quantum correlations grow into a fully determined temporal order of things.

KNOW NO BOUNDS

Because of these quantum effects, there is no singularity at the Big Bang, no sharp point where the density is infinite. Space-time forms a finite, four-dimensional surface with no boundaries or singularities. This surface is similar to that of a sphere on which one can travel without ever finding an edge. This feature

---

3. Ibid., 125.   4. Ibid., 11.
5. S. W. Hawking, *A Brief History of Time: From the Big Bang to Black Holes*, New York: Bantam Books, 1988.

of the Universe Hawking calls its "self-containedness," meaning that the Universe is nowhere open for any intervention coming from outside. This, he says, "has profound implications for the role of God as Creator."

In Hawking's opinion, the proper time for God to act would be the beginning of the Universe, where—by setting the rate of expansion and other initial conditions—he could determine the general structure and evolution of the cosmos. But if there are no boundaries and no singularities, there is no beginning at which God could act. Hawking writes:

Einstein once asked the question: "How much choice did God have in constructing the Universe?" If the no-boundary proposal is correct, he had no freedom at all to choose the initial conditions.[6]

Of course, even if the Universe is self-contained, God would still be free to choose the laws that govern it. But this freedom could also be illusory. If there is only one logically possible set of physical laws, God has no choice. Hawking writes:

There may well be only one, or a small number, of complete unified theories, such as the heterotic string theory, that are self-consistent and allow the existence of structures as complicated as human beings who can investigate the laws of the Universe and ask about the nature of God.[7]

Despite the there-may-well-be reasoning, the philosophical vistas opened by the model are worthy of contemplation. Hawking is aware that any physical theory, even the fully self-consistent and unified theory, "is just a set of rules and equations." The most important problem remains:

What is it that breathes fire into the equations and makes a Universe for them to describe? Why does the Universe go to all the bother of existing? Is the unified theory so compelling that it brings about its own existence? Or does it need a creator, and, if so, does he have any other effect on the Universe? And who created him?[8]

The final sentence of the book is this:

If we find the answer to that, it would be the ultimate triumph of human reason—for then we would know the mind of God.[9]

THE WHATEVER GOD

What Hawking did not openly say was said by Carl Sagan in his introduction to Hawking's book:

6. Ibid., 174.
8. Ibid.

7. Ibid.
9. Ibid., 175.

This is also a book about God or perhaps about the absence of God. The word God fills these pages. Hawking embarks on a quest to answer Einstein's famous question about whether God had any choice in creating the Universe. Hawking is attempting, as he explicitly states, to understand the mind of God. And this makes all the more unexpected the conclusion of the effort, at least so far: a Universe with no edge in space, no beginning in time, and nothing for a Creator to do.[10]

Yet even if the Universe is self-contained, and even if only one set of physical laws is logically possible, one hardly could stop asking: Where do these laws come from? What is their nature? This is not a gap in our scientific theories; all of science is marked with the problem. Any attempt to comment on it leads us into difficult questions concerning the relationship between physical laws and the mathematical structures that express these laws. These questions preoccupied Albert Einstein and many other great scientists.

The examples of Jastrow and Hawking are typical. The first example comes from the period when people were coming to terms with the firework beginning of the Universe. The second illustrates the present tendency to look for ultimate explanations in the (so far unknown) fundamental laws of physics. A few decades ago, religious interpretations of the Big Bang cosmology were an easy temptation, although the steady-state cosmology of that time could be considered a heroic struggle to defend the self-explanatory character of the Universe. In our day, the attitude prevails to fill in all gaps in science with the most audacious hypotheses, which too often have philosophical motivation as their only rational basis.

Jastrow's comments are a generic case of God-of-the-gaps theology. In the Big Bang, the history of the Universe (as contemplated backward in time) breaks down, creating an enormous gap in our knowledge. We do not know where the Big Bang comes from, we ignore its cause, we know nothing about the previous state of the world, we have no idea whether the world even existed before that critical event. Our ignorance is immense. It seems that only the hypothesis of God could help.

It is a hypothesis that will almost certainly turn out to be superfluous. God-of-the-gaps theology represents a lack of imagination, for what is now a boundary of science can soon be its well-explored region. This is both theological and scientific error. From the theological point of view, it reduces God to the rank of a dubious methodological principle; from the scientific point of view, it violates a rule never to go beyond natural phenomena.

It is only a difference in degree that separates Jastrow-like arguments from

10. Ibid., x.

the physico-theology of the seventeenth century, when, from the harmony of planetary motions, people inferred the existence of the omnipotent clock-maker; or from the marvelous machinery of the gnat's eye, they deduced the existence of the divine designer.

NO GAPS, NO GOD

The God-of-the-gaps theology is perhaps less transparent in my second example; nevertheless, it is there. Sagan clearly suggests that God should be rejected. For people accepting this, God is necessarily God of the gaps: There are (or will be) no gaps, therefore the hypothesis of God is superfluous. One could put it shortly: no gaps, no God.

This is clearly very bad theology. Is it equally bad science? It depends. If it inspires the search for solutions to hitherto unsolved problems, it can promote scientific progress. But if its only goal is to populate science with strange hypotheses in order not to leave any gaps for metaphysical ingredients, the road to correct solutions could be easily blocked by misleading ideas.

Hawking's works are lasting contributions to science, and he is too serious a researcher to allow himself to be guided by dubious ideologies. I suspect that philosophical comments in his book are reflections after the fact rather than principles guiding his scientific research. There is no doubt, however, that some researchers introduce metaphysical ideologies into their scientific work.

Twentieth-century science writings abound in such confusion. For instance, when quantum physicists discovered the uncertainty principle, many defenders of traditional philosophy claimed that humanity's free will was finally vindicated. Later on, some other writers—working from interpretations of quantum mechanics that seemed to emphasize conscious observers—developed the ideology that in the beginning of the Universe, when there were no other conscious observers besides God, his observing of the Universe was necessary for laws to operate.

Nowadays the so-called strong anthropic principle creates a vast field of possibilities for similarly minded authors. From the fact that extremely fine-tuned initial conditions are indispensable for a Universe such as ours, these authors build various versions of the old proof of God's existence from finality. They flesh out incomplete physical theories with the hypothesis of God or some other metaphysical doctrine.

There are equally many scientific theories that have been claimed not to leave any place for God. Many thinkers have used the theory of evolution as a weapon against religious interpretations of the world. In the eyes of such thinkers, the idea of God should be rejected because it is no longer needed to explain life. This kind of argument is always based on the tacit presupposition that a given scientific theory is truly self-explanatory—that no further assumption is needed to justify it.

In fact, such a claim can hardly be substantiated, for every scientific theory works on the assumption that the laws of nature are somehow given and enable the theory to operate. The theory of evolution assumes that the laws of probability permit natural selection. More sophisticated thinkers try to make science self-explanatory by invoking the methodological principle that in science what goes beyond experimental evidence does not count, ergo does not exist. This is the source of various forms of the positivist antireligious attitude. Yet this attitude is itself based on the assumption that methodological principles can serve as an ontology. A good methodology can easily turn out to be a bad ontology.

THE PROBLEM SITUATION

I do not say that metaphysics and theology are insignificant or meaningless; I am only arguing that they should not interfere with science. The best way of doing science is to stop thinking directly about any metaphysical preconditions or implications. In lieu of metaphysics, what should lead our research? In many sciences, experiments are the guide. But what about sciences so remote from laboratory experimentation as cosmology?

My answer is that this field should be guided by the same principle as any other branch of science. In doing research, we always face a certain "problem situation," as Karl Popper called it. A good scientific work poses new and often unexpected problems that are to be solved. Experimental data (if they are available) or experimental possibilities (if they are open) also define the state of the art. But when there are no well-defined problems and no broader effort to contribute to, experimental results are sterile and can only casually lead to valuable conclusions. In science, context is crucial.

There are local problem situations—the ones that affect only a particular area of research—and global problem situations—which have important repercussions in an entire branch of science. An example of a global problem situation is the one that evolved in physics a century ago. Seemingly, it concerned only a very technical problem about the electrodynamics of moving bodies, but people such as Henri Poincaré, Hendrik Lorentz, and Einstein realized its importance for the very foundations of physics. Their work resulted in the special theory of relativity.

When speaking of such achievements, we should distinguish between the context of discovery and the context of justification. In the context of discovery—the way scientists arrive at new ideas—philosophy certainly can play an important role. For instance, Einstein was strongly influenced by the philosophical views of Ernest Mach; without reading Mach's writings, he might never have started thinking about relativity.

But in the context of justification—when the theory is ready to fight for its place in science—no overt philosophical or theological premises should be taken into account. The only things that matter are empirical verification, mathematical elegance, and consonance with other physical theories. Einstein eventually abandoned Mach's philosophy, and his theory proved to be independent of any philosophical presuppositions.

Even if metaphysical ideas are fruitful in the context of discovery, scientists are most successful when they do not work with the aim of defending or destroying a given philosophical or theological doctrine. Historically, when this has happened, subjective goals have overpowered impartial objectivity. Metaphysics is most helpful when implicitly arrived at and critically examined.

As far as the origin of the Universe and of physical laws is concerned, the problem situation is formed largely by two major programs in theoretical physics: the quantization of gravity and the unification of physical interactions. Recently, observational astronomy has been the driving force in cosmology; observers of early galaxy formation and large-scale structure have outpaced the theorists.

Gaps in our knowledge can be twofold. There are gaps through a deficit, when we know nothing about something we would like to know about. In such a case, we are looking for a knowledge that could fill the gap. The initial singularity in nonquantum cosmology is an example. The histories of particles and observers break down at the edge of space-time, beyond which a great hole in our knowledge extends. The widespread evidence for dark matter is another example.

There are also gaps through an excess, when we do not know something because the true hole in our knowledge is filled with empty hypotheses and misleading models. In such a case, the gap becomes a trap. One does not realize when one starts hunting one's own shadow.

2 ON THEOLOGICAL INTERPRETATIONS OF PHYSICAL CREATION THEORIES

INTRODUCTION

In recent years many books and articles have appeared dealing with theological interpretations of physical theories. Very often it is claimed that the so-called new physics offers new horizons for theological reflection. On the one hand, such a situation should be welcomed as potentially opening ways for rapprochement between science and theology, which for many decades remained blocked by positivistic prejudices. On the other hand, it almost inevitably leads to dangers of pseudoscientific explanations and compromised God-of-the-gaps strategies in theology. A responsible methodological analysis of theological interpretations of scientific theories seems needed more than ever. The aim of this chapter is to contribute to this goal.

In section 2, the structure of physical theories is briefly reviewed to prepare the background for discussing, in section 3, their different types of interpretations. In section 4, the results of this analysis are applied to some cosmological models or theories (especially those implying a creation of the Universe) and their theological interpretations. Finally, section 5 touches briefly on the theological significance of the comprehensibility of the world as a precondition of any scientific theory.

Sometimes it is difficult to draw a sharp borderline between philosophical and theological interpretations of scientific theories. Although I will be interested mainly in theological interpretations, the majority of the following analysis remains valid, *mutatis mutandis,* for philosophical interpretations.

THE STRUCTURE OF PHYSICAL THEORIES

Any physical theory consists of: (A) a mathematical structure, (B) the domain of the theory—roughly speaking a part or an aspect of the world to which the theory refers, and (C) bridge rules between (A) and (B); they are also called coordinating definitions or interpretation (in a narrower sense) of (A). One usually says that (A) models (B).[1]

This is, of course, a very idealized scheme of a physical theory. Usually, (A) is not given in a ready-made state from the beginning. Very often, the mathematical structure of a given theory is only very roughly sketched by its creator, as, for example, the mathematical structure of classical mechanics in Newton's work (in fact, at the time the fundamental notions of calculus were not clearly elaborated). Sometimes, only certain equations are proposed describing some physical phenomena in terms of a few of their solutions, and the mathematical environment of these equations, the field of their solutions, and so forth, are discovered much later. This was the case with the general theory of relativity. Initially proposed by Einstein in the form of his field equations together with a few physical postulates, it gradually developed into the very elaborate mathematical structure associated with the rich physical interpretation. Until now, only rather "small" regions of the space of all solutions to Einstein's field equations are known. It is by no means an exception in the history of science that the solutions found in the beginning turn out to belong to a zero-measure subset in the set of all solutions. Einstein's static world model can serve as an example. It was discovered in 1917 as the first relativistic cosmological model, and now we know that it is only one, and in a sense very exceptional, world model in the set of all possible solutions.

When a mathematical structure is more or less a priori chosen to model some domain of reality, it is usually a sign of a crisis in physics. This happens when theoreticians nervously search for a theory without having adequate empirical guidelines. In the history of both classical and contemporary physics, it is usually an interplay between experimental results and some partial mathematical structures that gives rise to valuable new physical theories, as illustrated, for instance, by the early history of quantum mechanics.

Usually, the full mathematical structure of a physical theory is known only when this theory has been transcended by a new and more general theory, that is, when the limits of applicability of the old theory are already known. For in-

---

1. A word of warning seems necessary. The structure of physical theory was originally analyzed by neopositivists in a logically rigorous manner. I take the liberty of presenting it in a more colloquial style frequently used by physicists. For instance, strictly speaking, coordinating definitions can relate only theoretical statements with observational statements. Therefore, domain of theory (our element (B)) should be defined as a set of utterances about a part (or aspect) of the world. However, physicists prefer to speak directly of the world, presupposing that the experiments they perform establish a certain type of contact with reality. In such a context, the term "bridge rules" is often used. This straining a point in physicists' favor does not influence the outcomes of our discussion.

stance, the full mathematical (geometrical) structure of classical mechanics was discovered only after elaborating geometric details of the generally relativistic structure of space-time (by Cartan and others).

The most delicate element in the above scheme is the domain of a physical theory, that is, an aspect of physical reality to which the theory semantically refers. This domain can sometimes be given a priori (i.e., before the theory is created or constructed) in terms of common sense cognition and using ordinary language description; but in other domains this is impossible, as in the case of quarks, black holes, and quantum gravity. However, strictly speaking the only authentic sources of our knowledge about the domain of a theory are the results of experiments that are not independent of the mathematical structure of the theory (without this structure we would not know what to measure, how to measure, and how to interpret what has been measured); such results only sample aspects of reality, that is, give us information about the tip of an iceberg that remains totally hidden from us. We can believe only that the mathematical structure of the theory reflects or discloses (in some approximate way) the structure of the iceberg itself. For this reason some versions of the structuralist theory of explanation are not uncommon among working scientists; usually, this type of explanation is presupposed unconsciously by them.[2]

Bridge rules connecting elements (A) and (B) of physical theories can be almost straightforward, as for example in classical mechanics where our everyday sense perception is a reasonably reliable guide. In such a case, we can say that the theory in question has a natural interpretation. In more advanced theories of recent physics, bridge rules can be very complicated. They are certainly not one-to-one coordinating definitions, but are entangled in nuances of the mathematical structure, and their references are sometimes ambiguous. All discussions concerning various interpretations of quantum mechanics have their origin here.

To sum up:

(1) The structure of a physical theory is an organic totality. Elements (A)–(C), enumerated above, are *nonlinearly* mixed with each other.

(2) The structure of a physical theory is a *dynamic* entity; it evolves and has a history.

2. Roughly speaking, by the structuralist type of explanation I mean a standpoint according to which the world's structure (very often hidden from our direct perception) is approximated and disclosed by the mathematical structures of physical theories. According to structuralism, there is a certain resonance between the structure of the world and the structures of physical theories; this justifies the agreement, so often achieved, of theoretical predictions with the actual empirical data. For details see E. McMullin, "Structural Explanation," *American Philosophical Quarterly*, 15 (1978), 139–147.

(3) The italicized words suggest that physical theories should be treated as *dynamical systems* and perhaps investigated with the help of the dynamical system method. I think this suggestion should be taken seriously. Notice that in this approach Kuhnian normal science and scientific revolutions are naturally interpreted as stable states and bifurcation points of a dynamical system, respectively.[3]

INTERPRETATION STRATEGIES

I now offer a few remarks concerning theological (or philosophical) interpretations of physical theories. By an interpretation of this kind, I mean *any comment on a particular physical theory*. My understanding is, therefore, very broad; in fact, it presupposes only one limitation: the comment in question must concern a single, well-identifiable, physical theory. Usually such comments refer—even if this is not directly noticed by their authors—to the mathematical structure that is supposed to disclose the structure of physical reality. The relationship of such comments to the mathematical structure of a given theory can be threefold:

a) A comment can be inconsistent with or even contradict the mathematical structure of a theory. Such comments include those interpretations of the theory of relativity which claim that it presupposes an "ontologically" unique or absolute time, such as Bergson's[4] or Maritain's[5] "philosophical interpretations" of special relativity; Mach's original interpretation of Newtonian mechanics that claimed to incorporate into its conceptual framework the idea of the relativity of mass; and so forth.[6] Such interpretations are usually regarded by physicists as "hand-waving arguments" and should be treated as inadmissible.

b) A comment can be neutral with respect to the mathematical structure of a physical theory. For instance, the space-time of the special theory of relativity can be interpreted either as describing the block universe, with the past and the future on an equal footing, or as a process of becoming, with the "now" of

3. I have developed this point of view in the paper "Nonlinear Evolution of Science," *Annals of Philosophy* (Catholic University of Lublin), fasc. 3, 32 (1984), 103–125 (in Polish, with English summary).

4. H. Bergson, *Durée et simultanéité (à propos de la théorie d'Einstein)*, Paris: Alcan, 1922; the second edition in 1923 contains three new appendices.

5. J. Maritain, *Réflexions sur l'intelligence et sur sa vie propre*, Paris: Nouvelle Librairie Nationale, 1926, especially ch. 7.

6. See my analysis of Mach's views regarding this question: "Between Newton and Einstein: Mach's Reform of the Newtonian Mechanics," in *Newton and the New Direction in Science*, ed. G. V. Coyne, M. Heller, and J. Życiński, Cittá del Vaticano: Specola Vaticana, 1988, 155–173.

a given inertial reference frame as its only real state.[7] A good symptom indicating that the interpretation of a given theory is neutral with respect to its mathematical structure is the following. Suppose you are able to show that your interpretation does not produce inconsistencies with the mathematical structure of the theory you interpret. Try to say something contradictory with what your interpretation asserts. If this does not require changes in the actual mathematical structure of the theory, this means that both your interpretation and its negation can be referred to the given theory, and consequently your interpretation (and its negation as well) is neutral with respect to its mathematical structure. For example, suppose you interpret the space-time of the special theory of relativity as the block universe. This produces no inconsistencies with the mathematical structure of the theory, but you can also see that if you change to the "flowing time" interpretation, you need change nothing in this structure.[8] This means that both interpretations are neutral with respect to it.

c) A comment can be in strict agreement with the mathematical structure of a given physical theory. Such a comment can be regarded as an exegesis of the mathematical structure of the theory. It so closely follows this structure that any deviation from it would immediately lead to inconsistencies with the structure of the theory. An example (at least in the intention of the authors) of such an exegesis is the book by D. J. Raine and M. Heller, *The Science of Space-Time*,[9] in which interpretations (of type (c)) of different space-time theories (from Aristotle to general relativity) are studied. Such an exegesis can be a very difficult task for many reasons, for instance: (i) mathematical structures of many recent theories still evolve; (ii) everyday language, in which such comments are usually made, is often inadequate to the "internal logic" of more advanced mathematical structures. In this view, it is not true that only those things that can be clearly expressed in everyday language can be made understandable. For instance, everyday language cannot "clearly" describe nonlinear situations, but modern physical theories make such situations understandable by modeling them with the help of nonlinear mathematics.

Philosophical or theological interpretations of physical theories (such as, for example, creationistic interpretations of cosmology; see below, section 4)

7. See R. Penrose, "Singularities and Time-Asymmetry," in *General Relativity: An Einstein Centenary Survey*, ed. S. W. Hawking and W. Israel, Cambridge: Cambridge University Press, 1979, 581–638, 883–886, section 12.2.5. See also C. J. Isham and J. C. Polkinghorne, "The Debate over the Block Universe," in *Quantum Cosmology and the Laws of Nature*, ed. R. J. Russell, N. Murphy, and C. J. Isham, Vatican City State: Vatican Observatory Publications; Berkeley: The Center for Theology and the Natural Sciences, 1993, 135–144.

8. These two interpretations can be regarded as contradictory with each other in the sense that they cannot be true together.

9. D. J. Raine and M. Heller, *The Science of Space-Time*, Tucson: Pachart, 1981.

assume the form of comments on physical theories. If they are of type (a), they are pseudo-interpretations and therefore render a poor service to theology, making it ridiculous in the eyes of scientists. They cannot be of type (c), because physical theories, from their very nature, say nothing about religious matters (as more fully discussed below). Therefore, they can be only of type (b); that is, neutral with respect to the mathematical structure of a given theory. Interpretations of this type should be taken "seriously but not literally."[10] They can show more than the noncontradiction between a given scientific theory and a given philosophical (or theological) doctrine; if they are successful, they can be regarded as demonstrating a certain consistency or consonance among them.

A warning follows from these considerations: Our analysis of type (c) interpretations stressed the inadequate character of everyday language for interpreting the mathematical structures of physical theories. Careful analysis of many contemporary physical theories shows that the structure of the world (as it is approximated and disclosed by the structures of our theories) transcends the possibilities of our language and our imagination. In light of this fact, we must be aware of a sense in which type (b) interpretations are inadequate. In this case our imagination and our linguistic resources are more weakly guided by mathematical structures than is the case with interpretations of type (c). We must be ready to admit that what we believe to be a good comment, consonant with a given theory, could easily turn out to be a metaphor or an image adapted to our limited possibilities rather than truly approaching the nature of reality.

CREATION INTERPRETATIONS IN COSMOLOGY

Great confusion reigns in the philosophical literature dealing with cosmological matters. In the following, I will illustrate my analysis with examples picked up more or less at random from the manifold instances of such confusion.

It is more or less evident that authors will avoid interpretations that would be in open contradiction with the mathematical structure of a given physical model or theory. An example of such an open contradiction would be the claim that Einstein's static world model supports the idea of a temporal beginning of the Universe. Of course, it is possible to argue that God could create the static Einstein universe in a ready-made state at any instant of its existence, but this would be an interpretation superimposed, so to speak, on the model, requiring additional assumptions of an extrascientific character necessary to

10. See I. G. Barbour, *Myths, Models and Paradigms*, New York: Harper and Row, 1974, 7.

enforce this interpretation on the model's structure. Moreover, these assumptions would automatically qualify the interpretation as belonging to category (b) rather than category (a).

Usually, inconsistencies (or even contradictions) between proposed interpretations and a given model or theory are more cleverly disguised. When they are brought to light they are often unmasked as falling under category (a); this shows simultaneously that they cannot aspire to belong to category (c). There is a host of instances. The subject matter often inspires an eloquent rhetoric. A good example is Robert Jastrow's famous saying, quoted in the preceding chapter, about the scientist who is about to conquer the highest peak and is greeted there "by a band of theologians who have been sitting there for centuries." The point is that both scientists and theologians are aiming at the *same* peak; that is to say, the Big Bang theory and the biblical phrase "In the beginning God created heaven and earth"[11] are supposed to speak about the same event—the creation of the Universe. This is clearly stated by John A. O'Keefe in the afterword to Jastrow's book:

We see then, that the resemblance between our cosmology today and that of the theologians of the past is not merely accidental. What they saw dimly, we see more clearly, with the advantage of better physics and astronomy. But we are looking at the same God, the Creator.[12]

More examples of the same interpretative fallacy are described by Adolf Grünbaum. Some of them are "instructively articulate" as instances of the confusion of concepts.[13] The illegitimacy of such interpretations can be demonstrated in two ways: first, one could show that the authentically theological doctrine of creation says something different from what can be deduced from the Big Bang theory; second, one could appeal to a methodological analysis in order to show that theological questions transcend the limitations inherent in the very nature of the scientific method. In fact, each of these two ways cannot avoid using elements of the other one; they differ from each other in the point of departure rather than in the essence of the argument.

The best approach at elucidating this sort of methodological misunderstanding is a historical analysis of the development of the creation doctrine in theology. This method shows persuasively that the theological idea of creation is immensely richer than anything physics or cosmology is able to say. It is not

11. R. Jastrow quotes this biblical verse in the context of his interpretation; see *God and the Astronomers*, New York: Warner Books, 1980, 124.

12. Ibid., 158.

13. A. Grünbaum, "The Pseudo-Problem of Creation in Physical Cosmology," *Philosophy of Science*, 56 (1989), 373–394.

difficult to demonstrate that a proponent of such a theological interpretation says something different from what can be read out of a given scientific model or theory, and in this sense the interpretation in question transcends the structure of a given model or theory. To pursue this analysis further would exceed the limits of the present chapter; the reader is referred to the extant literature.[14]

It is interesting to notice that many creation interpretations of type (a) consist in imputing to theologians specific views never (or seldom) shared by them, the most common error being the identification of creation (in the theological sense) with the initiation in time of the existence of the Universe. There are so many instances of this error that there is no need to quote any of them.

The second way is based on the well-founded achievements of the modern philosophy of science, and consists in applying its results concerning the nature and scope of scientific theories to the particular case of cosmological theories. One could repeat here Grünbaum's analysis[15] with a slight change of emphasis: his results should not be understood as following from an a priori positivistic or "over-empiricist" idea of science (which, from the phraseology he uses, leads me to suspect he falls into), but as derived from sound methodological premises (as I believe he actually intended). The way he uses the term "pseudo-problem" with regard to the philosophical or theological doctrine of creation suggests an a priori assumption that the limits of the scientific method coincide with the limits of rationality.[16] Such an assumption constitutes an epistemological standpoint that necessarily follows neither from science nor from its philosophy. In fact, the present analyses are based on a conviction that this assumption is not true.

Grünbaum distinguishes two questions: first, "Does the physical Universe have a temporal *origin*, and—if so—what does physical cosmology tell us about it?" and second, "Was there a creation of the Universe, and—if so— what light can science throw on it, if any?" He argues that the first question is a

14. I especially recommend a short account by Ernan McMullin of the history of the creation and evolution doctrines presented in his introduction to the volume *Evolution and Creation,* ed. E. McMullin, Notre Dame: University of Notre Dame Press, 1985, 1–56. See also the paper by the same author, "Natural Science and Belief in a Creator: Historical Notes," in *Physics, Philosophy, and Theology: A Common Quest for Understanding,* ed. R. J. Russell, W. R. Stoeger, and G. V. Coyne, Vatican City State: Vatican Observatory Publications; Berkeley: The Center for Theology and the Natural Sciences, 1988, 49–79.

15. A. Grünbaum, "The Pseudo-Problem of Creation in Physical Cosmology."

16. This is also apparent in Grünbaum's attempt to reduce all questions transcending the scientific method to mere psychological discomforts. In his opinion, a question concerning the creation of the Universe "cannot be regarded as a well posed challenge merely because the questioner finds it psychologically insistent, experiences a strong feeling of puzzlement, and desires to answer it." Ibid., 821.

legitimate physical problem, whereas in the second question, "the genuine problem of the origin of the Universe or of the matter in it has been illicitly transmuted into the pseudo-problem of the 'creation' of the Universe or of its matter by an external cause." The above distinction of the two kinds of questions and their evaluation is well known,[17] and there is no need to repeat all arguments usually quoted on its behalf.

If creation interpretations of cosmology are inconsistent (or even contradictory) with this physical theory (as claimed by Grünbaum), that is to say, if they belong to category (a), they cannot be regarded as a legitimate exegesis of its mathematical structure, that is, they cannot be of type (c). The third possibility (of their being of type (b)) remains to be disputed.

In the above-analyzed creation interpretations falling under category (a), the error consists in identifying certain physical statements with some theological assertions (physicists and theologians "met at the top the same peak"). If, in such a contest, identity is replaced by a kind of consonance, the interpretation switches from category (a) to category (b), and no methodological objections can be raised against it. However, in the case of the Big Bang theory and the theological doctrine of creation, to say simply that God created the Universe in the Big Bang singularity and therefore these two ideas are "consonant" would be rather a trivial statement. To avoid triviality one should provide a comment showing a compatibility of these two doctrines (but not their identity). Usually, theologians point out that to create in the theological sense means something much more than to bring a thing into existence, the thing that *a moment ago* was just nothing. Even Grünbaum is ready to admit that "the view of *timeless* causation set forth by Augustine" evades his criticism, and he disregards it only because he finds it "either unintelligible or incoherent." However, these two reasons are not a matter of scientific methodology but rather of psychological temperament or of a priori assumptions.

Within interpretations of type (b) different strategies are possible, varying from claiming mutual independence of physical theories and theological doctrines, through dialogue or some kind of integrations, to a constructive consonance between them. Some of these strategies have been analyzed by Ian Barbour[18] and Willem Drees (the latter with special reference to cosmological problems).[19]

---

17. See, for instance, W. B. Drees, *Beyond the Big Bang: Quantum Cosmologies and God,* La Salle: Open Court, 1990.

18. I. G. Barbour, "Ways of Relating Science and Theology," in *Physics, Philosophy, and Theology: A Common Quest for Understanding,* 21–48; and in *Religion in an Age of Science: The Gifford Lectures 1989–1991,* volume 1, San Francisco: Harper & Row, 1990, 3–28.

19. W. B. Drees, *Beyond the Big Bang.*

A good example of an interpretation falling under category (c) is Chris Isham's paper[20] in which he makes a "step by step exegesis" of the Hartle-Hawking model of the quantum creation of the Universe. He clearly shows that the theological doctrine of creation and "creation" as a quantum process have hardly anything in common besides the name "creation." He warns, however, that "some attention should surely be paid to the shifting forms in which the archetypes of space and time are impinging on the scientific world." Evidently, as soon as we change from studying the structure of the Hartle-Hawking model to contemplate "the archetypes of space and time" in their role of shaping our intuitions concerning the creation of the world, we immediately leave the secure land of interpretations (c) and enter the territory of those belonging to category (b).

THE PHILOSOPHICAL AND THEOLOGICAL SIGNIFICANCE OF PHYSICAL THEORIES

The philosophical and theological significance of physical theories is not limited to categories (a), (b), and (c), with which we have dealt in the previous sections. Theology has always interacted—and, I think, will always interact—with the sciences in manifold ways. For instance, scientific ideas may be for theologians a source of inspiration to reach new theological insights or to invent more appealing metaphors; they might help to evoke the feeling of mystery ("if in physics things go so far beyond our imagination, what can we say about God?") or to create a suitable context for reconsidering or reinterpreting a traditional religious doctrine. Such interactions are unavoidable because our thinking (in theology and elsewhere) is unable to operate over long periods of time in isolation from the evolving stream of social knowledge. Therefore, such interactions are indispensable if theology is to fulfill its mission with respect to each generation. Usually, theology interacts, in one of these ways, with no particular theory but rather with an overall image of the world as it is drawn by science as a whole in each epoch. Consequently, the above analysis does not refer to this kind of interaction (because I have considered exclusively *interpretations of particular* physical theories).

Sometimes, however, a particular physical theory can enter into a fruitful interaction with a theological (or philosophical) doctrine. Let us consider two instances of such interactions.[21] First, it can happen that some part of a physical theory plus specific additional premises can provide reasonable grounds for

---

20. C. J. Isham, "Creation of the Universe as a Quantum Process," in *Physics, Philosophy, and Theology: A Common Quest for Understanding,* 375–408.

21. They were suggested to me by Nancey Murphy.

a theological conclusion. Second, a theological theory and a scientific theory might have implications that turn out to be mutually dependent or even equivalent. Neither of these cases is an interpretation of a scientific theory in the sense described at the beginning of section 3. Of course, one could interpret the theory in question "in the light" of additional premises or of the fact that its conclusions are somehow related to some theological conclusions. If this happens, interpretations fall into category (b) and are neutral with respect to the content of the theory. In both cases some external elements (with respect to the original implications) are needed (such as additional premises or theological implications) to make a comment possible.

Let me, finally, mention yet another way in which science can be relevant, and very much so, for philosophical or theological discourse. In my opinion, the very existence of physical theories and their effectiveness in processing our knowledge of the world are of much greater importance for theology than any theological interpretation of a particular theory. As it is well known, the question of why the method of using mathematical structures to model some aspects of the world works, and works so well, is a nontrivial philosophical problem.[22] This question is often expressed in the form: Why is the world mathematical? Perhaps it should be regarded as a special instance of a more general question: Why is the world comprehensible?[23] Having no possibility to enter the discussion of the problem in a more exhaustive way, I should refer the reader to the huge literature on this problem.[24]

In philosophy one can at most try to demonstrate the nontriviality of this problem and to conclude with Einstein that it is "the eternal mystery . . . which we shall never understand."[25] In theology one could go a step further and try to offer a theological interpretation of this result. For instance, one could say that the comprehensibility of the world and its existence are but two aspects of the *creation*. Owing to the act of creation the world exists, and through the act of creation the world is comprehensible. The rationality of the Creator is reflected in the created world. To use the old Platonic principle,

22. Only a very few positivistically minded thinkers, usually nonphysicists, would dismiss it as evoking purely emotional reactions.

23. I say "perhaps" on behalf of those who are inclined to identify the comprehensibility of the world with its mathematical character.

24. My preferred readings on this subject are: A. Einstein, "Physics and Reality," in *Ideas and Opinions*, New York: Dell Publ., 1978, 283–315, especially the beginning of this paper; E. Wigner, "The Unreasonable Effectiveness of Mathematics in the Natural Sciences," in *Communications in Pure and Applied Mathematics*, 13 (1960), 1–14; R. Penrose, *The Emperor's New Mind: Concerning Computers, Minds, and the Laws of Physics*, New York: Oxford University Press, 1989, especially chs. 3 and 4; J. D. Barrow, *The World Within the World*, Oxford: Clarendon Press, 1988, especially ch. 5.

25. Einstein, "Physics and Reality," in *Ideas and Opinions*, 285.

"God always geometrizes," and consequently every result of God's creative action always has a geometric (or more generally—mathematical) character.

To sum up, I think that legitimate theological interpretations of cosmological theories should be limited to type (b). Such interpretations are useful insofar as they help the Christian "to make his theology and his cosmology consonant in the contribution they make to his world-view."[26] Moreover, I strongly believe that Christians who want to look to the sciences for a deeper understanding of the creation should not take into consideration any particular cosmological model or theory, but turn instead to the most fundamental assumptions presupposed by every scientific endeavor.

26. E. McMullin, "How Should Cosmology Relate to Theology?" in *The Sciences and Theology in the Twentieth Century*, ed. A. R. Peacocke, Notre Dame: University of Notre Dame Press, 1981, 52.

3 THE SCIENTIFIC IMAGE OF THE WORLD

INTRODUCTORY REMARKS

Christian theology has always experienced a tension between two tendencies: on the one hand, fidelity to its sources; on the other hand, openness toward contemporaneity. Christianity is a historical religion in the sense that it took its origin from historical events, and it cannot cut off its links with these events under the threat of losing its identity. This circumstance directs efforts of many Christian theologians toward the past. Moreover, the centuries mediating between the present epoch and the "foundational events" also contribute to the actual religious convictions. History is not a channel passively transmitting to us doctrine and tradition; it actively enriches the heritage of the origin. Owing to this process, many opinions have entered Christian tradition that never belonged to its essence but rather are results of casual accidents of history. However, a curious property of history is that from time to time it undergoes violent accelerations, and during such periods the tendency appears (quite natural in these circumstances) to distance itself from the past. The acceleration of history in our time is greater than ever before, and this is why the tension between the past and the future must be taken very seriously.

Theology is always embedded in a broader context of culture, and together with the general culture it participates in all adventures of history. The general culture is especially sensitive to the world image that is, in a sense, obligatory at a given epoch. The world image constitutes, as it were, a background out of which the general culture takes its vital forces. But, reciprocally, the world image is a product of culture. Its stuff comes from various sources: philosophy, religious beliefs, scientific ideas (usually strongly simplified), imaginations fostered by art and literature. Moreover, the proportion of various components changes from epoch to epoch. Although the world image is a "fuzzy structure," it exhibits an extraordinary effectiveness in shaping artistic tastes, evaluation criteria, and intellectual preferences of a given epoch.

In spite of the fact that the world image in a given society undergoes sometimes almost continuous changes between one generation and the other, one can quite clearly distinguish its different phases in the history of Western culture. The medieval European culture was homogeneous to such a degree that one could speak about the unique, in principle, medieval image of the world. The origin of the empirical sciences in the seventeenth century was a great shock for the Western culture, which relatively quickly surrendered to the mechanistic worldview enforced by the common (at those times) interpretation of scientific theories. The mechanistic worldview had been very effectively assimilated by the Western culture, and in spite of the fact that in the beginning of the twentieth century this worldview completely lost its scientific foundations, it is even now powerfully present in the convictions of many people and in various products of our culture.

Our century began with the far-reaching revolution in the foundations of physics, and it is marked with the consequences of this revolution (or perhaps simply by its continuation). Scientific theories become more and more abstract, and more and more distant from the possibilities of our imaginative power. As a consequence of this, scientific theories much less influence the image of the world functioning in the general culture of our times than they did in the last three centuries. Perhaps we should say (in plural): "the world images functioning in the present cultures." The fact that the once homogeneous culture has split into many cultures is sometimes regarded as a symptom of crisis.

How does theology feel in this situation? Christian synthesis of philosophy, theology, and general culture in the Middle Ages was such an exceptional and aesthetically appealing achievement that Christian theology never got rid of the shock caused by the collapse of this synthesis. Traces of the medieval synthesis are still present in many theological treatises, mostly in the form of remnants of the Aristotelian world image and in the fear of changing to more modern worldviews.

The mechanistic world image rather superficially influenced theological disputes, but it certainly strongly shaped popular religious imagination. As far as theology is concerned, elements of the present scientific world image have to fight remnants of the Aristotelian cosmology rather than face its mechanistic successor. The presence of the actual scientific worldview in theology is rather weak. Except for relatively frequent references to the evolutionary vision of the Universe created by Teilhard de Chardin, theologians exhibit a strange inertia with respect to the authentic dialogue with the sciences. I emphasize the word "authentic" because declarations referring to the dialogue are many.

The above remarks are of necessity very sketchy. They serve only as an introduction to my main theme in this chapter, namely to the question of how the contemporary theologian should react with respect to the so-called scientific image of the world. In section 2, I will try to understand what does the "scientific image of the world" really mean and which are its mean properties. In section 3, my task will be to reconstruct the cosmological background of the present world image. This will lead, in section 4, to some conclusions regarding our main theme. The problem is important because every theologian, even if he or she refuses doing so, always is thinking in terms of a certain image of the world.

THE STRUCTURE OF THE SCIENTIFIC IMAGE OF THE WORLD

There are many images of the world, but among them one deserves our special attention, namely, the so-called scientific image of the world. It is not a well-defined concept. One could describe it as a global picture of the world obligatory for scientists of a given epoch. Of course, it changes from scientist to scientist, but, after a suitable "averaging," one can obtain quite distinct patterns forming such a world picture.

Some sciences (for instance, physics and astronomy) contribute more than other ones (for instance, geography or ornithology) to the scientific image of the world. The views of more influential scientists and popularizers (not necessarily of better ones) shape this image more than do those of other men of science.

The scientific image of the world exhibits one prominent feature: it constrains the scientists and intellectuals of the given epoch more (in a sense) than religious dogmas constrain the believers. The constraining mechanisms—although put into motion by no "external authorities"—are very powerful, because they are enforced by social factors acting invisibly but in a deeply efficient manner.

Let us enumerate some other features of the scientific image of the world.

An important role in it is played by elements that do not come from the sciences but rather from various preconditions that are assumed even before any science has been done. Such preconditions are usually assumed tacitly, for nobody in this epoch is able to think otherwise. In this sense, what is most certain for people sharing a given worldview is not what is explicitly asserted by them, but what they even cannot put into words. Many of such "preconditions" are of a metaphysical character.

Among preconditions of science in a given epoch one can find elements coming not only from the results of the sciences, but also from the method itself with the help of which the sciences are done. In this sense, for example, the limits of the method determine the limits of the image of the world (what is beyond method is beyond the image of the world), and the limits of the world image are its very "influential" property. However, in speaking about the limits of the scientific image of the world one must be tolerant. This image is shaped by an intellectual fashion rather than by any rules of scientific methodology, and very often what is at the verge of the scientific method is in the center of common fascinations.

Also to the scientific image of the world belong questions that can be asked within the sciences, even if the answers to some of them are not yet available.

Suggestions coming from considering such questions can form important aspects of the world image. In this sense, the world image certainly transcends the actual limits of science. But vice versa, there exist the forbidden questions, that is, the questions that are not allowed to be asked within the sciences. By filtering out certain ideas, they become an important factor structuring the image of the world (this factor played a significant role in the period dominated by the positivistic philosophy).

The scientific image of the world is far from being objective. Its elements are not impartially evaluated (according to the degree of their justification) by people accepting this image. For instance, elements referring to global features of the world are usually treated as more important than those referring to local ones. And doubtlessly, elements somehow enlightening the place and the role of humankind in the world are of the highest importance, because the world image is—as if from its nature—centered on human needs.

For many people (scientists included), science—by the intermediary of its image of the world—fulfills functions similar to those of religion: it provides life motivations, shapes ethical attitudes, and so forth. This refers not only to scientists who declare themselves as nonbelievers. Also, in the case of scientists-believers, elements coming from the scientific image of the world significantly contribute to their attitude toward the existential questions.

As we can see, the sciences themselves play a secondary role in forming the scientific image of the world. It is rather an interpretation of science, or even a set of interpretations, that forms the world panorama permeating the culture of a given epoch.

THE COSMOLOGICAL BACKGROUND
OF THE PRESENT WORLD IMAGE

Every scientific image of the world requires a scene, or a cosmological framework, on which it could develop. For many philosophers and theologians of the Middle Ages, such a cosmological framework was provided by a vulgarized version of the Eudoxian world model, with the Earth in the center surrounded by crystalline spheres to which the Moon, the planets, and the stars were attached. In modern times, this cosmic picture was replaced by the infinitely extending Euclidean space and the absolute time uniformly flowing from minus infinity to plus infinity. Both these cosmic images were products of a philosophical imagination rather than the results of any scientific theory. For the first time in the history of science we now have a truly scientific cosmology with its standard relativistic model and its numerous empirical tests. However, only some elements of this model (mixed with elements coming from other sources) can be found in the general image of the world of our times. I will take a closer look at them.

To simplify my task of reconstructing the present image of the world, I have adopted the following method. As it is well known, the journal *Scientific American* is widely read by many people interested in science and also by scientists who want to know what is going on in the "neighboring disciplines" to their particular fields of research. The November 1994 issue of this journal was devoted to the topic *Life in the Universe*. The collection of papers published in this issue by invited specialists in various fields can be regarded as an approximation to what could be thought of as the scientific image of the world "obligatory" at the end of the twentieth century (of course, many details presented in these papers should be omitted to obtain a sufficiently global picture). In the following, I simply collect the main features emerging from the reading of this issue of the *Scientific American*.

First of all, the Universe—both in its totality and in its parts—is an evolving system. The concept of evolution has entered the world image from biology (Darwin's theory), but has been extrapolated to the entire cosmos by the standard model of the Universe. Owing to this model, the evolution of the Universe is by many simply identified with its expansion (recession of galaxies).

The evolution of the Universe is not limited only to global changes; it also consists in the process of developing more and more organized structures. Nonlinear thermodynamics, the theory of dynamical systems and deterministic chaos, and various models of growth of complexity have significantly contributed to our understanding of this process. However, the above-mentioned quickly progressing branches of science are too recent and too technical to be able to shape the common "seeing of the world." Nevertheless, some of their results, suspected for a long time, certainly fulfill this role.

A typically twentieth-century feature of the world image is the belief that new structures emerge in the process of the cosmic evolution. The concept of emergence excludes the necessity of "external factors" (e.g., God's special action). New structures are the result of the laws of physics alone. However, they are not a priori contained in the initial conditions of the Universe. The "higher level" of organization results, in an unpredictable way, from the former "lower level," but the new level is autonomous; that is, it is ruled by new laws that did not exist in the previous states. In this sense, the future of the Universe is open. The openness of the Universe is the next characteristic feature of our worldview (as opposed to the strictly deterministic picture of the nineteenth century). Moreover, this feature plays a prominent role in the actual worldview for other reasons. Rigid determinism of classical physics has been transcended by the quantum mechanical paradigm and the discovery of deterministic chaos. Even in classical dynamical systems strict predictability of phenomena cannot be indiscriminately assumed any more.

Two tendencies seem to be pronounced in the contemporary progress of science: the tendency toward unity on the fundamental level (grand unification and superunification of physics), and the tendency toward the holistic view on the large scale (dynamical systems, nonlinear effects). Although these trends are still programs rather than achieved results, they already seem to change our manner of viewing the Universe.

Another interesting aspect of the present image of the world is what could be called a return to man. As is well known, in the Copernican revolution man was deprived of his central position in the Universe (see, however, Chapter 5), and the scientific revolution of the seventeenth century eliminated man from the scientific method. I doubt whether this state of affairs has substantially changed in our day, but various popular interpretations of scientific results tend to emphasize the above-mentioned "return to man." The role of observers in the theory of relativity, and especially in quantum physics, and the so-called anthropic principles in cosmology belong to those fields of research that are most often used to stress the role of man both in the Universe and in the scientific method.

THE WORLD IMAGE AND THEOLOGY

Should theology take into account the current scientific image of the world? The fact that the scientific world image is changeable and is far from being the result of strictly scientific investigations suggests the negative answer to this question. In such a view there is some true component, but one could quote at least three reasons against it:

First, speaking and thinking within a certain image of the world is unavoidable. The world image is present in the entire cultural climate and intellectual atmosphere of the epoch, and because theology is a part of this climate and this atmosphere, it cannot avoid speaking and thinking in terms of the current world image. If a theologian tries to speak contemporary language, he will sooner or later (perhaps unconsciously) make use of the elements of the actual worldview.

Second, if a theologian avoids using the actual image of the world, he very often implicitly makes use of an ancient, outdated picture of it. One could quote an almost infinite number of examples of this unhappy procedure.

Third, if a theologian uses the outdated world image (openly or implicitly), his pastoral efficiency is very limited. People to whom the scientific world image is dear are unable to accept theological truths remaining in conflict with this image. It was St. Augustine who remarked that if a Christian manifests his ignorance in scientific matters, he makes Christian doctrine ridiculed in the eyes of pagans. Nobody would willingly accept ridiculed beliefs.

How can one solve this dilemma? It seems that there is no other way than to accept the actual image of the world when doing theology, but to keep it under control. The theologian should be able responsibly to discern what in this image comes from a solid theory, what forms a scientific hypothesis, and what is an element of a current intellectual fashion rather than that of science. Of course, this puts a heavy burden on the theologian: he or she must remain in contact with actual scientific achievements. An interdisciplinary working group could be of great help.

In the Middle Ages the future professor of theology had not only to undergo an intensive training in philosophy, but also to teach philosophy before being appointed by the theology faculty. If we remember that in those times philosophy fulfilled the role in many respects similar to that of our sciences, obvious conclusions suggest themselves.

4 A PROGRAM FOR THEOLOGY OF SCIENCE

When doing science one investigates the Universe. This statement is almost tautologically true because the Universe can be defined as the totality of things that are investigated in the process of doing science. The Universe is given to the sciences in their method. In this sense the limits of the scientific method are the limits of the Universe. Everything that transcends the empirical investigation transcends, from the very definition, the Universe of the sciences. One of the main tasks of the philosophy of science is to determine the limits of the applicability domain of the empirical method or, equivalently, to determine the limits of the Universe. One can say even stronger and more precisely that all hitherto achievements of philosophy of science could be reduced to an attempt at understanding what the empirical sciences can do and with the help of which methods. The problem at stake here is the problem of limits. We should notice, however, that the limits in question are defined "from the side of the sciences," that is, by approaching them from within the domain controlled by the sciences. The other side remains inaccessible for the scientific method.

The basic theological tenet concerning the Universe is that it has been created by God. This statement should also be understood as a tautology if by the Universe we mean everything that has been created by God. Such an understanding of the Universe seems to be natural in theology.

It is therefore evident that the Universe of the sciences and the Universe of theology differ from each other, and this difference is a consequence of the fact that the methods of these disciplines polarize their vision of reality. The Universe of the sciences is but a part of the theological Universe. This is so not only because the Universe of the sciences coincides with what we call the "material Universe" and the theological Universe goes beyond the realm of matter, but also because the method of theology is able "to see" in the material Universe some aspects that are transparent for the scientific method and consequently do not belong to the Universe of the sciences. The material Universe, as contemplated by theology, is richer than the Universe as seen from the scientific perspective.

Precisely at this point there appears the possibility of doing theology of science. As a theological reflection upon the sciences, theology of science would investigate the consequences of the fact that the empirical sciences investigate the Universe, which has been created by God.[1]

Theology of science would have to be an authentic part of theology with all methodological peculiarities of a theological discipline. If one agrees that science is for the humanity an important value, one should regard theology of science as a subchapter of the theology of human values. The specific feature of this subchapter would consist in amply using the results of philosophy of science.

As this has been stressed above, philosophy of science analyzes the limits of the scientific methods, but from its very nature, it is unable to go beyond these limits. The awareness of the fact that the Universe has been created by God allows theology of science to see those aspects of the world that are inaccessible for both the sciences and their philosophy. In other words, theology of science is able to contemplate the limits of the scientific method "from the other side," that is, from the side about which the sciences "know nothing" at all.

In this short chapter, I would like to consider only two such aspects of the world that are important for theology of science but are entirely transparent for the scientific method, namely, the contingency of the world and values present in it.

The first of these aspects can be expressed in the following sentence: The Universe in its existence is entirely dependent on God as its Creator. Traditional theology, borrowing the term from traditional philosophy, called this aspect of the world its contingency. The thesis about the dependence of the world on God in its existence is an essential part of the Christian doctrine of creation (although this dependence can be, and in fact is, understood in manifold ways). There is a big discussion as to whether the scientific method presupposes the existence of the investigated object or not. I do not want to enter this discussion here.[2] Even if the scientific method presupposes the existence of the investigated object, it does not presuppose it as dependent on God. This constitutes

---

1. The idea of theology of science has been proposed in my book *The New Physics and a New Theology*, Vatican City State: Vatican Observatory Publications, 1996, ch. 7.

2. My personal point of view is that although this presupposition is very often made by scientists it is not the presupposition of the scientific method. For the scientific method, it is enough to assume that *if a given object exists* it has properties disclosed by the scientific method.

the domain of theology. And the reflection upon the sciences in the light of this presupposition is the task of theology of science.

The second of these aspects can be expressed in the sentence: The Universe is impregnated with values. At least from the times of the Vienna Circle, it is very well known that the scientific method is insensitive to values: normative and evaluating sentences do not belong to the scientific language.[3] However, this does not mean that values are not present in the world. From the theological perspective, the Universe is an implementation of the creative plan of God. This plan contains in itself not only those aspects of the world that the sciences attempt at deciphering with the help of their own methods, but also those aspects of reality that in axiology are called values. This set of problems could be included into the traditional theological treatise "on the goal of creation." In every rational activity goals weave themselves into the systems of values being values themselves. To contemplate the sciences in the light of values would constitute another task for theology of science.

Sometimes it can also happen that the philosophical reflection on science reveals a problem, but only dimly and to a certain extent, whereas the problem could be seen in a brighter light when looked upon from the theological perspective. A typical example is provided by the problem of the so-called rationality of the world. It can be expressed in the form of the famous Einstein question: Why is the world so comprehensible? The very existence of science and the successes of its method testify to the fact that the world *can be* rationally investigated. The method of science presupposes the property of the world owing to which it answers questions addressed to it, provided they are formulated in the correct language (typically in the language of mathematics). Philosophical reflection upon the Einstein question convincingly discloses its nontrivial character but is unable to go any further. However, when contemplated in the light of theological principles, this question can be put into the broader context showing its deeper meaning. The world has been created by God according to God's rational plan. Science is but a human endeavor to decipher this plan. The rationality of the world remains very close to the concept of Logos—the immanence of God in his creation.

In the opinion of many contemporary theologians, the characteristic feature of the entire theology consists in a specific anthropological point of view. In fact, this point of view could be reduced to the statement that the principal goal of the Revelation is not to teach people the knowledge of the Universe; that is, not to satisfy their innate curiosity of the world, but rather to introduce

---

3. It is interesting, with respect to this assertion, to read the paper by Ernan McMullin published in *Philosophy of Science Association*, ed. P. Asquith, T. Nickles, and E. Lansing, 1983, 3–25.

them into the sphere of saving values. The Revelation is of the existential rather than informational character. With this in mind, it is clear that the task of theology of science cannot consist in giving us this information that we would like to have but that cannot be provided by the sciences. The task of theology of science is the same as that of theology in general, with the proviso that it is directed to the specific subject of this theological discipline; that is, to the critical reflection on those Revelation data that allow us to look at science as a specifically human value.

PART TWO

FROM THE HISTORICAL PERSPECTIVE

Relations between science and religion are not designed on the desks of philosophers of science and theologians; they are shaped by historical processes. Without studying the history of both science and theology, it is impossible to comprehend properly the nature of these relations. Moreover, quite often the profound study of a given case is able to not only disclose apparent aspects of a conflict but also to show mutual interactions that remain invisible for the "naked eye." This is why, after some methodological analyses in Part One, a historical study should follow. To give justice to such a study, a few volumes should be written. In what follows we focus— and very selectively, indeed—on only two processes, both of great importance for the issue in question. First is man's place in the scientific image of the world of a given epoch. We should not forget that it is precisely the human being in whom two methodologically different "planes"—the plane of religious needs and the plane of the scientific activity—cross each other. Often, tensions and conflicts between science and religion are but consequences of the current "philosophy of man." Second is the evolution of the concept of rationality as it was shaped by Christian theology, on the one hand, and the ways of doing science, on the other, and their mutual interactions. I am inclined to think that the concept of rationality is the next in importance, after man's place in the Universe, as far as the science and religion dialogue is concerned.

Common wisdom asserts that the Copernican revolution degraded man from his central position in the Universe. In fact, the medieval image of the world was never anthropocentric but rather theocentric. Man was in it a marginal being. It is true, however, that this margin should be attributed a privileged character—not only because of the Earth's geometrical central position but, first, because of the overwhelmingly anthropomorphic architecture of the medieval world. The origin of modern science and its subsequent evolution shifted these "proportions": geometrically, man had obtained an "average position," but the image of the world gradually became more and more anthropocentric. Modern philosophy of science, and philosophy in general, is certainly "man oriented." We could truly speak of the shift "from the privileged margin to an average center." This is the subject matter of Chapter 5.

In twentieth-century philosophy and theology, the important role in this shift was played by the vision of the world proposed by Teilhard de Chardin, on whom we concentrate in Chapter 7. But before critically examining his views, we must first study, in Chapter 6, the evolution of the concept of rationality and its influence on shaping relationships between the Church and its theologians, and the world of science and its manifold ways of forming people's attitudes toward the world (only in this context can Teilhard de Chardin's views can be correctly placed). My main thesis in Chapter 6 is that the biblical idea of Logos, and its subsequent theological elaborations, could be thought of as a religious counterpart of the concept of rationality. This does not mean, however, that all conflicts between science and theology are automatically precluded. The struggle for understanding, both from the theological and scientific sides, is a human activity and is strongly conditioned by many historical factors. In this respect, the role of "bridge people" in the dialogue between science and religion cannot be overestimated. One of them was Georges Lemaître, the founder of the Big Bang cosmology and a Roman Catholic priest. In Chapter 8, we briefly present his profile as a man of faith and a man of science. Although he left only a few written remarks concerning the dialogue between science and religion, his engagement in the scientific research has probably built more solid bridges between these two fields of human activity than many learned treatises concerning the subject.

5

FROM THE PRIVILEGED MARGIN
TO AN AVERAGE CENTER

A DREAM FOR THE OVERTURE

It is a commonplace to assert that the Copernican revolution has denied man his central position in the world, and that as a result of this revolution the geocentric Universe has been replaced by the world satisfying what is often called the Copernican principle. According to this principle, the world presents (statistically) the same image irrespective of the place from which it is viewed. The Copernican ideological revolution[1] has doubtlessly introduced one of the most drastic changes into the image of the world ever enforced by a scientific achievement. Consequences of the "Copernican shift" are felt to the present days. Copernicus himself in his *De Revolutionibus* hardly touched upon such philosophical (or ideological) issues. These aspects of the Copernican revolution were developed much later by others, mainly by imputing to Copernicus views never shared by him.

If the essence of the Copernican revolution consisted in moving the observer from the Earth to another (typically located) celestial body, it is Johannes Kepler who should formally be attributed the authorship of this revolutionary shift. In his *Somnium seu Astronomia Lunaris*[2] he, for the first time, looked at the Universe from a celestial body other than the Earth. No wonder that the first space travel had to be undertaken to the nearest celestial body—the Moon. *Somnium* was, in a sense, the work of Kepler's life. Yet when a student in Tübingen, he wrote down some ideas concerning the

1. It was Karl Popper who has distinguished between *scientific revolutions* and *ideological revolutions*. Scientific revolution is "a rational overthrow of an established scientific theory by a new one," whereas ideological revolution comprises "all processes of 'social entrenchment' or perhaps 'social acceptance' of ideologies which incorporate some scientific results." The Copernican revolution was for Popper a scientific revolution as far as it overthrew a dominant scientific theory, and an ideological revolution insofar as it changed man's view of his place in the Universe. See K. R. Popper, "The Rationality of Scientific Revolutions," in *Problems of Scientific Revolutions* (The Herbert Spencer Lectures, 1973), ed. R. Harre, Oxford: Oxford University Press, 1975, 88.

2. J. Kepler, *Somnium: The Dream or Posthumous Work on Lunar Astronomy*, trans. E. Rosen, Madison: University of Wisconsin Press, 1967.

problem of how the motions of various celestial bodies would appear to an inhabitant of the Moon, "who directly comprehends by his senses the proper motion of his dwelling place just as little as we inhabitants of the earth do that of ours."[3] Later on, his imagination, doubtlessly stimulated by Plutarch's *De Facie in Orbe Lunae*,[4] from time to time returned to the subject of the voyage to the Moon. Finally, during the pauses in the printing of the *Ephemerides* (which started in the beginning of 1630, the year of the astronomer's death), Kepler attended to the printing of his *Somnium*. The supervising of the printing was completed by Jacob Bartsch, Kepler's last student and his son-in-law. The work appeared in 1634.

Dreams had already a good position in the philosophical literature. At the end of Cicero's *Republic*, the story is told called *Somnium Scipionis*. In a dream Scipio Africanus Major carried Scipio Africanus Minor up to a height.

Scipio now noticed that the stars were globes which easily outstripped the Earth in size. Indeed the Earth now appeared so small in comparison that the Roman Empire, which was hardly more than a point on that tiny surface, excited his contempt.[5]

Somnium Scipionis was very influential in the Middle Ages, and the doctrine that medieval thinkers read out of it was the insignificance of the Earth as compared with cosmic standards.[6] The message of Kepler's *Dream* was different. Kepler wrote:

The purpose of my *Dream* is to use the example of the moon to build up an argument in favor of the motion of the earth, or rather to overcome objections from the universal opposition of mankind.[7]

Friendly spirits take the hero of the story to Levania (name given by Kepler to the Moon) and show him its inhabitants and its geography, but first of all the celestial phenomena observed from it.

Here [Kepler] attends to all the phenomena which are presented by the sun, the earth, the planets as regards their motions, their light and their sizes for the dwellers of the moon, both on the side turned toward us and on that turned away. The alternation of day and night, the length of periods of time, seasons, the alternation of heat and cold— all these he includes in his consideration.[8]

Numerous footnotes supplement the story with tedious calculations and details making out of it something more than a piece of literary art.

3. M. Caspar, *Kepler*, New York, 1959, 362.
4. *Plutarch's Moralia: Concerning the Face which Appears in the Orb of the Moon*, vol. XII, trans. H. Cherniss, Loeb Classical Library, London, 1957.
5. C. S. Lewis, *The Discarded Image*, Cambridge, 1988, 26.
6. Ibid., 23–28.   7. J. Kepler, *Somnium*, 36.
8. M. Caspar, *Kepler*, 364.

Kepler's conclusion is that "Levania seems to its inhabitants to remain just as motionless among the moving stars as does our earth to us humans."[9] The entire work should be regarded as supporting the Copernican theory "not only by putting the Earth in motion but also by regarding the moon as an Earth."[10]

The imaginary voyage of the Earthly observer to the Moon, in such a detailed way described by Kepler, triggered one of the most far-reaching processes in the history of human culture. Not only Western philosophy but also Western theology and its relationship to science will be strongly affected by this process. However, to understand its scope and its significance we must go back to the times when the Earth still occupied its central position in the Universe.

LAUGHTER FROM THE SPHERES

In describing the medieval (or pre-Copernican) image of the world, I will follow, albeit in a selective way, analyses of C. S. Lewis presented in his *The Discarded Image*. Although in the author's intention it is only "an introduction to medieval and Renaissance literature," one can learn more from it about the medieval cosmological views than from many professional textbooks of the subject. I will not be interested in cosmological speculations of philosophers and astronomers but in what is called by Lewis "the Model." "This is the medieval synthesis itself, the whole organisation of their theology, science, and history into a single, complex, harmonious mental Model of the Universe."[11] This Model is present in the works of art and literature rather than in philosophical or scientific treatises of those times. In every period, philosophical or scientific treatises help "to provide what we may call a backcloth for the arts." This backcloth is highly selective. It borrows from science and philosophy only those elements that seem to be intelligible to a layman and appeal to his imagination and emotion.

Thus our own backcloth contains plenty of Freud and little of Einstein. The medieval backcloth contains the order and influences of the planets, but not much about epicycles and eccentrics.[12]

Such a backcloth always has an enormous inertia; it dies more laboriously and more slowly than do scientific models.

C. S. Lewis considers the Model as an achievement to be set beside *Summa* of Aquinas and Dante's *Divine Comedy*. All three are supreme works of art in

9. J. Kepler, *Somnium*, 17.
10. S. J. Dick, *Plurality of Worlds*, Cambridge, 1984, 78.
11. C. S. Lewis, *The Discarded Image*, 11.
12. Ibid., 14.

which "we see the tranquil, indefatigable, exultant energy of passionately systematic minds bringing huge masses of heterogeneous material into unity."[13]

Of all three perhaps the Model was, in a sense, a central work—"that in
which most particular works were embedded, to which they constantly referred, from which they drew a great deal of their strength."[14]

There is no doubt that the Model was geocentric, but it was neither geometric nor anthropocentric. Alanus ab Insulis, in his *De Planctu Naturae*, expressed this clearly. He compared "the sum of things to a city. In the central
castle, in the Empyrean, the Emperor sits enthroned. In the lower heavens live
the angelic knighthood. We, on Earth, are 'outside the city wall.'"[15]

How, therefore, could the Model be geocentric?

Because, as Dante was to say more clearly than anyone else, the spatial order is the opposite of the spiritual, and the material cosmos mirrors, hence reverses, the reality, so
that what is truly the rim seems to us the hub.[16]

Chalcidius, the author of the *Commentarius* to Plato's *Timaeus* (widely read in
the Middle Ages), gave another unexpected answer to the question of why the
Earth is central: "It is so placed in order that the celestial dance may have a centre to revolve about—in fact, as an aesthetic convenience for the celestial beings."[17] "To be geocentric" in our present meaning implies spherical symmetry,
which is a geometric concept; in the medieval intuitions our central position in
the Universe was only indirectly related to geometry, and geometry decisively
broke down when it was incompatible with ascribing to the humanity a lower
place in the cosmic hierarchy. "The Medieval Model is, if we may use the word,
anthropoperipheral. We are creatures of the Margin."[18]

It is only from the perspective of distant centuries that the Copernican revolution looks like a degradation of man. For the medievals, man was never an
important element of the cosmic order. Lucan, a Roman author of the first
century (A.D. 34–56), in his *Pharsalia* describes how the soul of Pompey ascends
to the heavens. The ascension is similar to that of Scipio in Cicero's *Republic*.
When Pompey arrived "to the great frontier between air and aether . . . he
looked down and saw the mockeries done to his own corpse, which was having
a wretched and hugger-mugger funeral. They made him laugh."[19] This motive
reappears in the later literature: Boccacio uses it for the soul of Arcita, and
Chaucer for the soul of Troilus. C. S. Lewis concludes:

13. Ibid., 10.   14. Ibid., 12.
15. Ibid., 58.   16. Ibid., 58.
17. Ibid., 55.   18. Ibid., 58.
19. Ibid., 32–33.

I think that all three ghosts—Pompey's, Arcita's, and Troilus'—laughed for the same reason, laughed at the littleness of all those things that had seemed so important before they died; as we laugh, on waking, at the trifles or absurdities that loomed so large in our dreams.[20]

The medieval Model was "anthropoperipheral." Insignificance of man was, from the very beginning, built into its architectonic design, but—strangely enough—it was made almost entirely of anthropomorphic elements. The main stuff out of which the Model was composed consisted of elements of human imagination.[21] Even if this imagination sometimes worked in a seemingly geometric framework (the center of the world, celestial spheres, etc.), it violated—with no hesitation—all geometric standards if they did not fit the imaginative scheme. The main methodological rules according to which the Model was devised were rules of esthetics. The perfection principle, inherited from Platonic and Neoplatonic philosophy but strongly rearranged by the Christian sense of beauty and moral righteousness, dominated the entire edifice, leaving no place for the principle of simplicity that later on had to play so important a role in modern science. The tendency to order and classify everything could be thought of as only a feeble shadow of future mathematical modeling of natural phenomena. Our laws of nature were anticipated by various "sympathies, antipathies, and strivings inherent in matter itself."[22] Of course, the Model was supposed, by its creators and its users, to be coherent, but a suitably trained imagination was able to compose even contradictory elements into an apparently coherent whole (as we have seen, the humankind occupied a simultaneously central and peripheral position in the world). There was negligible empirical control over the Model and over consequences it could imply—just as there is no empirical control over a work of art. It is enough if it is beautiful, inspiring, or excites metaphysical emotions. The medieval Model of the world fulfilled all these functions. And even more—it was a *locus theologicus* of those times, in the following sense:

To all historians of ideas Whitehead once gave an ingenious advice:
    When you are criticizing the philosophy of an epoch, do not chiefly direct your attention to those intellectual positions which its exponents feel it necessary explicitly to

---

20. Ibid., 24.
21. One can speak of a "characteristically medieval type of imagination": "It is not a transforming imagination like Wordsworth's or a penetrative imagination like Shakespeare's. It is a realising imagination. Macaulay noted in Dante the extremely factual world-painting; the details, the comparisons, designed at whatever cost of dignity to make sure that we see exactly what he saw. Now Dante in this is typically medieval." Ibid., 206.
22. Ibid., 92.

defend. There will be some fundamental assumptions which adherents of all the variant systems within the epoch unconsciously presuppose. Such assumptions appear so obvious that people do not know what they are assuming because no other way of putting things has ever occurred to them. With these assumptions a certain limited number of types of philosophic systems are possible, and this group of systems constitutes the philosophy of the epoch.[23]

In this sense, the medieval Model, or at least some of its elements, constituted the "philosophy of the epoch." As a background conceptual system, it was also omnipresent in the medieval theology. A separate study would be needed to show its all-penetrating, and consequently not easily detectable, action.[24] Even the great theological plan preserved in almost all theological treatises of the Middle Ages (God—Creation—Redemption—Sacraments—Eschatology) reflects a cosmic order into which the "economy of salvation" is harmoniously inscribed.

There were two main sources of the medieval Model—Greek philosophy and Christian faith—just in this order: first the pagan philosophy and then the religious belief. Elements of the first, very selectively inherited from Antiquity, were a backbone of the Model; elements of the second provided a normative framework rather than a stuff out of which the Model was constructed. The Greek philosophy reached the Middle Ages through a very casual selection of texts, often only pieces of the originals. A general collapse of culture, a great gap in the evolutionary chain of development during the dark centuries separating Antiquity from the Middle Ages, created a great reverence for any scrap of written material. Let us once more quote C. S. Lewis:

If, under these conditions, one has also a great reluctance flatly to disbelieve anything in a book, then here there is obviously both an urgent need and a glorious opportunity for sorting out and tidying up. All the apparent contradictions must be harmonised. A Model must be built which will get everything in without a clash; and it can do this only by becoming intricate, by mediating its unity through a great, and finely ordered multiplicity.[25]

WITHOUT THINKING ABOUT THOUGHT

The Copernican revolution certainly struck a serious blow to the medieval Model. This is especially true if by the Copernican revolution we understand not only the work of Copernicus himself but also all these processes to which it gave a powerful momentum. To these processes belong:

23. A. N. Whitehead, *Science and the Modern World,* Collins-Fontana Books, 1975, 65.
24. Such a study has been undertaken by N. M. Wildiers, *Weltbild und Theologie vom Mittelalter bis Heute,* Zürich, Einsiedeln, Köln, 1974; especially Part I.
25. C. S. Lewis, *The Discarded Image,* 11.

(1) unification of the "earthly physics" and the "physics of heavens,"
(2) dehierarchization of the Universe,
(3) geometrization and infinitization of space,
(4) mathematization of science,
(5) its mechanization, and
(6) increasing of the role of controlled experimentation in science.

All these processes were many times subject to a thorough analysis[26] and there is no need to repeat it here. Let us notice that to these six major processes I have not included the one commonly attributed to the Copernican revolution, namely, depriving the humankind of its privileged central position in the Universe. As we have seen, people of the Middle Ages did not attach a great significance to the central position of the Earth, and before the geometrization of space had been completed, such a position could be understood in manifold (also metaphorical) ways. Of course, I do not deny that the realization that the Earth had been degraded to the role of an average planet had enormous impact on the imagination of people, but this came much later as a result of all the above-enumerated processes. And this was but a part of a more complicated pattern of radically changing man's relationship to science and the Universe.

I am inclined to ascribe a predominant role in this pattern to the mathematization of science. The process itself was by no means a new one. For a long time it was present in astronomy; it created an Archimedean tradition in the so-called classical sciences (optics, acoustics, statics). In Antiquity and in the Middle Ages it was paralleled and often dominated by a mystical approach to numbers and to mathematics in general. The intensification of this attitude in the fifteenth century could be regarded as a presentiment of what had to come. In the works of Galileo and Newton a method of a dialogue with nature in the language of mathematics was finally established. Again, there is a host of fine analyses of this phenomenon, and I will not try to summarize them here. I want only to stress some of its features directly connected with the present topic.

Experimentation with nature and the mathematical method of constructing models of natural phenomena not only began to eliminate the anthropomorphic approach to the world but also turned out to be possible owing to the gradual elimination of the "cognizing subject" from the scientific method. It is not only that "nature can be thought of as a closed system whose mutual

---

26. Some aspects of these analyses I have presented in the paper "Anthropic Ideology Throughout the Ages," in *Historia et Theoria Scientiarum*, 2 (1992) 54–76.

relations do not require the expression of the fact that they are thought about."[27] The point is that the precondition for the success of the modern scientific method was that Galileo and Newton had "to think about nature without thinking about thought."[28] I do not claim that the mathematical-empirical method will never be able to think about its own thinking about nature. In fact, there are symptoms that this begins to be the case. Gödel's theorems in metamathematics seem to imply that thinking about our mathematical inquiries is an important limiting factor, and some interpretations of quantum mechanics pretend that thinking about quantum processes is indispensable for them to be measurable. I insist only on saying that the elimination of the "conscious subject" from the scientific method was a precondition for the *classical* science. Taking into account all subtleties of the functioning of the Universe was simply too difficult (both in fact and in principle) for the young science to deal with. Simplifications, idealizations, and step-by-step approximations are sine qua non conditions of the scientific method, and at first stages of its development these conditions had to be very restrictive. Elimination of man was but a part of the idealization strategy being a crucially important component of the scientific method. It is a source of constant astonishment that the strategy of idealizations, even such a crude one as getting rid of the thought that the world is being thought about, works, and works so efficiently. However, it does, and it is, so to speak, an empirically corroborated fact.

I think that it is not Galileo or Newton but Descartes who, as a symbolic personage of this process, stands at the crossroads. His strict dichotomy—"extended matter" for physics and "conscious substance" for philosophy—did not create modern physics, but it did separate modern philosophy from physics to come.

It is interesting to notice that with this "elimination of man" from the scientific method, another important process coincides, namely, that of "arithmetization" of human life by a clock-measured time. With the invention of the mechanical clock, "time was no longer associated just with cataclysms and festivals but rather with everyday life."[29] The process had begun within the mercantile class, but it soon spread among other strata of the society. As put by Lewis Mumford:

Time-keeping passed into time-saving and time-accounting and time rationing. As this took place, Eternity gradually ceased to serve as measure and focus of human actions.[30]

27. A. N. Whitehead, *The Concept of Nature,* Cambridge, 1971, 3.
28. Ibid.
29. G. J. Whitrow, *Time in History,* Oxford, 1988, 110.
30. After Whitrow, ibid.

The timeless medieval world with everything (human beings included) at the assigned place irreversibly vanished. Personal existence began to be regarded "as being essentially based on the present moment."[31]

Husserl[32] accused the classical science of "treason of the human cause." I do not think he was right. One cannot blame a train that it does not fly; flying is not its business. However, Husserl's objections might be regarded as justified as far as they reflect a dangerous split the successes of modern science have made in the consciousness of many modern people.

STRANGENESS AT THE CROSSROADS

One of the main symptoms of this split was a separation of the ways of science from those of religion. The medieval synthesis seemed to be irreversibly lost. I will come back to some external or "institutional" aspects of this separation in Chapter 6. I would like now to focus on a heart of the matter.

In the previous section I turned the attention of my reader to an "elimination of a human subject" from the scientific method. Some philosophers (including Husserl) claim that when analyzing the scientific method one must ultimately take into account the fact that, after all, this method is actually executed by human individuals and that everything in the sciences is basically dependent on our sensory perceptions. In a sense, this is trivially true. (However, in a sense only, because what if we ask which are the sensory data in a modern accelerator experiment giving a long series of numbers on its computer outputs?) If we want to go beyond trivial statements, we must say that there are neither sensory perceptions nor personal convictions that really count, but *interindividual* (or *intersubjective*) exchanges of information. Doing science is perhaps the only human activity that has succeeded in developing such a high degree of practically identical understanding of scientific theories and methods by people of a very different cultural background. The key feature of this "practically identical understanding" is that it does not require (moreover, it is not concerned with) having a similar insight into a given theory or method; its essence consists in enabling people a fruitful cooperation and contributing to a common stock of results.

On the other hand, religion, from its very meaning *(religare)*, is an intimate nexus between an individual and God. I do not want to imply that religion has no social or institutional aspects; it certainly has, and they seem indispensable for its full authenticity, but they become empty and senseless with no reference

31. Ibid., 170.
32. In his *Die Krisis der europäischen Wissenschaften und die transzendentale Phänomenologie*, Hamburg, 1982.

to this basically individual *nexus*. Moreover, religion is an answer to the existential problems of man, and these problems are always intimately individual; they do not primarily concern any information exchange between people, but a "drama of existence" that always engages the deepest layers of the human personality.

This contrast between the interindividual character of science and the fundamentally individual character of religion has introduced a "strangeness" between science and religion. A strangeness could be more disastrous than open hostility. A strange thing very often means a contemptible thing. I think this is one of the main reasons for the split between ways of science and ways of religion in modern times.

In the Middle Ages a real conflict between religion and the image of the world was a priori excluded, because the image of the world had been constructed with the aim to provide a background for both the religious doctrine and the existential drama of man. The human drama inscribed into the cosmic architecture of the Model remained in harmony with the universal design.

In the world dominated by the modern sciences, a conflict between science and religion was potentially present from the very beginning; by eliminating the human existential problems from the domain controlled by the scientific method, these problems were sentenced to insignificance.

The fact, very often alluded to by historians of science and historians of theology, that the medieval image of the world had so strictly coalesced with Christian theology that the collapse of the former seemed to denote the collapse of the latter, is but a secondary effect. The old image of the world acquired an enormous "theological inertia," for the new image was able to offer only strangeness when a synthesis was looked for. One had to wait more than two centuries, until philosophical reflection on the scientific method was mature enough, to comprehend that methodological differences need not be equivalent to mutual exclusion, and that a respect of competence combined with tolerance could be better than premature syntheses.

However, before this happened, new philosophical interpretations, substitutes of a synthesis, accumulated around science. After a relatively short period of the so-called *physico-theology*—which on the one hand can be thought of as a posthumous child of the medieval synthesis and, on the other hand, as an expression of a religious fascination with new scientific achievements—positivistic, materialistic, and finally atheistic interpretations took over. All these interpretations created an atmosphere in which the worship of God was gradually replaced by the worship of man. One could risk a statement that the medieval world was anthropoperipheral but anthropomorphic, whereas the mod-

ern world, proud of its freedom of anthropomorphic elements, was transformed into an anthropocentric structure. Man has become its quasi-absolute
value.

COSMOTHEOROS

In the last decades of the seventeenth century, the possibility of intelligent
life on other planets excited public interest. A treatise, *The Plurality of Worlds*,
written by Bernard le Bovier de Fontenelle[33] and published in 1686, gained
enormous publicity and became a first best-seller popularizing the new science
(in fact, more Cartesian than the Newtonian one). Only a little less popular
was a treatise written by Christiaan Huygens bearing the title *Cosmotheoros or
Conjectures concerning the Celestial Earths and their Adornments (Kosmotheoros, sive,
de terris coelestibus earumque ornatu conjecturae)*.[34] I think the work by Huygens
closes, in a sense, a period opened by Kepler's *Dream* or, better, these two
works form a kind of parentheses comprising a process that in the meantime
has reached a certain maturity. Both works were published posthumously, and
both could be thought of as comments to purely scientific accomplishments of
their authors. Kepler had undertaken his journey to the Moon "to build up an
argument in favor of the motion of the Earth."[35] Huygens, the other way
round, used the Copernican theory to render a similarity more probable between other planets and our Earth. Other planets must have a vegetation and
animals because without them "we should think them below the earth in
beauty and dignity; a thing that no reason will permit." Huygens' method of
reasoning is always the same and is best expressed in the following sentence:
"From the nature and circumstances of that planet which we see before our
eyes, we may guess at those that are further distant from us."

Huygens criticized Kepler's story about the Moon's inhabitants, "but he
carried out for the planets much the same program that Kepler had for the
moon."[36] He described astronomical phenomena in a detailed way as they are
seen from each of the planets (Jupiter with its many moons and Saturn with
its spectacular rings provided Huygens with especially rich possibilities).

Kepler was yet unable to forget the old medieval cosmic harmony. Although he destroyed perfect circular orbits of the planets, he tried to replace

33. B. le Bovier de Fontenelle, *Entretiens sur la pluralitée des mondes*, ed. Alexandre Calame,
Paris, 1966.
34. All quotations in this section come from the English translation: *The Celestial Worlds Discover'd: or, Conjectures concerning the Inhabitants, Plants and Productions of the Worlds in the Planets*,
London, 1698 (Facsimile reprint, London, 1968).
35. J. Kepler, *Somnium*, 36.
36. S. J. Dick, *Plurality of Worlds*, 130.

them with symmetries of Euclid's regular solids into which the planetary orbits could be inscribed or onto which they could be circumscribed. Under Huygens' pen the old world was annihilated completely. The cosmographical mystery of Kepler "is nothing but an idle dream taken from Pythagoras or Plato's philosophy." To replace this "private design" Huygens proposes another picture:

What a wonderful and amazing scheme have we here of the magnificent vastness of the universe! So many suns, so many earths, and every one of them stocked with so many herbs, trees and animals, and adorned with so many seas and mountains!

And what about ourselves, our planet, our Sun? The new picture of the world compels Huygens to conclude "that our star has no better attendance than the others." Here we have the modern cosmological principle stated for the first time in its full. We occupy an average place in the Universe. This will be a paradigmatic statement for about three hundred years to come; it will remain unchallenged until the stronger versions of the present anthropic principle. In the medieval Model we were creatures of the margin, acquiring all our significance from the Spiritual Center of Everything; in the modern world we are just average, and being average we have no hope for anything else anywhere in an infinite vastness of average places. We have made the modern world in our own image and similitude.

6 SCIENTIFIC RATIONALITY AND CHRISTIAN LOGOS

INTRODUCTION

The empirical sciences constitute a specific type of rationality. For many people it is the only admissible type, or at least a kind of ideal model that should be imitated by other species of rational knowledge as far as it is possible. However, the evolutionary line that has led to this type of rationality has been woven from two threads (strongly interacting with each other), one of which goes back to Greek philosophy, and the other one to the Christian doctrine of creation. Theological reflections on creation, especially in the Middle Ages, stressed the contingency of the world. Because the architecture of the world is entirely dependent on God's will, it cannot be discovered a priori by any kind of speculative thinking. This opened the way to the empirical investigation of nature. If modern science and Christian theology have their roots so strongly interacting, the split between them in modern times might seem to be an unexpected surprise. But in fact it was well established by the events and processes of history.

In this chapter I will argue that, in spite of all the differences and conflicts, the deep philosophical affinity between the scientific spirit of rationality and the Christian approach to the created world still exists and still continues to exercise its influence on the very foundations of scientific thinking. Rationality is a value, and the choice of this value (on which all science is based) is a moral one. Without a religious attitude toward the world and toward science (so often emphasized by Einstein), such a choice is reduced to a blind game of purely conventional preferences. From the theological perspective, there is an intimate relationship between the spirit of rationality and the Christian idea of the Logos. The philosophy of science discovers that all science is based on the assumption of rationality, and it completes its analyses by elaborating the consequences of that discovery. It is here that a theology of science should take over.

In section 2, I will examine the Greek roots of scientific rationality. Section 3 elucidates the role of Christian theology in shaping Western ways of looking at nature. The split between the world of science and the world of Christian thought that took place in modern times is briefly considered in section 4. Starting from section 5, I move from the historical perspective to analyze the present situation touching on some key methodological aspects of the problem. My central thesis on the relationship between scientific rationality and the Christian Logos is discussed in section 6.

FAITH IN REASON

One of the essential tenets of scientific rationality is the deep conviction that nothing should be accepted without sufficient proof or argument. But what kind of proof or argument should be admitted? This is a secondary, although extremely important, question. In actual scientific practice, it is answered by the method of trial and error rather than by any a priori prescription.

However, independent of what one assumes as a sufficient proof or argument, no proof or argument can be given to validate the claim that one should direct one's thinking with the help of *any* proofs or arguments, that is to say, that one should be rational. Any proof or argument in favor of this claim tacitly assumes that one wants to be rational. The decision to be rational is, therefore, a choice.

Rationality is undoubtedly a value. This becomes manifest as soon as one confronts rationality with its opposite, irrationality. We instinctively treat irrationality as something degrading and almost inhuman. Some philosophers would say that to be rational follows from human nature, from the very fact that we are equipped with the faculty of thinking and choosing: If rationality is a value, then the decision to be rational is a *moral* choice.

Freedom is a part of that morality which constitutes the rational attitude of man toward the Universe. The only admissible force is that of proof or argument. Any view imposed by external coercion is irrational, because it is imposed and not inferred from evidence. It seems also that an internal freedom is presupposed by rationality; without being free to choose between possible paths of reasoning, the process of constructing any proof or argument could hardly be imagined.[1]

It was Karl Popper who saw this in a very clear light. He wrote: "The choice

1. S. W. Hawking and G. F. R. Ellis, speaking of free will, note: "This is not something which can be dropped lightly since the whole of our philosophy of science is based on the assumption that one is free to perform any experiment." *The Large Scale Structure of Space-Time,* Cambridge: Cambridge University Press, 1973, 189.

before us is not simply an intellectual affair, or a matter of taste. It is a moral decision." Moreover, "it is, in many senses, the most fundamental decision in the ethical field." Because it cannot be argued for or demonstrated, Popper calls it "the faith in reason."[2]

This moral choice gradually matured in the evolution of Western thinking. The adherence to the empirical method of investigating the world may be thought of as a final step in this process. All the successes of this method can be considered as arguments revealing the correctness of that choice. However, this does not change the fact that the empirical method cannot prove itself, and that it still remains a moral choice.

The history of science is nothing else than an attempt to reconstruct, in all its shades and details, the maturation of this choice, its victories and its defeats—in a word, our struggle to develop the astonishing capability of being rational.

There is no doubt that at the beginning of this process lies the discovery of the ancient Greeks that it is worthwhile to ask the world difficult questions and search for answers with no help from outside. The analysis of this event is too well known to be repeated here. I would like only to stress its extraordinary character. We have challenged the reality that surrounds us and that is inside us. We have decided to understand this reality, and we have presumed that this can be done. With no help, either from the gods or from some hidden forces, we have stood alone against the silent Universe.

The Greek type of rationality is, first of all, an ethos of thinking. Any thesis has to be clearly stated and must be argued for. This is a well-defined process of thought, and not just any process. It ought to proceed in agreement with the rules of rationality. It is no wonder that the Greeks put a lot of effort and ingenuity into codifying these rules. Greek logic was by no means just a set of technical details appended to Greek philosophy; it was its moral code.

This part of the scheme of rationality should be considered as perhaps the greatest achievement of the Greeks. The geometric system of Euclid, discussed and improved through the centuries, has finally led to modern axiomatic systems that can be thought of as expressing the spirit of rationality, freed of any "matter." It tells us how to deduce one truth (expressed in a set of propositions) from another truth in an absolute and reliable manner. Although, from time to time, some philosophers try to proceed on their own, by discarding the rules of logic they will certainly be relegated to the marginal ar-

2. K. Popper, *The Open Society and Its Enemies,* vol. 2, London: Routledge and Kegan Paul, 1974, 232–233.

eas of the history of philosophy, in spite of a possible short-lived fascination with their originality.

Axiomatic systems are "freed of matter": they are not yet the process of thinking. They constitute a structure that has to be filled with "matter," that is, with the content of thought. The structure is filled in with this content through assumptions or axioms from which the chain of logical deductions begins. Here the Greeks had serious problems—the more so, for they were not aware of their problems' existence. They highly esteemed thinking itself and instinctively believed that it was the process of thinking that should establish the starting point of deduction. However, if thinking is to be correct, it has to be governed by the rules of logic. The only way out of this vicious circle was for the Greeks to appeal to self-evidence. But it was the self-evidence of thinking rather than of observation. Usually, our eyes see what thinking orders them to see (or, to be more strict, we try to interpret data in accordance with what the brain has previously registered). Thinking, on the other hand, is usually entangled in the language that is supposed to express it. No wonder that Greek philosophies were based on analyses of common language; and because common language is strictly connected with everyday life, some Greek philosophers (e.g., Aristotle) believed that their philosophies were based on experiment. It was true at least to a certain extent. We should remember, though, that we cannot impose on the Greeks our concepts of experiment and experimentation. With only a few exceptions (Archimedes was the most eminent one), the difference between scientific experimentation and everyday experience was for the Greeks rather loose and ill-defined.

The ethics of thinking, which the Greeks succeeded in imposing upon all antiquity, was also their aesthetics of thinking. Rules of thinking are simultaneously rules of beauty: the discipline of form, the harmony of deductive movement, the proportion of structure. In Plato's dialogues or Lucretius' hexameters, the literary framework of thought is almost as important as the thought itself; but even Aristotle's coarse phrases are beautiful, for an imposing edifice is being constructed out of them, as if of heavy pieces of granite.

FROM THEOLOGY TO SCIENCE

Christianity appeared within the evolutionary chain of Jewish thinking. However, it was not the Old Testament mentality that shaped the intellectual form of the new religion. The Greek type of rationality, not especially caring about experimental details and always hastening to comprehensive syntheses, seemed to provide a suitable background for theological speculations.

Could transcendence be put into syllogisms? Application of the Greek pattern of rationality to theological questions had, sooner or later, to produce scholasticism. The truth concerning God and God's activity could hardly be expected to appear at the end of long chains of distinctions and exclusions, but such a method of doing theology constituted an excellent exercise in applying logic. Owing to medieval theology, Europe has learned a great deal of the Greek ethics of thinking.

Logical thinking is more secure if it is defended against extralogical influences. It is rote manipulation with symbols that replaces the psychology of thinking and eliminates the possibility of error in the process of inferring logical consequences from their assumptions. Medieval thinkers excelled in inventing subtle formalisms. It seems that they stressed the mnemotechnical aspects of symbols too much. Perhaps they aimed at problems that were too difficult. The fact is that their formalisms were not efficient enough. It was art for art's sake, rather than as a tool for solving real problems.

Mathematics is very close to logic. In both disciplines the rules are practically the same. From the historical point of view, if logical chains began with something that could be expressed in numbers (that could be measured), logic was considered to be mathematics. For a long time mathematics served astronomy well. Without mathematics there would have been no astronomy. The heavens, when contemplated in the light of first principles, remain dark and silent. They speak only when addressed in the language of numbers. As soon as measurement began to enter the philosophy of nature (faintheartedly in the beginning, but gradually with more and more self-confidence), it was transformed into the modern natural sciences, with the role of logic replaced by that of mathematics. Progress in mathematics soon became an integral aspect of the evolution of science.

However, the role of Christianity in the origin of modern science cannot be reduced to sharpening and transmitting the Greek heritage to our times. Many historians of science agree that Christianity added to this heritage something substantial, something that doubtlessly contributed to the fostering of the empirical method. It is no surprise that this new element was supplied by the Christian teaching on the creation of the world.

Medieval interpretations of the doctrine of creation almost unanimously agreed that the existence of the Universe should be considered an effect of the free will of the Creator. This free decree of the divine will concerned both the world's existence (the world did not have to be created) and the plan of creation (the world's architecture could have been very different from what we actually observe). The world bears the trait of contingency in both its existence and in its structure. This last point is of great significance. The structure of the world cannot be deduced from self-evident, or otherwise a priori, premises. The only way leading one to knowledge of the world is to open one's eyes and see what can be seen of the world. In other words, one has to experiment with the world.

Does this mean abandoning the Greek conviction about the world's rationality? Not at all. The structure of the universe is the implementation of God's creative plan, and this plan is fundamentally rational. However, its rationality transcends the possibilities of the human mind to such a degree that it cannot be deduced from self-evident axioms. The only realistic strategy is the empirical method. One must start experimenting with nature and only then try to fit theoretical structures to the results of this experimentation. If the theoretical structures lead to conclusions that turn out to be in agreement with the results of other experiments, there is a good probability that these structures approximate the structure that constituted God's plan of creation.

If Christianity played such an important role in paving the way for the experimental sciences, one might expect that the origin of the sciences would initiate a period of symbiosis between scientific and religious thinking. This was not the case. The succeeding age was marked with conflict, not with harmonious coexistence.

TWO STREAMS OF KNOWLEDGE

What was the cause of these dramatic conflicts? There are many studies on this subject. My working hypothesis is that it was the institutionalization of the Church's teaching that was one of the main factors responsible for splitting the way of the Church from the way of science. Traditional structures had reached such a high degree of specialization that they were unable to adapt themselves to new conditions. By institutionalization I mean not only a subordination of philosophy and theology to Church authorities, but also what may be called an "invisible college" (to use a well-known expression in a slightly different context); that is, ways of thinking elaborated by long tradition, a balancing of influences among different schools and systems, consolidated methods of collecting and transmitting information, unwritten codes of behavior for people involved in the ways of knowing. The sciences were born in an entirely new situation no longer controlled by Church authorities. From the very beginning they started to create their own "invisible college." Conflicts were unavoidable.

The conflicts abounded with drama. Incessant series of successes by the new sciences generated totalitarian tendencies. Church thinkers found themselves on the defensive and responded by triggering mechanisms of isolation.

Two circumstances favored this process: first, the great inertia of institutional-ized structures in collecting and transmitting knowledge (mentioned above); and, second, the extreme specialization of the new sciences. The point is that the understanding of scientific theories (let alone creative work in science) re-quires protracted studies and great intellectual effort. Proper assessment of sci-entific theories by an outsider is practically impossible. On the other hand, sci-ence is democratic, in the sense that everybody has the right to participate, with the condition, however, that a budding scientist would devote enough ef-fort and time to acquire the necessary skills and knowledge. In this way theolo-gians and philosophers of the epoch, busy with their own problems, found themselves somewhat excluded from the possibility of a competent dialogue with the empirical and mathematical sciences, always accelerating in their progress and specialization.

In the long run, this separation and isolation turned out to have important consequences. The stream of knowledge split into two branches. In each of them progress went on independent of the other. Within the empirical sci-ences it quickly developed into a chain reaction. Technology, as the natural continuation of the sciences, began to change both social and individual lives. Some totalitarian and positivistic tendencies in the sciences became promi-nent, and theology in the eighteenth and nineteenth centuries had its own ups and downs. The exaggerations of scholasticism contributed to theology's questionable reputation. Neoscholasticism and neothomism should be consid-ered as attempts to exit from this impasse. One must admit that they were par-tially successful, but only within the Church's stream of knowledge, with neg-ligible effects as far as dialogue with the empirical sciences was concerned. The impact of neothomism on people engaged in doing science was confined to conversions. These are still occurring, but much less frequently. Some scien-tists were converted to metaphysics, but it usually had almost no effect on ei-ther the sciences themselves or the milieu of a given scientist.

Progress requires a certain continuity, and there is no continuity of knowl-edge without education. No wonder, then, that both the scientific and the ecclesiastical streams of knowledge have developed their own educational sys-tems, surprisingly different and independent of each other. Many contempo-rary Roman Catholic universities have excellent departments of mathematics, physics, biology, and so forth, and, of course, their own philosophy and theolo-gy faculties. I know of a very few examples of interaction between them. Usu-ally, two independent streams of knowledge flow through the same university campus.

WHAT SHOULD BE DONE?

Here I stop my analysis. It is not my goal to go into details of the present relations between the Church and the world of science. There are many good accounts of these questions and the interested reader should refer to them. Everything I have said so far was intended as an introduction to the question, What should be done in order to improve these relations?

A possible answer could be, Nothing should be done. Both science and the Church benefit from the separation. Philosophy of science has taught scientists to respect the limits of the scientific method. Outside these limits there is ample room for philosophical or even religious belief. On the other hand, the Church has learned not to interfere in the internal affairs of the sciences. The Church is expected, from time to time, to stress the value of science as a human endeavor. If this *savoir vivre* is preserved, there will be no conflicts and perhaps even some mutual appreciation.

I am not quite happy with this solution—if it is a solution at all. An agreement of noninterference proves to be sometimes necessary and is a temporarily efficient means of resolving conflicts. The point is, however, that in the present situation the conflict-frontier cuts through the interior of the human person (especially of the person who believes and also does science). The human personality cannot be split into different zones of influence.

The other extreme would be equally dangerous. Differences in aims, languages, and methods, well-established limits of competence, and full respect for the different nature of the other side should always be kept in mind and never trespassed. The answer to the question, "What should be done?" can be reached only under the condition that these methodological differences are strictly respected. There can be no return to the period when theology and the sciences seemed to constitute the same field of human activity. Methodological anarchy solves nothing. The answer should be sought by respecting the individuality and integrity of both the sciences and religion.

THE CHRISTIAN LOGOS

Why should we do science rather than engage in some other sort of intuitional creativity? How is an appeal to emotion and intuition worse, as far as our cognitive relations with the world are concerned, than an appeal to reason? In the name of which ideals should we prefer "the awareness of our limitations, the intellectual modesty of those who know how often they err"[3] to a confidence in human nature that simply knows what is good and what is bad?

3. Ibid., 227.

As we have seen, there are no rational motives compelling us to choose between these two possible options. Rationality is a moral choice. But to choose without any motives whatsoever is heroic, and to be heroic day after day is very hard. No wonder, therefore, that the "spirit of rationality" becomes tired from time to time and gives way to different forms of irrationality. This is what happens nowadays. "The conflict between rationalism and irrationalism has become the most important intellectual, and perhaps even moral, issue of our time."[4]

The moral choice for rationality could be, after all, based on an illusion. A mortal game in which losers become fools and winners are declared wise—a struggle for power, in fact—is what science really means in the eyes of many. The degradation of the natural environment and the prospect of atomic annihilation are only external symptoms of a much deeper crisis. If the choice of rationality is not a choice of value but only part of a blind game with nature, it is ultimately an immoral choice. In that case it is fundamentally my own choice that matters. I could have chosen differently. I become a final criterion of my choice; it is up to me to decide how to use the technological achievements of science. With no moral norms besides myself, I may use them to further my own egoistic goals.

It was Einstein who asked the question, "Why is the world comprehensible?" Why? Einstein was not able to answer the question; he could say only, "The eternal mystery of the world is its comprehensibility. . . . The fact that it is comprehensible is a miracle."[5] The question ends with astonishment. The philosophy of science can do nothing more. It is the theology of science that has to take over and go deeper in seeking the answer to this question.

In light of Christian theology, the choice of the rational method in science is not an unrestricted choice. It is, of course, the doctrine of the creation of the world that is responsible for this constraint. The world is a realization of the rational plan of the Creator; and there is no other way of unraveling the structure of the world except through rational attempts to decipher God's plan. Let us focus on this point for a moment.

The world is for me impregnated with meaning.[6] There are various objects such as a table or a star. I need the table; I can eat or write on it. I also need the star; it can be a source of inspiration for me or an object of intensive study. Both the table and the star constitute values for me.

Only something that has a meaning can be a value, and something can

4. Ibid., 224.

5. A. Einstein, *Ideas and Opinions,* New York: Dell, 1978, 285.

6. The following passage is taken from my book *The Justification of the World,* Cracow: Znak, 1984, 94–96, in Polish.

have meaning only for somebody. A table is but a set of physical fields and particles. It becomes the table for somebody who enters into a cognitive nexus with it and identifies it as a table.

The environment of meanings and values is even more important for us than air or food. Without air and food we must die; without an environment of meaning and values we would not even be human.

Once the world, through a long process of evolution, gave birth to human beings, it ceased to be as it had been before. Through human beings the world has been filled with meaning and entered into a complicated fabric of values we have woven out of our ability to think and to will. The process of knowing the world is itself a great value for us. Because it is a value, we want to know what the world would be like without our value-creating presence. To attain this goal we have elaborated an empirical method for investigating the world that consciously prescinds from value and meaning. This strategy is very difficult to implement. Science cannot avoid using human language, which by its very nature is full of anthropomorphic meanings and values. To minimize this, the empirical sciences adopt, as much as possible, the language of mathematics. Although this language is man-made, it has been created in such a clever manner that its only content is its form. Once the form of this language has been established, we no longer have any power over it.

The world of physics, of astronomy, and of biology is maximally dehumanized. It is true that nowadays we reappear in this world as observers, and through our interpretive activities we influence the investigated object (especially, e.g., in quantum physics). However, we are observers who measure (i.e., translate what we see into numbers), restraining ourselves from any act of evaluation. Silence about values is the price paid for the efficacy of the scientific method. As a result, in the minds of many thinkers, an image of the world devoid of any value has been established.

In the light of the Christian doctrine of creation, this is simply not true. Without human beings the world would have no "human-made" meaning and value, but we are not even the principal creators of meanings and values. The structure of the world is a realization of God's plan and, as such, is totally impregnated with Meaning and Value. Capital letters are intended here to remind us that the words "Meaning" and "Value" are powerless to express the full significance of God's plan. To use Plato's metaphor, meanings and values created by us are only shadows of That Meaning and That Value. "The Word (Logos) was with God. Through Him God made all things; not one thing in all creation was made without Him."[7] And not only that: "the Logos was made flesh."[8] The

---

7. John 1:1–3.   8. John 1:14.

doctrine of the incarnation of the Logos certainly has its theological significance as far as the relationship between humankind and rationality is concerned. The Logos made flesh is a profound theological reality, far from being completely explored by theologians, and in the present context opens new vistas for reflection.[9]

All science is based on the spirit of rationality. To follow this spirit was a choice of humanity. Was this a moral choice or just a blind game with values? The answer given by religion to this question should not be seen simply as a service that faith can render science. It is immensely more than that. My metaphysical hypothesis is that the spirit of rationality participates in the Christian Logos. In the course of human history, the Logos assumed the flesh of scientific rationality. The theological perspective allows us to understand this not only as a literary metaphor. "That Christ is the Logos implies that God's immanence in the world is its rationality."[10]

Only by living in a world of Value and Meaning is it truly worth taking up science.[11]

9. I am grateful to Nicholas Lash for turning my attention to this aspect of the problem.

10. This formulation I owe to Olaf Pedersen. It certainly deserves to be more fully elaborated.

11. See M. Heller, *The World and the Word—Between Science and Religion,* Tucson: Pachart, 1986, 175.

7 TEILHARD'S VISION OF THE WORLD AND MODERN COSMOLOGY

INTRODUCTION

In Teilhard de Chardin's vision of the world one can distinguish two layers. Although closely interwoven with each other, they are clearly visible. The first layer consists in a very specific interpretation of scientific data; the second layer, in a certain mysticism that gives a peculiar atmosphere to Teilhard's work. He was a biologist, and there is no doubt that his vision of the world borrowed its main features from biology. However, no global vision of the world, claiming to be based upon or oriented toward the sciences, can avoid taking information from physics in general, and from cosmology in particular.

To push anything back into the past [these are opening sentences of *The Phenomenon of Man*] is equivalent to reducing it to its simplest elements. Traced as far as possible in the direction of their origins, the last fibers of the human aggregate are lost to view and are merged in our eyes with the very stuff of the Universe.[1]

To deal with "the stuff of the Universe" is, in Teilhard's opinion, the task of physics and cosmology.

The importance of the physical ingredient of Teilhard de Chardin's vision of the world is obvious. In fact, the entire first part of *PhM* is devoted to contemplating the past of the Universe "as it must appear to an observer standing on the advanced peak where evolution has placed us."[2] Since Teilhard's times this peak has grown higher, and today we see better the details of the world's history. It would be of great interest to compare critically our present understanding of the physical world with that which has entered Teilhard's way of seeing. This is precisely the aim of the present chapter.

To make this goal practicable I will focus on *PhM,* only occasionally referring to other writings of Teilhard.

---

1. T. de Chardin, *Le Phénomène Humain,* trans. B. Wall, London: Collins-Fontana Books, 1974, 43. In the following I abbreviate the title of this book to *PhM*.
2. Ibid., 39 (from the Foreword).

When reading *PhM* one can relatively easily trace Teilhard's information source concerning current cosmological ideas. The manuscript of *Le Phéno-mène Humain* was ready in 1938 (and first published in 1955); at that time the most elaborated cosmological theory was that of Georges Lemaître. By 1955 the steady-state cosmology was also on the market. Because, however, it pre-sented the stationary rather than the evolutionary Universe, it did not fit Teil-hard's scheme. No wonder, therefore, that Teilhard's knowledge of cosmology was based mainly on Lemaître's writings. In a footnote at the end of the first chapter of *PhM* one reads:

Nowadays, for various convergent reasons, notably Relativity combined with the cen-trifugal retreat of the galaxies, physicists prefer to turn to the idea of an *explosion* pul-verising a primitive quasi-atom within which space-time would be strangulated (in a sort of natural absolute zero) at only some milliards of years behind us.[3]

This is a clear echo of Lemaître's views on the primeval atom and its subse-quent decay ("pulverisation") that gave origin to the Universe and its present variety of forms. Teilhard also mentions an "unresolved simplicity" that is "at the very bottom" of things—typical elements of Lemaître's cosmology.[4] Le-maître's idea of the primeval atom, the simplest possible state of matter, initi-ating the evolution of the Universe certainly pleased Teilhard's aesthetic taste as dual with respect to his key concept of the maximum complexification state fulfilling the history of the Universe. If the latter is called Omega by Teilhard de Chardin, the former is sometimes referred to as Alpha.[5]

In this present chapter, I do not intend to trace vestiges of cosmological ideas spread in Teilhard's writings; my goal—I think—is more ambitious. Teil-hard's vision of the world is doubtlessly based on three views that he arrived at by reflecting on contemporary physics and cosmology. They are (1) the view on matter as a stuff of the Universe, (2) the view on evolution in time as a fun-damental feature of the Universe, and (3) the view on a special type of energy that is responsible for the complexification of the Universe. About a half of the century elapsed since Teilhard de Chardin had formulated his vision of the

3. *PhM*, 52, see also p. 328: "The astronomers have lately been making us familiar with the idea of a Universe which for the last few thousand million years has been expanding in galaxies from a sort of primordial atom."
4. Lemaître writes: "The best we can do is to call it [the initial state of the Universe] an Atom, rather in the Greek sense of the word than of this very complicated thing which is a modern atomic nucleus. . . . The beginning of cosmology is therefore expanding space starting from zero and filled up with the pieces of the Primaeval Atom, presumably small, more or less stable, atoms, such as these which are observed today in actual physics." "The Primaeval Atom Hypothesis and the Problem of the Clusters of Galaxies," in *La structure et l'évolution de l'univers*, Bruxelles: R. Stoops, 1958, 8.
5. See, for instance, *PhM*, 283.

world, and it seems reasonable to confront these three Teilhard's tenets with the recent developments in physics and cosmology. This is what I intend to do in the subsequent sections.

STUFF OF THE UNIVERSE

Teilhard's vision of the world starts with matter and ends with Spirit as two poles of the same reality. At the Alpha point, matter originates and through the growth of multiplicity and gradual complexification attains its final state at the point of Omega, where Spirit dominates and completes the evolution of the Universe. Teilhard de Chardin underwent a similar line of development in his personal life: from the early fascination with matter (iron, crystals, rocks), through the "cosmic sense" that apprehends separate things as elements of a wider whole, to the experience of a single all-embracing Form or Spirit, the final goal of the evolution.[6]

In the vision of the world presented in *PhM*, "the stuff of tangible things reveals itself with increasing insistence as radically particulate yet essentially related, and lastly, prodigiously active."[7] In the physicist's analysis, matter "tends to reduce itself into something yet more granulated" and is "in an unending state of disintegration as it goes downward."[8] In this process, "beyond a certain degree of depth and dilution," we lose the familiar properties of our macroscopic world: light, color, warmth, impenetrability, and so forth, and "indeed, our sensory experience turns out to be a floating condensation on a swarm of the indefinable."[9] Although matter itself, at its fundamental level, certainly is not a tangible thing, it is "the substratum of the tangible Universe."[10]

In spite of its "radically particulate" character, matter reveals its holistic aspects: "Considered in its physical, concrete reality, the stuff of the Universe cannot divide itself, but as a kind of gigantic 'atom,' it forms in its totality . . . the only real indivisible."[11]

Precisely, because of its holistic aspects, matter, as it reveals itself to Teilhard's intuition, is far from being an inert stuff of the mechanistic philosophy; "matter reveals itself to us *in a state of genesis* or becoming."[12] The process of *granulation* "gave birth to the constituents of the atom and perhaps to the atom itself."[13] The holistic aspect of matter does not consist in a repetition of the same pattern; different pieces of matter become a whole by the structural

---

6. See T. M. King, *Mysticism of Knowledge*, New York: The Seabury Press, 1981, ch. 1.

7. *PhM*, 44.   8. Ibid., 44–45.

9. Ibid., 45.   10. Ibid.

11. Ibid., 47.

12. Ibid., 53, italicized by Teilhard de Chardin.

13. Ibid.

interaction of everything with everything. This interaction is at the basis of the creative process of complexification, the key concept to understanding Teilhard's system (see below). In this sense, matter is "prodigiously active."

When reading Teilhard's writings one has a strong impression that the entire system was constructed by him to overcome the "temptation of matter." One should not forget that in Teilhard times positivistic and materialistic tendencies were much more alive in the sciences than they are nowadays (even now they are still quite strong in the biological sciences). The strategy chosen by Teilhard (the choice certainly being conditioned by his personal experience) consisted in affirming matter rather than "fighting it"—however, not as an independent absolute but as the other pole of spirit. Teilhard writes:

> The difficulties we still encounter in trying to hold together spirit and matter in a reasonable perspective are nowhere more harshly revealed. Nowhere is the need more urgent of building a bridge between the two banks of our existence—the physical and the moral—if we wish the material and spiritual sides of our activities to be mutually enlivened.[14]

This perspective should be kept in mind if we try to understand why Teilhard so strongly insisted on the "tangible" character of matter in spite of its "disappearance" on deeper levels of "granulation." Even if matter in itself is not a tangible thing, it is "the substratum of the tangible Universe."

To a contemporary theoretical physicist Teilhard's "temptation of matter" or his "involvement in matter" is something difficult to understand. The "stuff of the Universe" as seen through the eyes of modern physical theories has very little in common with the traditional concept of matter; it has become so abstract and so far away from the sensory perception that to many philosophizing physicists it looks more like a "pure form" than a substratum of what can be seen and touched. To elucidate this intuition I will not comment on the host of enunciations by outstanding physicists similar to that of John Barrow:

> We must recognize that "things" like photons and neutrons cannot be "real" in the same way that we think that chairs and tables are real. They are more like shadows: arising from a combination of light and the observer's situation.[15]

Neither will I develop Misner's idea that "the world's hardware is its software."[16] Instead, I will briefly present some results of the modern quantum

---

14. Ibid., 67–68.

15. J. Barrow, *The World Within the World*, Oxford: Clarendon Press, 1988, 150.

16. This is the main thesis of Charles Misner's paper *The Immaterial Constituents of Physical Objects*, delivered at the UNESCO Symposium in Munich, September 1978.

field theory relevant to our understanding of the concept of the "stuff of the Universe."

Quantum field theory is not only the most successful physical theory (its predictions concerning electron-photon interactions are correct to within one part in 10^8), but it is also the most adequate theory explaining three of the four fundamental physical interactions, namely, electromagnetic, nuclear weak, and nuclear strong interactions (it does not refer to gravity). It is more fundamental than the ordinary quantum mechanics because it is relativistic, and the ordinary quantum mechanics is to be recovered from it by a suitable limiting process (quantum field theory is essentially quantum mechanics with an infinite number of degrees of freedom). There are strong reasons to believe that, in the present state of the development of physics, one cannot understand the "stuff of the Universe" without referring to quantum field theory.

Quantum field theory is a relativistic theory, that is, its laws are the same in all inertial reference frames. This means that the empirically testable predictions of quantum field theory cannot change if we make a transition from one inertial frame of reference to another inertial frame of reference. Mathematically, such a transition is performed with the help of the so-called Poincaré transformation. Here we have reached the key point of my argument.

From the point of view of the majority of physics textbooks, Poincaré transformation is just a set of equations allowing one to change from one inertial reference frame to another inertial reference frame. For a mathematical physicist, however, Poincaré transformations should be looked upon from a much wider perspective. First, one defines an abstract mathematical structure, called a Poincaré group. It is an abstract structure because it embodies certain purely formal symmetries implemented in the concept of the group operation. At this stage, there are no equations that would "describe" these symmetries. The equations appear only when the abstract Poincaré group is *represented* in a concrete mathematical space. We deal with a group representation when transformations between points of this space, called *representation space,* are given (now in the form of equations), and if these equations reflect (in the precisely defined meaning of this term) the abstract symmetries of the group.

In the theoretical structure of quantum field theory, an important role is played by the space of states. Elements of this space, the state vectors, model possible states of the considered quantum system. From the mathematical point of view, the state vectors are elements of a Hilbert space, and it is this space that is treated as a representation space for the abstract Poincaré group.

In general, any abstract group admits an infinite number of possible representations (even in the same representation space many different representations of the same group can be defined). From among many possible representations of the Poincaré group (in the Hilbert space), only the so-called unitary representations have physical meaning. And here we meet the miracle of quantum field theory. Every group representation can be decomposed into the so-called *irreducible representations*—in a sense, the smallest representations of the given group. It turns out that irreducible unitary representations of the Poincaré group describe properties of the physical fields, that is, of what in modern physics best corresponds to the everyday concept of matter.

We remember St. Anselm of Canterbury's ontological proof of God's existence: God is the most perfect being. What exists is more perfect than what does not exist. Therefore God exists. It is commonly believed among philosophers that this "proof" is not valid because there is in it a jump from the purely logical or formal order (what can exist) to the ontological order (what actually exists). Something similar seems to intervene in our case. Purely formal, abstract symmetries of the Poincaré group, when unitarily represented in the Hilbert space, become measurable physical fields. What is an inadmissible jump in St. Anselm's proof seems to be the essence of the physical method.

Of course, we could neutralize the above reasoning by stressing that irreducible unitary representations of the Poincaré group are not physical fields themselves, but they *model* physical fields. This is certainly true; however, the concept itself of modeling is in these circumstances a very peculiar concept. There is no "thing" given to us independently that we could model with the help of some mathematical structures. The only access we have to physical fields is through their mathematical models. What is inherent in the unitary representations of the Poincaré group that distinguishes it from all other symmetries (and their representations) and makes them apt to model the existing things?

Teilhard de Chardin wanted to overcome the "temptation of matter" with the help of his concept of the bipolar stuff of the Universe (matter and spirit as two aspects of the same reality). Contemporary philosophizing physicists seem to have just the opposite problem: how to save matter against idealistic or Platonic interpretations of modern physical theories?

I do not want to say that Teilhard's intuitions in this respect were totally wrong. I only suggest that progress of physics has disclosed horizons that go beyond this field of possibilities that Teilhard had at his disposal.[17]

17. In some cases the new horizons have substantiated Teilhard's rather vague intuitions. For instance, in the view of nonlocality of quantum phenomena (revealed in Aspect's experiments), Teilhard's claim that the "total" character of matter "is something quite other than a mere entanglement of articulated inter-connections" (*PhM*, 48–49) seems today to be fully justified.

TIME AND EVOLUTION

If we had to choose a single word to characterize Teilhard's vision of the world, our choice would certainly go to the word "evolution." His way of seeing the reality is evolutionary from the beginning to the very end. "Is evolution a theory, a system, or a hypothesis?" asks Teilhard de Chardin. And he immediately answers:

It is much more: it is a general condition to which all theories, all hypotheses, all systems must bow and which they must satisfy henceforward if they are to be thinkable and true. Evolution is a light illuminating all facts, a curve that all lines must follow.[18]

Strangely enough, exactly at this point Teilhard's thinking meets serious difficulties when confronted with the perspectives opened by the achievement of contemporary cosmology.

One of the most far-reaching discoveries of the present science of the Universe is that not everything has to have a single history. Three concepts are strongly interrelated: time, history, and evolution. History presupposes time. A linear course of events measured by time is history. And if one can find a parameter or criterion that would indicate an increase of a certain quantity along this course of events, one is entitled to speak about evolution. The point is that in the theory of relativity, in general, there is no unique time and no unique history. There might be two sources of this phenomenon.

The first source is very well known from special relativity; general relativity adds to this phenomenon its own peculiarities. Time, and consequently history, is not an invariant concept. It depends on the choice of a reference system. Two different observers, remaining in two different states of motion, can contemplate two different histories of the same process. A typical example is the process of a gravitational collapse. When viewed by an observer taking part in the process, it ends up catastrophically with the final crunch in the infinitely great tidal forces. However, when regarded by an "external" observer, the history of the collapsing object is infinitely long only asymptotically approaching the "no-return" surface.

The second source of the non-uniqueness of time is even more striking (and it is typically generally relativistic). It can happen that the entire space-time manifold cannot be covered by a single coordinate system, and local time coordinates cannot be combined to form a universal (global) history. This happens notoriously if closed timelike curves occur in a given space-time manifold. Moreover, such situations are generic, in the sense that if we wanted to

18. *PhM*, 241.

choose a world model (being a solution to Einstein's equations) at random, the chances to pick up a model with a global history would be negligibly small.

It follows that evolution is not an "ontological *a priori*"; it is not "a general condition to which . . . all systems must bow and which they must satisfy . . . if they are to be thinkable and true." For a global time to exist, and consequently for an evolution to occur, certain preconditions must be satisfied. The present theory of relativity knows a beautiful mathematical theorem that precisely specifies these preconditions.[19] It is not a surprise that they require a certain degree of causality (excluding the existence of temporal loops) together with a stability of this property (in the sense that small perturbations should not destroy it).

A surprising fact is that these preconditions are satisfied in the actual Universe. The initial conditions from which our world took off had to be very finely tuned to produce the world with a global history on the background of which the evolution could proceed. A tiny deviation from these initial conditions would have destroyed the possibility of global time and evolution. This should be considered as another instant of "anthropic coincidences" to which we owe our own existence.[20]

This is not yet the end of the story. According to the present paradigm, the initial conditions of the actual Universe were established as the consequences of the quantum gravity era of the very young Universe. So far there is no final theory of quantum gravity, but a few existing models quite clearly suggest that in the primordial state of the Universe there was no time (at least in the present meaning of this term). In the widely popularized Hartle-Hawking world model,[21] time emerged from purely spatial dimensions of quantum era; in other models of quantum cosmology[22] there were quantum correlations that gave origin to a temporal ordering of events.

19. See S. W. Hawking and G. F. R. Ellis, *The Large Scale Structure of Space-Time*, Cambridge: Cambridge University Press, 1973, pp. 198–201. For a more accessible review with the same philosophical comments, see my paper: "Time and History, The Humanistic Significance of Science," *Eur. J. Phys.*, 11, 1990, 203–207.

20. See J. D. Barrow and F. J. Tipler, *The Anthropic Cosmological Principle*, Oxford: Clarendon Press, 1986; J. Leslie, *Universes*, London: Routledge, 1990.

21. See the original paper: J. B. Hartle and S. W. Hawking, "Wave Function of the Universe," *Phys. Rev.*, D28, 1983, 2960–2975, and its popularization: S. W. Hawking, *A Brief History of Time*, New York: Bantam Books, 1988.

22. See, for instance, C. J. Isham, "Quantum Theories of the Creation of the Universe," in *Quantum Cosmology and the Laws of Nature*, ed. R. J. Russell, N. Murphy, and C. J. Isham, Vatican City State: Vatican Observatory Publications; Berkeley: The Center for Theology and the Natural Sciences, 1993, 49–89.

Let us employ a metaphoric language of Teilhard to express our conclusions. Evolution is not "a curve that all lines must follow." Contemporary theoretical physics suggests just the opposite: all lines must be organized into a very special pattern to give rise to the evolutionary processes. Teilhard always took science seriously. There are strong reasons to believe that if he lived today and knew the recent developments in cosmology, he would modify his views. Instead of the aprioristic inevitability of time, he would contemplate the fine tuning that enabled the evolution to start and develop.

BY REASON OF COMPLEXITY

A driving force of the Teilhardian evolution is a growth of complexity. It is not an abstract evolution that leads the Universe through the process of transmutations. It is the increase in complexity that makes the evolution a decisive factor of the cosmic process. However, we should not forget that in Teilhard's times thermodynamics studied mainly equilibrium structures with the second law (entropy growth in irreversible phenomena) completely dominating the scene. To a structure with growing complexity there corresponds a negligibly small number of configurations in the space of all possible outcomes. It is, therefore, an "extremely improbable" state. From the point of view of equilibrium thermodynamics, complexification processes should be regarded as a miracle. This "miraculous" aspect of biological evolution was emphatically expressed by Prigogine and Stengers:

Thus any attempt at extrapolation from thermodynamic descriptions was to define as rare and unpredictable the kind of evolution described by biology and the social sciences. How, for example, could Darwinian evolution—the statistical *selection* of rare events—be reconciled with the statistical disappearance of all peculiarities, of all rare configurations, described by Boltzmann? As Roger Caillois asks: "Can Carnot and Darwin both be right?"[23]

To proceed with his vision of the world Teilhard de Chardin had to overcome this discrepancy between Carnot and Darwin. To this end he developed the following strategy. Things have their external aspect as well as their internal aspect. Ordinary physics deals with the external aspect of things, but "a kind of phenomenology or generalized physics" is to be created that would be able to deal with both aspects of things. Teilhard de Chardin argues:

It is impossible to deny that, deep within ourselves, an "interior" appears at the heart of beings, as it were seen through a rent. This is enough to ensure that, in one degree or another, this "interior" should obtrude itself as existing everywhere in nature from all

23. I. Prigogine and I. Stengers, *Order Out of Chaos,* London: Fontana, 1984, 128.

time. Since the stuff of the Universe has an inner aspect at one point of itself, there is necessarily *a double aspect to its structure,* that is to say in every region of space and time—in the same way, for instance, as it is granular: *co-extensive with their Without, there is a Within to things.*[24]

To the *without* and *within* of things there correspond two types of energy: a tangential energy that "represents 'energy' as such, as generally understood by science,"[25] and a radial energy that draws the Universe "towards even greater complexity and centricity—in other words forwards."[26]

From the point of view of physics, the idea of "two energies" is completely arbitrary. Moreover, it turned out to be non-necessary in order to explain the origin and growth of structures in the Universe. One should admire Teilhard's intuition, which directed his thinking to the problem of complexity. In his days, however, any speculation to solve this problem had to be premature. In contemporary nonlinear thermodynamics there is no longer any contradiction between Carnot and Darwin, and we should turn to the scientific explanation of the growth of complexity.

It is not possible here for me to go into details of the contemporary theory of the growth of complexity.[27] I will focus only on its mathematical foundation. It was changing from linear dynamics to nonlinear dynamics that enabled physicists and mathematicians to cope with the problem of complexity. A typical property of linear equations (which model linear dynamical systems) is that the sum of their two solutions gives us the new solution. Consequently, a totality modeled by a linear equation can be nothing more than the sum of its parts. A typical example is wave motion. A particular wave is described by a solution of the very well-known *linear* differential equation called the wave equation. This equation has many other solutions. Each of them describes waves with different characteristics (length, amplitude, velocity of propagation). If we add two such solutions we obtain a new wave that is a composition of the original two waves (such a "superposition" of solutions is responsible for the phenomenon of interference of two waves). If the Universe were only a linear system, nothing really new could emerge out of its dynamics.

Nonlinear equations are totally different in this respect. Two of their solutions do not lead to a new solution. If we "superimpose" two solutions of a

24. *PhM,* 61, italicized by Teilhard de Chardin.

25. *PhM,* 71.

26. *PhM,* 70. In fact, Teilhard assumes that there is only one energy that "is physic in nature," but it can be divided into two components—tangential and radial.

27. I refer the reader to recent popular and semipopular literature, for instance: I. Prigogine and I. Stengers, op. cit.; P. Davies, *The Cosmic Blueprint,* New York: Simon and Schuster, 1988; I. Stewart, *Does God Play Dice?* London: Penguin Books, 1990.

nonlinear equation, they can produce an extra-effect that was not present in any of the original solutions. In consequence, even a simple non-linear equation can exhibit a very complex and unexpected behavior. For instance, Einstein's equations of gravitational field are strongly nonlinear. Each of their solutions corresponds to a particular gravitational field (e.g., coming from the Sun, or a planet, or a star). If we combine two such gravitational fields we do not obtain a simple sum of them. The two original fields interact with each other, and the interaction itself acts as a source of a new gravitational field. This new gravitational field enters into interaction with the already existing fields and is itself a source of a new field—and so on, and so on. We must solve the equations to see the final outcome of this nonlinear network of interactions.

Nonlinear equations very often exhibit another interesting property. To select a particular solution of a given equation one must choose the initial conditions of this solution. If I throw a stone, its trajectory depends on the position of my hand and on the direction I am aiming at. The trajectory of the stone is a solution of the equation of motion; a concrete position of my hand and the chosen direction determine the initial conditions of this solution. It can happen that a slight deviation from the original initial conditions selects a solution that is only slightly different from the original solution. In such a case nothing interesting happens. However, if slightly modified initial conditions lead to drastically different solutions, the predictability breaks down (although the motion remains fundamentally deterministic), and the solution can produce a highly structured pattern. We never have an absolute control over initial conditions. We can select physical magnitudes only within a certain "box of errors," and if the initial conditions taken from this box lead to drastically different solutions, we cannot guess in advance what will develop from the selected initial conditions. This phenomenon is called deterministic chaos. The name is not particularly well chosen, because the processes denoted by it are at the basis of the origin and evolution of highly organized structures, which in themselves are not chaotic at all. But the name is not entirely bad, for these highly organized structures often present "chaotic shapes": there are no two identical cells in the same organism; there are no two identical trees in the same species.

We cannot claim that we already have understood all mechanisms underlying the growth of complexity in the Universe, but we can claim that the old contradiction between Carnot and Darwin has disappeared. Prigogine and Darwin go smoothly together.[28] Nonlinear thermodynamics—that is, thermodynamics making use of nonlinear equations—provides physical principles of

---

28. The problem of the relationship between Prigogine's theory of structure formation and Teilhard's thought was analyzed by J. F. Salmon, "Teilhard and Prigogine," *Teilhard Studies*, no. 16, Chambersburg: Anima Press, 1986.

the growth of complexity, including the biological evolution. There is no need for any type of nonphysical energy.

CONCLUSION

Schrödinger once wrote:

A scientist is supposed to have a complete and thorough knowledge, at first hand, of *some* subjects and, therefore, is usually expected not to write on any topic of which he is not a master. This is regarded as a matter of *noblesse oblige.*[29]

In this sense, any synthesis based on the sciences is always, and always will be, premature. On the other hand, there is inscribed in our cultural genes a sort of instinct for an all-embracing, unified vision of the world and our place in it. Schrödinger continues:

I can see no other escape from this (lest our true aim be lost forever) than that some of us should venture to embark on a synthesis of facts and theories, albeit with second-hand and incomplete knowledge of some of them.[30]

This is why, although any synthesis is always premature, it is indispensable.

Moreover, science of the last decade of the twentieth century contains in itself, if not germs of a synthetic vision, then at least some elements of a large-scale perspective. In the present chapter I have touched upon three such elements: the nature of the stuff of the Universe, the roots of time and evolution, the nonlinear strategies of the origin and growth of structures. The stuff of the Universe, in the eyes of contemporary physics, has decidedly become something more similar to a structure or form than to inert pieces of material substratum. Directedness of time and history no longer seem to be an ontological a priori of any existence, but rather an outcome of finely tuned initial conditions. And the growth of complexity is now regarded as a process emerging out of physical laws rather than a foreign element in the body of physics. Contemporary physics tends to a Grand Unification—not only in the technical meaning of this term to combine all fundamental forces into one theoretical structure, but also in the sense of elaborating general concepts allowing us to ask more far-reaching and more overall questions.

In this chapter, I have focused on some *physical aspects* of Teilhard's synthesis. I do not claim that physics is enough to create a synthetic vision of reality. Teilhard had his own ways of going beyond the realm of physics. He attempted "to see and to make others see." This is why I like to call his synthesis a vision of the world. Some people have better eyes than others.

29. Preface to E. Schrödinger, *What Is Life?* Cambridge: Cambridge University Press, 1969 (in one volume with *Mind and Matter*).
  30. Ibid.

8 LEMAÎTRE—PRIEST AND SCIENTIST

TWO COMMITMENTS

Being both a Roman Catholic priest and a scientist may seem to combine two professions that can function interchangeably: on Sundays one is a priest; on weekdays one works as a scientist. However, these professions, if treated seriously, require total commitment. Moreover, both professions cannot be done in isolation from the two respective communities: the Church and the so-called world of science. Georges Lemaître was a dedicated priest and an outstanding scientist. No wonder that his life was marked with many problems arising on the borderline between his two fields of life commitment. To understand his personality and his work better, we should outline the atmosphere that prevailed, in the first half of the twentieth century, in both the world of science and the world of Church teaching. Lemaître belonged to the group of the very few people who, from their own experience, knew these two worlds and could contribute to their mutual rapprochement.

THE WORLD OF SCIENCE

At that time, the world of science was dominated by the positivistic approach to the problem of human knowledge. The influence of Mach writings on physicists was still enormous. Conventionalism of Poincaré and Duhem and their deep insight into the nature of scientific theories were soon overshadowed by the logical positivism of the Vienna Circle. Philosophers belonging to this group of thinkers were impressed by great advances made by the theory of relativity and quantum mechanics, and they put a lot of effort into interpreting both of these theories in a positivistic manner. The Copenhagen interpretation of quantum mechanics, developed by Bohr and his school, clearly contained some features of the positivistic thought, and, through its great influence on working physicists and philosophers of science, significantly contributed to the strengthening of logically-positivistic influences. Einstein himself, after creating his special theory of relativity, considered himself a disciple of Mach, and only during his work on general relativity did he realize that he was no longer following positivistic recipes of doing physics. Soon after, he began his lonely campaign against the Copenhagen interpretation of quantum mechanics and commonly accepted ideas concerning science and its methods.

In these circumstances, not only were religious views regarded, in the scientific circles, with an almost open hostility (see, e.g., the case of Duhem and his struggle against such an attitude), but even doing cosmology was looked upon with mistrust and suspicion. The courage required to face the problem of the Universe was not something easily recommended by positivistically minded philosophers of science. Besides that, Lemaître was often accused of infiltrating religious elements into cosmological theories. Although his Primeval Atom model was proposed by him as a solution to some problems connected with the age of the Universe and quantum mechanical description of its early phases, he was notoriously accused of introducing the Christian idea of creation into the cosmological framework.

Foreseeing such objections, Lemaître was careful not to mix his religious convictions with his work as a scientist. He emphasized that, just as there is no Christian way of running or swimming, there is no Christian way of doing science. He stressed that even in the beginning of the Universe God was a "hidden God" and not a concept that could be grasped by a scientific theory. In his 1958 Solvay Conference paper he wrote:

As far as I can see such a theory remains entirely outside any metaphysical or religious question. It leaves a materialist free to deny any transcendental Being. He may keep, for the bottom of space-time [i.e., the initial singularity], the same attitude of mind he has been able to adopt for events occurring in non-singular places in space-time. For the believer, it removes any attempt to familiarity with God, as were Laplace's chiquenaude or Jeans' finger. It is consonant with the wording of Isaias speaking of the "Hidden God," hidden even in the beginning of creature.[1]

ESSENCES AND PHENOMENA

In the first decades of the twentieth century, the intellectual life of the Roman Catholic Church was permeated with the phobia of modernism. The condemnation of this premature attempt to conform the Roman Catholic way of thinking with modern trends in world philosophy was still alive. Although modernism was not directly related to scientific research, the area of possible contact with science was felt to be a sensitive field of potential conflicts.

---

1. G. Lemaître, "The Primaeval Atom Hypothesis and the Problem of the Clusters of Galaxies," in *La structure et l'évolution de l'univers,* Bruxelles: R. Stoops, 1958, 1–31.

Since the encyclical letter *Aeterni Patris* of Leo XIII, neothomism was a quasi-official philosophy of the Roman Catholic Church. It was taught in seminaries and Roman Catholic universities. The Catholic University of Louvain, with which Lemaître was connected during the whole of his scientific life, was one of the most important centers of the neothomistic movement. Approximately at that time (first three decades of the twentieth century), the neothomistic philosophy elaborated its own approach to the sciences. To protagonists of this approach belonged Jacques Maritain, but relatively quickly it was accepted by neothomists of many European countries.

The neothomistic approach to the sciences, the sort of the neothomistic philosophy of science, had two roots. The first root, typical for this philosophical school, went back to Aristotle and St. Thomas Aquinas. Both these thinkers developed a theory of knowledge based on the fundamental distinction of the three degrees of abstraction: physical and mathematical sciences were placed by them on the first and second degree of abstraction, respectively; whereas the third degree of abstraction was reserved for metaphysics. Maritain and others applied this theory of knowledge to the modern sciences and supplemented it with suitably modified elements of the current philosophy of science. This was the second root of the neothomistic approach to the sciences. However, the current philosophy of science was mainly of the positivistic (and neopositivistic) origin. One of its principal tenets was that science deals only with phenomena (which can be reached by experiments), totally discarding the "essential aspect of things." The underlying philosophy subsumed that no essences exist; one can meaningfully speak only about phenomena. Neothomists took over this doctrine, but modified it by claiming that whereas science investigates phenomena, philosophy penetrates into the essences of things.[2]

During his training for priesthood at the seminary in Malines, Lemaître certainly learned this approach to the sciences and, as can be seen from some of his writings, he accepted it, at least partially, in thinking about science and its relationship to philosophy and theology. His insistence upon not mixing theology with science was not only a strategic idea in his contacts with other scientists; it was a consequence of his methodology of science and theology allowing him to avoid a too easy concordism.

Because of its specific subject-matter, the Universe as a whole, cosmology often provokes metaphysical and theological reflections. In this field, the temptation of concordism is usually greater than in other branches of science. As it is well known, even Pius XII did not succeed in avoiding it. He was interested in

2. The above analysis is based on chapter 4 of my book *The New Physics and a New Theology*, Vatican City State: Vatican Observatory Publications, 1996.

astronomy and had a substantial knowledge of it. In November 1951, during the solemn audience at the end of the Study Week organized by the Pontifical Academy of Sciences, Pius XII delivered his much discussed talk in which he explored some philosophical and theological implications of modern cosmological theories. He was inclined to identify the initial singularity appearing in some world models with the creation of the Universe, and he argued that modern theories substantiate evidence of God's existence by providing new basis for the "proof *ex motu*" and the "proof from the orderliness" characterizing all parts of the Universe.

Lemaître did not attend this Study Week, which was devoted to the "Problem of Microseism," but he took part in the solemn audience and listened to the Pontiff's talk. It goes without saying that Lemaître was rather embarrassed with these views expressed in such an official way. No wonder that when he learned that the pope would deliver an address to the Eighth General Assembly of the International Astronomical Union in September 1952, he contacted the Cardinal Secretary of State and Father Daniel J. O'Connel, the Director of the Vatican Astronomical Observatory, who was a close confidant of Pius XII in scientific matters. Owing to their combined influence, the papal address, delivered on 7 September 1952, contained no direct references to the relationship between science and theology. Never again did Pius XII publicly discuss any theological implications of cosmological theories.

LEMAÎTRE'S HERITAGE

In the sixties logical positivism almost totally disappeared from the philosophical scene. One of the main sources of its disappearance was progress in physics, which—one could say—falsified predictions of the Vienna Circle philosophers by adopting the way of development forbidden by them. Important factors of this process were advances in cosmology and their strict fusion with other branches of physics. For instance, the modern theory of unified interactions is unthinkable without cosmological models of the very early Universe.

Contemporary philosophy of science, liberated from the burden of positivistic interpretations, clearly distinguishes scientific and philosophical methods of research, but fully acknowledges their interactions with each other in history and in present times. Many outstanding physicists and cosmologists (Hawking, Penrose, Davis, Barrow) do not hesitate writing books dealing with scientific, philosophical, and even theological matters.

The relationship between science and theology certainly enters a new phase. Growing mutual interest seems to be slowly replacing old hostilities. There are new institutions and societies (to mention only the European Society for the Study of Science and Theology), the aim of which is to explore possible fields of mutual interactions.

Also, in the Roman Catholic Church the attitude toward science seems to be undergoing substantial changes. An official letter of Pope John Paul II to George V. Coyne, the director of the Vatican Observatory, witnesses to these changes. Among other important things we read in it:

Some theologians, at least, should be sufficiently well-versed in the sciences to make authentic and creative use of the resources that the best-established theories may offer them. Such an expertise would prevent them from making uncritical and overhasty use for apologetic purposes of such recent theories as that of the "Big Bang," in cosmology.[3]

In this century theologians have written thousands of books and articles about mutual relationships between theology and science. In the vast majority of them, science is treated as it can be treated by "learned outsiders." Such books and articles can at most change the attitude of other theologians to science (which is an important factor), but they cannot change the real relationship between science and theology. Lemaître has left us only a very few remarks concerning this subject-matter, but his work in cosmology and his presence in the world of science contributed more to the improvement of interactions between the Roman Catholic Church and science than many learned theological treatises and official declarations.[4]

3. The full text of this letter can be found in *Physics, Philosophy, and Theology: A Common Quest for Understanding*, ed. R. J. Russell, W. R. Stoeger, and G. V. Coyne, Vatican City State: Vatican Observatory Publications, 1988, M1–M14.

4. Long after this chapter had been written, an excellent book appeared extensively dealing with Lemaître's life and work, with special emphasis on his views on science and religion: D. Lambert, *Un atome d'Universe: La vie et l'œvre de Georges Lamaître,* Bruxelles: Lessius-Racine, 1999.

PART THREE

THE WORK OF CREATION

In the previous parts, we looked at the science-religion relation-ships (or science-theology relationship) from the methodological and historical perspectives. We should not forget that these per-spectives only pave the way for the real encounter. Although sci-ence and theology use different languages and employ different methods, they often speak on the same subject. Therefore, con-frontations—not necessarily conflicts—are unavoidable. On the theological side there exists a time-honored doctrine on the two books—the Book of Nature and the Book of Revelation—given to humanity by God. Overlapping pages of these two books are espe-cially important for the science-theology dispute. The greatest overlap occurs when theology explores the Work of Creation and science tries to decipher the structure of the Universe with the help of mathematical and empirical methods.

Old discussions concerning the creation and the beginning of the Universe revived and took new strength together with the ap-pearance of relativistic cosmology and its world-models presenting an expanding universe with the "singularity" initiating their evolu-tion. Should the initial singularity (popularly called Big Bang) be identified with the "moment of creation" or understood as a loop-hole in our present knowledge that will, sooner or later, be filled in with solid scientific theories and well-working models? This is the main topic of Chapter 9. To go beyond the commonplace state-ments and superficial comparisons, we must penetrate into the geometric structure of current models of the Universe and its space-time. The effort one must invest in such an enterprise will amply be remunerated with a superb panorama and unexpected vistas. Remembering our methodological analyses, carried out in Part One, we cannot expect that scientific theories would directly tell us something about God and God's action in the world. This does not mean, however, that the theologian has nothing to learn from the scientific enterprise. On the contrary, the way scientific theories say nothing about God is significant—the progress in science teaches the theologian that our language and our concepts inscribed into the language are inadequate when referred to God. Our everyday vocabulary and our common sense concepts break down in the domains evading direct control by our sense perception, as, for instance, in the domain of quantum mechanics; how much more something similar must happen when we dare speak on the Infinite Transcendence.

This line of reasoning is further developed in Chapter 10. The chapter deals with the evolution of concepts in both science and theology. As mentioned above, it was quantum mechanics that first disclosed the inadequacy of our everyday concepts when they are applied to the quantum world. New concepts, which had to be elaborated, are generalizations of old ones that are now reduced to the rank of "special cases." The goal of Chapter 10 is to look at the development of some recent physical theories and the "adventures" of concepts involved in them, and to try to derive from them a lesson for theology.

For a long time, a great issue in theology was whether and how to refer our temporal concepts to God. The medieval answer to this question was the doctrine on God's atemporality. This doctrine is now frequently rejected by theologians, especially those connected with the so-called process theology, as depriving God of God's creative activity. Strangely enough, the idea of an atemporal stratum in the world's structure reappears recently in some important models of fundamental physics. Should this fact have some impact on theological thinking? Physical models teach us that atemporality does not necessarily mean static, motionless state; dynamics and timelessness can go together. This opens a vast field of speculations concerning timelessness and causality, timelessness and purpose or chance—the great themes of natural theology.

In presenting illustrative material from physics in Chapters 9 and 10, I have amply borrowed it from my own research in the domain of the so-called noncommutative geometry and its application to physics. This is a brand new field of investigation, less known even to scientists working in other areas of physics. Therefore, it seemed reasonable to present "noncommutative models" in a more detailed way than it is done in other cases, and to permit, in Chapters 9 and 10, more repetitions than is tolerated elsewhere in this book.

From the theological point of view, the Work of Creation is not limited to the initiation of the world's existence but is also present in its "everyday functioning." In this respect, looking at "ordinary" scientific theories is even more important that exploring those regions (or boundaries) of space and time where our theories break down and could suggest a beginning. The very existence of scientific theories and their success in explaining physical reality testify to the comprehensibility of the world. Einstein used to say that the world's comprehensibility is a mystery we will never comprehend, but from the theological point of view the comprehensibility of the world can be reduced to the rationality of its Creator. In this perspective, the goal of the scientific endeavor is but to decipher the "Mind of God" (Einstein's expression as well). Is this a theologically unavoidable conclusion? And what if, as claimed by some authors, at the very bottom of physical reality there reigns probability and pure chance, and there are some averaging mechanisms that produce apparent order out of fundamental chaos? To analyze this question from various sides and angles is the goal of Chapter 11.

Recent developments in science have discovered two types of elements shaping the structure of the world: the cosmic elements, such as symmetry and predictability, and the chaotic elements, such as randomness and unpredictability. Both are equally "mathematical," and both provoke the question of why the world is so comprehensible. They are but two aspects of the same Logos immanent in the structure of the Universe.

9 COSMOLOGICAL SINGULARITY AND THE CREATION OF THE UNIVERSE

INTRODUCTORY REMARKS

It would be difficult to find a popular book or an article on cosmology in which the author says nothing about the Big Bang and the creation of the Universe. It would be even harder to find a book or an article in which this problem was dealt with in a responsible manner from the point of view of both science and theology. The goal of the present chapter is to improve the statistics in this respect. However, this purpose cannot be achieved by repeating commonplace statements about the Big Bang as being a point with an infinite matter density at which the Universe and time began. One must go a little bit deeper into a mathematical definition of the *initial singularity* (a geometric counterpart of the Big Bang) and the conditions of its existence, for only then can one correctly decipher its physical content and its philosophical (or theological) significance. We will examine this question by starting with the first appearance of the singularity problem in twentieth-century cosmology, and ending with the most recent results concerning the geometric nature of singularities.

EARLY DISPUTES

It is interesting to notice that cosmological singularity started making trouble in our science of the Universe even before it had been formally discovered. Its appearance was acknowledged not earlier than in the work by Alexander Friedman in 1922.[1] It should be noted, however, that in his first paper on cosmology in 1917, Albert Einstein[2] had met with the same difficulty that is responsible for the singular behavior of the Universe in certain of its states. The problem at stake is that of gravitational instability, the same problem with which Newton had to cope when he pondered why

1. A. Friedman, "Über der Krümmung des Raumes," *Zeitschrift für Physik* 10 (1922) 377–386.
2. A. Einstein, "Kosmologische Betrachtungen zur allgemeinen Relativitätstheorie," *Sitsungsberichte der preussischen Akademie der Wissenschaften* 1 (1917) 142–152.

"Matter evenly scattered through a finite Space would not convene in the midst." He gave as his opinion

that there should be a central Particle, so accurately placed in the middle as to be always equally attracted on all Sides, and thereby continue without Motion, seems to be a Supposition fully as hard as to make the sharpest Needle stand Upright on its Point upon a Looking-Glass. And if the question is asked with respect to an infinite universe it becomes even harder: For I reckon this is as hard as to make not one Needle only, but an infinite number of them (so many as there are Particles in an infinite Space) stand accurately poised upon their Points.[3]

Initially Einstein himself (and many other cosmologists after him) believed that the appearances of singularities in the cosmological models considered at that time were by-products of the overstrong simplifying assumptions that were required to construct these models. The suspicion was that the so-called cosmological principle (the assumption of spatial homogeneity and isotropy of the Universe) was responsible. The understanding that this is not the case and that the real cause lies in the gravitational instability emerged rather laboriously. An important hint was given by Georges Lemaître,[4] who demonstrated that in a certain class of anisotropic world models the tendency toward the appearance of singularities is even greater than in isotropic ones, but the decisive step was made much later by Roger Penrose and Stephen Hawking (and some others), who proved several theorems on the existence of singularities.[5] It turned out that to remove singularities from the theory of gravitation is "as hard as to make an infinite number of Needles stand accurately poised upon their Points." However, this does not mean that this cannot be done, as we will see.

Long before this stage of the dispute ended, heated philosophical and even theological polemics had begun. Lemaître[6] tells us that when he was discussing with Einstein the Primeval Atom hypothesis, Einstein's reaction was: *Non, pas cela, cela suggere trop la création* (No, not this; this too much suggests the creation). From the very beginning philosophical views interfered with doing cosmology. Many authors shared Einstein's reluctance to accept any kind of beginning of the Universe. Some people did this for good methodological reasons, but some others never tried to hide their antireligious attitude. For instance, in William Bonnor's view, theologians had long awaited such an occa-

3. *Isaak Newton's Papers and Letters on Natural Philosophy*, ed. I. B. Cohen, Cambridge, Mass.: Harvard University Press, 292.

4. G. Lemaître, "L'univers en expansion," *Annales de la Société Scientifique de Bruxelles* A53 (1933) 51–85.

5. S. W. Hawking and G. F. R. Ellis, *The Large Scale Structure of Space-Time*, Cambridge: Cambridge University Press, 1973.

6. G. Lemaître, "Renontres avec A. Einstein," *Revue des Questions Scientifiques* 129 (1958) 129–132.

sion as a superdense state in the beginning of the Universe, for now they could claim that the biblical account of creation is right, and Bishop Usher was mistaken only by a few years.[7]

In these discussions arguments taken from science were mixed with those of purely theological origin. For instance, Arthur E. Milne argued that

the creation of the universe demanded creation at a point-singularity. For the creation by God of an extended universe would require an impossibility, the impossibility of the fixation of simultaneity in the void—impossibility, that is, to a rational God. The paradox follows that the Deity himself, though in principle all-powerful, is yet limited by his very rationality.[8]

The strategy of this argumentation is rather transparent. We have a scientific result (the point-singularity) and a theological idea of God (as a rational Being), and we make a *post hoc* deduction of this scientific result from this theological idea (God's rationality implies the point-singularity). Apart from a methodological incoherence of such strategies, there are always at least two implicit dangers involved in them: First, the results of science are of their very nature provisional—and in cosmology even more so than in other physical disciplines because of the high degree of extrapolation always present in cosmological theories. In fact, later on it emerged that classical singularities are not parts or elements of space-time, and consequently such concepts as that of "point" (in its usual meaning) are not applicable to them. Second, any "deduction" of a scientific result from theological premises can be only apparent (for instance, one can overlook some other important premises), and if the idea of God as a rational Being is true, the deduction in Milne's argumentation is indeed only apparent, inasmuch as the point-singularity concept, being meaningless, is not a scientific result.

If we look at these early polemics from the present perspective, we can quite clearly see that they were based, perhaps with a very few exceptions, on two often tacit presuppositions, one of which was purely scientific and another purely theological. The scientific one asserted that singularities (in particular the initial singularity) can be removed from cosmological models. Even those who claimed that the initial singularity is a permanent element of our image of the Universe (among them Milne and Lemaître) were unable to prove this claim. The theological presupposition consisted in identifying the beginning of the Universe with its creation: if the Universe had a beginning, it had to be cre-

7. W. Bonnor, *The Mystery of the Expanding Universe* (Quoted after Polish translation, Warsaw: PWN, 1964, 134).

8. A. E. Milne, *Modern Cosmology and the Christian Idea of God*, Oxford: Clarendon Press, 1952, 157.

ated by God; and vice versa, if it was created by God, it had a beginning. This presupposition was made by both defenders and opponents of the theological concept of creation. However, one should distinguish the theological meaning of creation from other meanings, as when this term is used by cosmologists as a synonym of physical origin, or even of initial singularity. The confusion of these meanings and the linguistic carelessness of many cosmologists significantly contributed to various misunderstandings. For instance, how is one to understand the following statements made by Jayant Narlikar:

> At an epoch, which we may denote by t=0, the Universe explodes into existence. . . . The epoch t=0 is taken as the event of "creation." Prior to this there existed no Universe, no physical laws. Everything suddenly appeared at t=0.[9]

It is important not to overlook the quotation marks around "creation." To many theologians and philosophers who are not experts in physics, this could appear to be a true theological account of creation ("the Universe explodes into existence"!). Strictly speaking, however, the issue here is the technical problem of the violation of the principle of energy conservation, as it could be guessed from the following:

> The most fundamental question in cosmology is, "Where did the matter we see around us originate in the first place?" This point has never been dealt with in big-bang cosmologies in which, at t=0, there occurs sudden and fantastic violation of the law of conservation of matter and energy. After t=0 there is no such violation.[10]

However, the suspicion arises that confusions of meanings, like the one above, could be intended, at least to some extent and at least by some authors. Science sells better if it is shown to conquer realms traditionally controlled by theology.

The first of the foregoing presuppositions, that singularities can be removed from cosmological models, was later made the subject matter of intensive studies. The quite unexpected results significantly changed the atmosphere of the Creation dispute. Unfortunately, the second presupposition, that beginning = creation, is still "on the market" and continues to cause confusion in discussions of the philosophical and theological implications of cosmology. We will deal with these problems in the subsequent sections.

CLASSICAL BEGINNING

An important breakthrough in discussions about the beginning of the Universe took place in the sixties when the singularity theorems were proved.

9. J. Narlikar, *The Structure of the Universe,* Oxford: Oxford University Press, 1977, 125.
10. Ibid., 136–137.

They are of purely mathematical character but have a natural physical interpretation. First, one defines a model of space-time. Its intended goal is to describe space-times encountered in the special and general theories of relativity; but from the mathematical point of view, such a model refers to any space considered in differential geometry, provided it satisfies the required conditions. On such a space one imposes further conditions that geometrically mimic properties of a gravitational field. Then, a quite long chain of mathematical deduction shows that the foregoing sets of conditions (together with another geometric condition, which can be interpreted as saying that the considered space-time is singularity-free), inevitably lead to a contradiction.

The key point is how to define singularity and what is meant by saying that a space-time is singularity-free. This is a big issue in relativistic physics, and, as we will see, it leads to sophisticated mathematical problems. Happily enough, what is needed to prove the singularity theorems is not the true singularity definition, but only a working criterion for a given space-time to be free of singularities. What becomes apparent is that such a criterion is provided by the so-called geodesic completeness of space-time (in the null and timelike sense). Geodesics are "the straightest curves" in a given space-time.[11] In the theory of relativity, null and timelike geodesics describe the free motion of photons and massive particles (or observers), respectively. The geometric concept of geodesic completeness represents the situation in which such motions could be indefinitely continued (in both time directions). This means, of course, that the history of any photon or particle will never cease to happen, and consequently that space-time has no edges or singularities.

This is a good working criterion for a given space-time to be singularity-free without the necessity of knowing the physical nature of singularities. However, by reversing the former reasoning, we could guess something about singularities themselves. If a (null or timelike) geodesic cannot be prolonged,[12] a certain history of a photon or particle must break down, and this occurs exactly because of the singularity (quite often it happens that not only one, but all histories, break down at a singularity). If a history cannot be prolonged, it ceases to happen; and what does it mean that the history of a particle ceases to happen? It means that this particle emerges out of nothingness, or disappears into nothingness. For instance, at the initial singularity in the Friedman world model, all histories of photons and particles emerge from nothingness in this

11. Every straight line in the Euclidean space is a geodesic. For the precise definition, see any textbook on differential geometry.

12. Let us notice that the usual concept of length has no invariant meaning in relativity theory.

sense. This strongly resembles the theological concept of creation out of nothing *(creatio ex nihilo)*. In such a context the last paragraph of the well-known
monograph on the singularity theorems is hardly surprising:

> The Creation of the Universe out of nothing has been argued, indecisively, from early
> times; see for example Kant's first Antinomy of Pure Reason and comments on it. . . .
> The results we have obtained support the idea that the universe began a finite time ago.
> However, the actual point of creation, the singularity, is outside the scope of presently
> known laws of physics.[13]

However, we should not forget that all conclusions of this sort are always
model dependent. The model in question is provided by the geometric model
of space-time, mathematical conditions of the singularity theorems, and their
physical interpretation. The latter is given by the theory of general relativity,
which, as a classical theory, does not take into account quantum gravity effects.
Because there are strong reasons to believe that these effects play the decisive
role in the early, superdense states of the Universe, the problem of the existence
of the initial singularity crucially depends on the future theory of quantum
gravity. This conclusion does not come from any trustworthy theory, but rather
from a combination of the present classical theory of gravity and various methods of quantizing physical fields. Based on such knowledge, we conclude that
when the energy density approaches that of the Planck threshold,[14] quantum
gravity effects become dominant. The singularity theorems are proven mathematical theorems; as such, they will always remain true. We can only hope that
the future theory of quantum gravity will violate one of the conditions appearing in these theorems, and in this way will free cosmology from singularities
(the so-called energy conditions are the most frequent candidates for being bro-
ken down by quantum gravity effects). Taking all these issues into account, it
would be premature to claim that the singularity theorems prove the beginning
of the Universe, let alone its creation.

There are also strong reasons preventing one from identifying the initial singularity with the "moment of creation." The nothingness out of which the histories of particles or observers emerge has nothing in common with the "metaphysical nonbeing" of philosophers and theologians. The singularity theorems
have been proven within the conceptual environment of the precisely defined
model of space-time, and saying that some histories suddenly end at the final
singularity means only that the curves representing these histories have reached

---

13. Op. cit., 364.

14. The Planck threshold is characterized by the Planck length: $(\hbar G/c^3)^{1/2} \approx 10^{-33}$cm; the Planck
time: $(\hbar G/c^5)^{1/2} \approx 10^{-44}$ s; and the Planck density: $c^5/\hbar G/^2 \approx 10^{93}$ g/cm^3. All these magnitudes are
constructed out of fundamental constants: velocity of light c, Planck's constant $\hbar$, and the New-
tonian gravitational constant G.

the edges of the model. It is true that, in the case of the initial singularity, these histories emerge out of nothingness, but it is nothingness from the point of view of the model. The *nothingness*, in this sense, is only what the model says *nothing* about. What is outside the model, the model itself does not specify.

This is the kind of interpretation I am calling the "exegesis of the mathematical structure" of a given physical theory.[15] It is a minimum interpretation closely following the mathematical formulae constituting the body of the theory under interpretation. Everybody who understands these formulae and their functioning in the given theory must accept this interpretation. Of course, one may superimpose any interpretative comments on this theory as long as they do not contradict its mathematical structure. However, strictly speaking, the theory itself remains neutral with respect to such comments. One might even superimpose on the same theory some other comments that contradict the previous ones (provided they do not contradict the mathematical structure of the theory). For instance, in our case, one can claim that the emergence of all histories of particles and observers from the initial singularity in the Friedman world model should be understood as the creation of the Universe by God from nothing *(ex nihilo);* or alternatively, that the Universe lasted from minus temporal infinity and that the initial singularity in the Friedman model is but a geometrical expression of the fact that all information from the previous cycle of the world's evolution has been lost (the Universe has forgotten its presingularity past). Neither of these interpretative comments contradicts the mathematical structure of the model, and any serious discussion between these two philosophies should look for support in departments of human speculation other than cosmology. The well-known criticism by Adolf Grünbaum[16] strikes at the theological doctrine of creation only if one forgets the above methodological analysis. It is not true, however, that the theologian as theologian has nothing to learn about creation from modern cosmological theories. This problem is discussed in the subsequent sections.

SPACE-TIME BOUNDARIES

For the time being let us set aside theological interpretations and stick to the "exegesis of mathematical structures." The singularity theorems are not the last word in the problem of the beginning of the physical Universe. The major question concerning the nature of singularities remains open.

In the singularity theorems, singularities are understood as "end-points" of curves representing histories of particles or photons. Can we be more precise

15. See above, Chapter 2.
16. A. Grünbaum,"The Pseudo-Problem of Creation in Physical Cosmology," *Philosophy of Science* 56 (1989) 373–394; "Pseudo-Creation of the Big Bang," *Nature* 344 (1990) 821–822.

about that? The "end-point" itself of such a curve is inaccessible for our research, because precisely at this "point" our model breaks down. However, we can use here a trick often used in geometry. Because a given end-point is determined by all curves that end at it, in all calculations we can treat interchangeably the end-point and all curves that end at it. Or, simply, we can identify end-points with such classes of curves. This means that by investigating the geometry of such classes of curves we are, in fact, investigating the set of end-points; and this of course is done from inside our model of space-time. The set of all end-points, in this sense, forms what is called the *singular boundary* of space-time.

In such a manner all singularities of a given space-time are represented as points of its singular boundary. If there are no singularities, the space-time has no singular boundary. In fact, the singularity theorems reveal themselves as theorems concerning the existence of singular boundaries. Notice, however, that although the boundary points are defined from within, they do not belong to the space-time itself (they do belong to the space-time boundary), and consequently it is meaningless to speak about them as of points in the usual sense. In fact, they can have a highly complicated structure that strongly depends on details of the boundary construction.

There are several known constructions of space-time boundaries. One of the first belongs to Hawking[17] and Geroch[18] and is called *g-boundary*; *g* is here an abbreviation for "geodesic," and it means that in this boundary construction only the geodesic curves have been taken into account. In general relativity, timelike and null geodesic curves represent histories of freely falling particles (or observers) and photons, respectively.[19] The importance of the *g*-boundary of space-time stems from the fact that in the singularity theorems only the completeness (or incompleteness) of space-time with respect to geodesic curves is taken into account. Precisely this issue is the source of another interesting problem. In the Universe there can exist particles the histories of which are not geodesic curves. For instance, a rocket moving with a bounded acceleration is a perfectly physical body[20] (although it is not "freely falling"), and the

17. S. W. Hawking, *Singularities and Geometry of Space-Time,* unpublished essay submitted for the Adam Prize, Cambridge University.

18. R. Geroch, "Local Characterization of Singularities in General Relativity," *J. Math. Phys.* 9 (1968) 450–465.

19. "Freely falling particles" is a technical term meaning particles that move in a given gravitational field under the influence of no other forces.

20. The condition that the acceleration should be bounded is essential. A rocket moving with unbounded acceleration would require an infinite amount of fuel that could hardly be regarded as physical.

space-times exist that are geodesically complete, but incomplete with respect to curves of bounded acceleration. To have a reasonable singularity definition, a criterion concerning such curves should be included in the definition.

A space-time boundary construction satisfying this requirement was proposed by Bernard Schmidt.[21] It is mathematically elegant and physically appealing. Schmidt does not consider directly space-time itself, but rather a larger space of all possible local reference frames that can be defined in this space-time. This larger space is called a *frame bundle* (over space-time). It is very much in the spirit of relativity theory for which reference frames are "more real" than points in space-time. One can meaningfully speak about curves in the frame bundle space, and it turns out that the standard notion of length refers to them correctly. The boundary points of a given space-time are defined in terms of classes of the frame bundle curves having finite lengths. The corresponding space-time boundary is called a *bundle boundary* or, for short, *b-boundary* of space-time; and it takes into account both geodesics and other curves in space-time.

Shortly after its publication Schmidt's b-boundary began to be viewed as the best available description of singularities. It had, however, one serious drawback: to compute b-boundaries of more interesting (nontrivial) space-times effectively was extremely difficult. Only a few years later, B. Bosshardt[22] and R. A. Johnson[23] were able to say something more concrete about the structure of the b-boundaries of such important cases as the closed Friedman world model and the Schwarzschild solution (describing a symmetric black hole)—and their results proved disastrous. It turned out that in both these cases the corresponding b-boundary consisted of a single point. This looks especially pathological in the case of the closed Friedman universe, in which there are two singularities: the initial singularity and the final singularity. In the b-boundary construction they coalesce to a single point; that is, the beginning of the Friedman universe is simultaneously its end. Moreover, in both the closed Friedman and Schwarzschild solutions, from the topological point of view the entire space-times together with their b-boundaries reduce to a single point.[24] Something is really going wrong.

21. B. Schmidt, "A New Definition of Singular Points in General Relativity," *General Relativity and Gravitation* 1 (1971) 269–280.

22. B. Bosshardt, "On the b-Boundary of the Closed Friedman Model," *Communications in Mathematical Physics* 46 (1976) 263–268.

23. R. A. Johnson, "The Bundle Boundary of the Schwarzschild and Friedman Solutions," *J. Math. Phys.* 18 (1977) 898–902.

24. Technically, the singularities are not Hausdorff separated from the rest of space-time.

There were many attempts to cure the situation, but with no substantial effect.[25] During the next several years the beautiful, but now useless, b-boundary construction, almost forgotten, waited on the libraries' shelves for a better time.

MALICIOUS SINGULARITIES AND A DEMIURGE

The situation described in the preceding section suggests that perhaps overly coarse tools were used to deal with a very subtle object. Is there any possibility of finding a subtler tool? The standard way of dealing with spaces in differential geometry is by means of local coordinate systems, but it has been demonstrated by L. Koszul[26] that one can *equivalently* develop differential geometry in terms of functions defined on a considered space. Later on Geroch[27] has shown that this method works, in principle, also when it is applied to space-times of general relativity. By using it we obtain nothing essentially new (and this method is usually much harder than the standard one), but it turns out that it can be quite naturally generalized. With some refinement of technology, functions can be defined on spaces that are not necessarily smooth (in the traditional sense)[28]—that is, on spaces that contain some sorts of singularities. The suitable geometric technology has been elaborated, and the corresponding spaces are known under the name of *differential* or *structured spaces.*[29]

Now it may be possible to reconstruct Schmidt's b-boundary in terms of structured spaces. The results of this procedure are encouraging. Milder kinds of singularities can be fully analyzed if this new method is employed. For instance, a space-time containing the so-called cone singularity (which models an infinitely long one-dimensional "cosmic string") can be regarded as a structured space (the singularity is a part of this space) and effectively studied with the help of the theory of these spaces. As far as stronger singularities are concerned, such as the ones in the closed Friedman and Schwarzschild solutions, the situation is much subtler. We recall that now space-time is modeled by a family of functions defined on it, and to have the full description of space-time this family must be sufficiently rich. In the case of space-times with strong sin-

25. For more details see, for instance, C. T. J. Dodson, "Spacetime Edge Geometry," *Int. J. Theor. Phys.* 17 (1978) 389–504; *Categories, Bundles, and Spacetime Topology,* Orpinton: Shiva Publishing, 1980.

26. L. Koszul, *Fibre Bundles and Differential Geometry,* Bombay: Tata Institute of Fundamental Research, 1960.

27. R. Geroch, "Einstein Algebras," *Comm. Math. Phys.* 9 (1972) 271–275.

28. In this approach, in fact, the very notion of smoothness is generalized.

29. See M. Heller and W. Sasin, "Structured Spaces and Their Application to Relativistic Physics," *J. Math. Phys.* 36 (1995) 3644–3662; strictly speaking, structured spaces are even more general than differential spaces.

gularities, the family of functions defining them contains only constant functions, far from enough for a satisfactory model of space-time (with singularities). Constant functions, in particular, do not distinguish points, because the value of such a function on each point is the same. This explains why the space-times of the closed Friedman model and the Schwarzschild solution together with their b-boundaries collapse to the single points. Singularities that produce such pathologies have been called *malicious singularities*.

It is possible to say even more. Consider the closed Friedman world model. As long as one deals with its space-time without taking into account its two singularities (the initial and the final ones), a sufficiently rich family of functions is defined on it,[30] and everything is as it should be. If, however, one tries to "extend" these functions to the singular boundary, all functions, with the exception of the constant ones, vanish, and everything collapses to a single point.

The following interpretative comment illustrates this situation.[31] For beings living inside the closed Friedman model everything is all right. By studying cosmology they can learn about the existence of the initial singularity in their past, and they can predict the final singularity in their future. Neither of these singularities is directly accessible to them; however, they have learned about the singularities by collecting information from within the space-time in which they live. If they had directly "touched" one of the singularities (tried to "extend" to them the corresponding family of functions), space-time with singularities would immediately have been reduced to a single point. Suppose further that the world under consideration has been created by a Demiurge in the initial singularity. To create the world, the Demiurge must "touch" the singularity (must deal only with constant functions), and therefore for the Demiurge the beginning of the world is simultaneously its end. Theologians always claimed that God is atemporal and everything happens instantaneously for God.

Remember, however, that such metaphoric interpretations are good only as didactic tools illuminating some aspects of the model. The story is evidently not yet finished; what we need are better tools to deal with the malicious nature of strong singularities. For the time being, one could summarize the situation by noting that although the method of structured spaces has provided insight into the nature of the problem and explained the source of difficulties in which the b-boundary construction is involved, it is still not powerful enough to solve completely the problem of malicious singularities.

30. This family contains all smooth functions (in the usual sense) on space-time.
31. It is only noncontradictory with the mathematical structure of our model.

POINTLESS SPACES

Happily enough, one generalization of geometry is still possible. It starts with a simple step. Multiplication of functions has a simple property: the order of functions in their product is irrelevant. Suppose two functions, f and g, are defined on a space X, and we want to multiply them. We do this in the "pointwise" manner. Let x be a point of X. First we compute $f(x)$—the value of the function f at the point x; then we compute $g(x)$—the value of g at x. These two values, $f(x)$ and $g(x)$, are numbers. We multiply them in the usual way and treat the result as the value of the product $f \cdot g$ at the point x, that is, as $(f \cdot g)(x)$. We can express this rule in the short formula $(f \cdot g)(x) = f(x) \cdot g(x)$. And we repeat the same for all points of the considered space X. Because in the multiplication of numbers the order is irrelevant ($7 \cdot 3 = 3 \cdot 7$), the same is true as far as multiplication of functions (defined above) is concerned. We express this by saying that multiplication of functions is *commutative* or that it satisfies the *axiom of commutativity*.

If, in the theory of differential spaces, we rejected the axiom of commutativity, we would obtain a new generalization of geometry, called *noncommutative geometry*. The problem is, however, that the multiplication of functions is always commutative (with the foregoing definition of multiplication); and to pass from commutative (that is, standard) geometry to noncommutative geometry we must change from functions to some other mathematical objects (such as matrices or operators), which are not multiplied "pointwise" (this would lead us back to commutativity). In other words, such objects are not permitted to "feel" points; and if we define a space with the help of such mathematical objects, this space turns out to be a pointless space, that is, a space in which the concept of point has no meaning. In fact, noncommutative spaces are, in principle, purely global constructs in which local notions (such as that of point and its neighborhood) cannot even be defined.

It came as a surprise that in spite of this "strange" property, differential geometry can be done in noncommutative spaces, albeit in a highly generalized sense. The seminal work of Alain Connes[32] soon matured into a new field of research in mathematics and mathematical physics.[33]

Noncommutative geometry has two sources. One is evidently the standard differential geometry of which it is a vast generalization. It should be remembered that the tendency toward generalizing concepts and methods has always

---

32. A. Connes, *Noncommutative Geometry*, New York and London: Academic Press, 1994.

33. See, for instance, J. Madore, *Noncommutative Differential Geometry and Its Physical Applications*, Cambridge: Cambridge University Press, 1999.

been a powerful driving force of mathematical progress. The second source of noncommutative geometry is none other than quantum mechanics. This fact might surprise an outsider, but it is well known to every physicist that in this physical theory observable magnitudes are represented by mathematical objects called *operators in a Hilbert space,* which multiply in a noncommutative way. In fact, the famous Heisenberg uncertainty principles are but the consequence of this noncommutativity. These properties of quantum mechanics were certainly an inspiration for the creators of noncommutative geometry. However, the real connections between noncommutative geometry and the mathematical structure of quantum mechanics go further than that. Every noncommutative space can be represented as a theory of operators in a Hilbert space. Roughly speaking, this means that every noncommutative space can be described in terms of some operators in a certain Hilbert space. One could even suspect that the "strange behavior" met in quantum mechanics (such as nonlocality manifesting itself in the Einstein-Podolsky-Rosen experiment) is the consequence of this structural affinity of quantum mechanics with noncommutative geometry (which from its very nature is nonlocal).

To formulate a mathematical problem correctly, very often one must define a space in which this problem unfolds. The structure of this space does not depend on the mathematician's will, but is implied by the nature of the problem. It happens quite often that the structure of the "space of the problem" is highly sophisticated—sometimes even pathological (from the point of view of standard geometrical methods). The aim of generalizing the usual (commutative) concept of space to the concept of noncommutative space was to find a tool for dealing with such pathological spaces. In fact, the new geometry efficiently deals even with such spaces with which the standard geometrical methods are hopelessly ineffective.[34]

As explained in the preceding sections, relativistic space-times with malicious singularities (such as the Big Bang singularity in the closed Friedman world model) are, from the geometric point of view, highly pathological spaces. Therefore, it seems natural to apply noncommutative methods to their analysis.

NONCOMMUTATIVE STRUCTURE OF SINGULARITIES

Indeed, relativistic space-times with all kinds of singularities can be described as noncommutative spaces. All major difficulties met so far in their

34. A beautiful example of such a space is provided by the so-called Penrose's tiling, a tiling of the Euclidean plane that has two basic tiles: kites and darts. Every finite patch of these tiles occurs infinitely many times in any other tiling of the plane so that any two tilings are locally indistinguishable. The space of all such tilings is a noncommutative space.

study disappear in the degree of generalization that leads to the very concept of noncommutative space.[35] As already shown, in this generalization process local concepts, such as those of points and their neighborhoods, become meaningless. In many situations they are replaced by the concept of *state,* a global notion. Even within the commutative context, if we are speaking about a state of a given system, we do not mean a "well localized" part of it but rather a certain characteristic referring to the system as a whole. Our everyday language also conforms to this way of speaking. If, for example, we speak about the state of an enterprise, we mean by that certain of its global characteristics, such as the increasing production rate or general income. The same intuitions are incorporated into the concept of the state of a physical system.

If we change to the noncommutative description of a space-time with singularities, we lose the possibility of distinguishing points and their neighborhoods, but we can still meaningfully speak about states of the system. Here, however, all states of the Universe are on an equal footing; there is no longer any distinction between singular and nonsingular states. Moreover, each state can be described in terms of operators in a certain Hilbert space in an analogous way, as is usually done in quantum mechanics.

With the use of this method, it was possible to prove several theorems characterizing various types of singularities, including malicious singularities, which occur in relativistic cosmology and astrophysics.[36] These theorems are important also because they disclose the way the singularities originate. As we already know, in the noncommutative regime the question of the existence of singularities is meaningless: we can speak only about the states of the Universe, and there is no distinction between singular and nonsingular states. However, when we change from the noncommutative description of the Universe to its usual (commutative) description, the ordinary space-time, with its points and neighborhoods, emerges, and some states degenerate into singularities.

This opens a new conceptual possibility. We could speculate that noncommutative geometry is not an artificial tool to use in coping with classical singularities in general relativity, but it somehow reflects the structure of the quantum gravity era. The fact that operators in a Hilbert space (which are mathematical objects typical for quantum mechanics) enter the very core of the noncommutative description of singularities could suggest that singularities "know something" about quantum effects. The tempting hypothesis is that

---

35. This has been shown in M.Heller and W. Sasin, "Noncommutative Structure of Singularities in General Relativity," *J. Math. Phys.* 37 (1996) 5665–5671.

36. M. Heller and W. Sasin, "Origin of Classical Singularities," *General Relativity and Gravitation* 31 (1999) 555–570.

below the Planck threshold there is the quantum gravity era that is modeled by a noncommutative geometry and, consequently, is totally nonlocal. In this era there is no space and time in their usual meaning. Only when the Universe passes through the Planck threshold, a "phase transition" to the commutative geometry occurs, and in this transition the standard space-time emerges together with its singular boundary. In fact, such a scenario of the very early Universe has been proposed.[37]

One often asks, Will the future theory of quantum gravity remove the initial singularity from our image of the Universe? Usually, either a "yes" or a "no" answer is given to this question, and they are supposed to be mutually exclusive. In light of the proposed scenario a third possibility should be taken into account: The Planck era is atemporal and aspacial, and the above question, as referred to this era, becomes meaningless. From the point of view of noncommutative geometry everything is regular, although drastically different from what we usually meet in space-time. As already shown, the singularities are formed in the process of the transition through the Planck threshold when space-time emerges out of noncommutative geometry. This process could also be explained in the following way.

Usually, we think of the Planck era as being hidden in the prehistory of the Universe when its typical scale was of the order of 10^{-33} cm. However, the Planck era could be found even now if we delve deeper and deeper into the strata of the world's structure until we reached the threshold length of 10^{-33} cm. After crossing this threshold we would find ourselves in the Planck "stratum" with its noncommutative regime. On this fundamental level, below the Planck scale, all states are on an equal footing; there is no distinction between singular states and nonsingular states. Only the macroscopic observer, situated in space-time (and thus well beyond the Planck threshold), can say that his Universe started from the initial singularity in its finite past, and possibly will meet the final singularity in its finite future.

METHODOLOGICAL CONCLUSIONS

Having reviewed the story of the singularity problem in twentieth-century cosmology, including some of its interpretations as the beginning of the Universe, we can now draw out of it a few methodological conclusions referring to the relationship between theology and natural theology (or philosophy, in

37. M. Heller, W. Sasin, and D. Lambert, "Groupoid Approach to Noncommutative Quantization of Gravity," *J. Math. Phys.* 38 (1997) 5840–5853; M. Heller and W. Sasin, "The Emergence of Time," *Physics Letters* A250 (1998) 48–54; M. Heller and W. Sasin, "Noncommutative Unification of General Relativity and Quantum Mechanics," *Int. J. Theor. Phys.* 38 (1999) 1619–1642.

general), from one part; and scientific theories and models from the other. Here and in the rest of this section, by interpretation I do not mean the "exegesis of the mathematical structure" of a given theory or model but rather an interpretation that is "superimposed" on this theory or model.

1. As we have seen, it is usually the latest scientific theory or model that gives rise to theological or philosophical interpretations, and very often these interpretations are announced with such conviction as to suggest that the theories or models are indubitable results of science. For instance, after proving several theorems about the existence of classical singularities, Hawking (with his co-author George Ellis) expressed the view that these theorems support "the idea that the universe began a finite time ago." Later on, when Hawking (with his colleague Jim Hartle) produced the now well-known model of the quantum origin of the Universe, he switched to the interpretation that is best encapsulated in the following quotation:

So long as the universe had a beginning, we could suppose it had a creator. But if the universe is really completely self-contained, having no boundary or edge, it would have neither beginning nor end: it would simply be. What place, then, for a creator?[38]

2. One could do theology or natural theology without any contact with scientific theories or models, and in fact many theologians and philosophers prefer this way of pursuing their disciplines. However, in such a case there is danger that instead of scientific theories or models, some pseudo-scientific ideas or outdated concepts will serve as a background for theological or philosophical speculations. The point is that neither theology nor philosophy can be studied without a "cultural environment" of a given epoch, and a general image of the world constitutes a vital element of this environment. If the image of the world is not taken (critically) from the sciences, it will certainly infiltrate theological or philosophical speculations from various intellectually suspect sources of human imagination.

3. In many theological or philosophical interpretations of cosmological theories or models, both theologians and cosmologists (especially the latter) often present the image of God creating the world and playing with the laws of physics, for instance, by throwing dice in order to decide which model of the Universe should be brought into existence. Incidentally, very often in such situations, the laws of physics seem to be exempt from God's omnipotence, and in any case God is supposed to be constrained by the laws of probability and statistics. Sometimes this picture of the world plays the role of a metaphor or a

38. S. W. Hawking, *A Brief History of Time,* New York: Bantam Books, 1988.

heuristic tool in some abstract analyses. If such an image of the Creator is taken more seriously, one can hardly recognize the God of theology or Judeo-Christian belief whose functions can by no means be reduced to those connected with "manufacturing" the world. It seems that such images of the Creator are laden more with the deistic concept of Deity than with the Judeo-Christian idea of God. This is why in such contexts I prefer to speak of a Demiurge rather than of the authentic God. However, this does not mean that the theologian has no lesson about God to learn from scientific theories. Such theories can disclose some unexpected "ways of existence" (e.g., the atemporal character of a noncommutative regime), which, by analogy, could be used in theological speculations about God.

4. A mathematical model could be of some importance for theological or philosophical analyses even if it is not empirically verified, and even if it will never be. Any mathematical model, provided it is correctly constructed, shows that the set of assumptions upon which it is based is not contradictory, and as such it can either falsify or corroborate some philosophical idea. For example, our noncommutative model unifying general relativity and quantum mechanics tells us something philosophically interesting, even if it will never find any empirical support. Its message is that existence in space and time is not the necessary prerequisite for the unfolding of physics. In particular, this model falsifies the doctrine, common among philosophers, that existence in time is the condition sine qua non for the possibility of any change and dynamics. Change and dynamics, in a generalized sense, however, are possible even in the absence of local concepts such as that of point or time instant (see the next section).

5. One should never forget about the temporary and transitory character of all physical theories and models. Even if some of them have successfully undergone the confrontation process with empirical data, they always can become a "special case" of a future more general theory, or of a model. The new conceptual environment could make their present philosophical or theological interpretation no longer attractive, or even highly artificial.

6. Scientific theories or models are per se neutral with respect to theological or philosophical interpretations. They can be interpreted in various ways as long as these interpretations do not contradict their mathematical structure. This does not mean that all such interpretations are on an equal footing; only that they cannot be refuted by arguments taken from these theories or models alone (because we suppose that these interpretations are not contradictory with their mathematical structures). Theological or philosophical interpretations of scientific theories or models can, of course, critically compete with

each other. Popper's "criterion of disputability" clearly applies to them: any rational interpretation should be open for discussion and criticism by its rivals.

THEOLOGICAL AND PHILOSOPHICAL CONCLUSIONS

Having in mind all the above methodological warnings, we can finally ask about a theological (and philosophical) lesson to be learned from the singularity problem as it evolved in twentieth-century cosmology.

1. It has built a strong case against the Newtonian concept of creation, that is, against the idea of an absolute space and an absolute time existing "from forever" (a kind of *sensoria Dei*) and God creating energy and matter at certain places of the absolute space and at the determined instant of the absolute time. Even classical singularities could hardly be reconciled with such an idea of creation. At classical singularities space-time breaks down, and the Newtonian concept of creation could be saved only by claiming that classical singularities are but an artifact of the method rather than the authentic element of the theory. Such a possibility, however, is practically excluded by the theorems about the existence of singularities.

2. The modern theologian should consider the possibility of going back to the traditional doctrine that the creation of the Universe is an atemporal (and aspatial) act. Starting from the second half of the nineteenth century, some physical theories (thermodynamics, statistical mechanics, certain data from the theory of elementary particles) suggested that time is essentially a macroscopic phenomenon connected with statistical properties of a great number of physical individuals (particles); and many contemporary quantum gravity-proposals and models of the very early Universe describe the Planck era as timeless and spaceless. The most radical in this respect seems to be the noncommutative model described in the previous sections, in which all local concepts are excluded by the very nature of noncommutative geometry. It would be inconsistent to regard creation as the process immersed in time while simultaneously asserting that the beginnings of the Universe are atemporal.

3. Some theologians and philosophers (especially those of the Whiteheadian school) claim that the existence "in transient time" is an ontological necessity. The fact that atemporal mathematical models of the physical world (in its Planck era) have been constructed falsifies this claim. The main argument of these theologians and philosophers that a timeless God would be a static being with no possibility of acting is erroneous. It is interesting to look in this respect at the noncommutative model of the Planck era. In physics we usually describe motion in terms of vector quantities. For instance, the velocity of a moving point is a tangent vector to the curve describing the trajectory of this point.

The curve is parametrized by a time parameter; and to represent the velocity of the moving point at a given time instant, we choose the tangent vector to this curve at the point corresponding to this time instant. In physical models based on a noncommutative geometry there are no points and time instants and, consequently, no vectors tangent at a given point. All of these concepts are local, and as such have no counterparts in the noncommutative setting. However, a standard (commutative) dynamical system (for instance, a body in motion) can be described in terms of vector fields, and vector field, being a global concept, has its noncommutative generalization, called the *derivation of a noncommutative algebra*. We cannot go here into detail, but it is enough to remember that vector fields on the usual (commutative) space are also derivations of a certain algebra (the algebra of smooth functions on this space). One can meaningfully speak of a noncommutative dynamics (without reference to local concepts such as that of point or time instant) provided that one describes noncommutative dynamics in terms of derivations of the corresponding algebra. Therefore, a generalized dynamics is possible even in the absence of the usual notion of time. Notice that this noncommutative dynamics is not the usual dynamics simply transferred to a new conceptual environment, but rather dynamics in the truly generalized sense. One of the essential features of this generalization consists in replacing all local elements with their global counterparts (if they exist).[39]

As always in similar situations in physics, the correspondence with previous theories is important. This is the case as far as the temporal properties of our model are concerned. It can be shown[40] that, as we cross the Planck threshold, first some temporal order appears and only then does space-time emerge, eventually with its singular boundary (depending on the model).

4. The latter property discloses a certain relativity of the concept of the beginning of the Universe. If we regard the initial singularity as a physical counterpart of the theological notion of the beginning of the Universe, we must say that from the perspective of the macroscopic observer the Universe had its beginning a finite number of years ago; but from the perspective of the fundamental level (supposing it is essentially noncommutative), the very concept of the beginning is meaningless. In the light of this result it could be interesting to go back to another traditional doctrine, strongly defended by St. Thomas

39. Theologians would certainly notice an analogy between this generalization process and the way of forming concepts referring to God in the traditional theology. I have in mind especially the so-called *via emminentiae*, a concept that is known from everyday usage as ascribed to God, but only after it has been purified from all negative connotations, and after all its positive connotations have been strengthened to their possible maximum.

40. M. Heller and W. Sasin, "The Emergence of Time," *Phys. Lett.* A250 (1998) 48–54.

Aquinas, that the beginning of the Universe and the creation of the Universe are two completely distinct concepts. Because the creation of the Universe is but a dependence of the Universe in its existence on the Primary Cause, one can think, without any danger of contradiction, about the created Universe existing from minus time infinity. The dependence in existence does not require the initiation of existence.[41]

I emphasize again that the noncommutative model does not prove or imply this traditional doctrine concerning the beginning and creation; it only shows its logical consistency.

TIMELESSNESS AND TIME

This final section explores, as a corollary of the foregoing analyses, the traditional doctrine of the relationship between the temporal existence of the Universe and God's eternity, and its consequences for our understanding of creation. To this end I cite the recent essay by Ernan McMullin[42] in which this author goes back to the traditional doctrine on time and eternity in order to cope with another important problem—that of purpose and contingency in the evolutionary process.

In the Platonic myth of creation, a Demiurge transformed independently existing chaotic stuff into the ordered Cosmos. In Aristotle's physics, the world always existed and only needed to be put into motion by the First Mover. St. Augustine saw God in a totally different way, namely, "as a Creator in the fullest sense, a Being from whom the existence of all things derives" (p. 104). Such a being must be above all constraints; and it cannot be denied that existence in time is one of the most far-reaching constraints. It limits one's existence to the transitory "now" surrounded by two kinds of nothingness: the nothingness of all those things that formerly existed but do not now exist; and the nothingness of all those things that do not yet exist. Perhaps it is even immersed into the third kind of nothingness—that of all those things that could have existed but never will.

Therefore, God should be regarded as being "outside" time created, though the metaphor is an imperfect one. Calling God "eternal" is not a way of saying that God is without beginning or end, like Aristotle's universe. "Eternal" does not mean unending duration; it means that temporal notions simply do not apply to the Creator as Creator (p. 105). The objection that this would make God

---

41. See *Aquinas on Creation*, ed. S. E. Balner and W. E. Carrol, Toronto: Pontifical Institute of Medieval Studies, 1997.

42. E. McMullin, "Evolutionary Contingency and Cosmic Purpose," *Studies in Science and Theology* 5 (1997) 91–112. In the rest of this section page numbers refer to this paper.

"static," devoid of all dynamics, was neutralized by the famous Boetius "defini-tion" of eternity. His formulation, "Eternity is the whole, simultaneous, and perfect possession of boundless life,"[43] emphasizes the abundant activity of the perfect and unconstrained life. Accordingly, one should understand the act of creation:

> Time is a condition of the creature, a sign of dependence. It is created *with* the crea-ture. . . . The act of creation is a single one, in which what is past, present or future from the perspective of the creature issues as a single whole from the Creator. . . . Cre-ation continues at every moment, and each moment has the same relation of depen-dency on the Creator. (p. 105)

Such an understanding of God's eternity and creation has further conse-quences for many theological problems, including the problems of design and chance. If God exists outside time and space,

> God knows the past and the future of each creature, not by memory or by foretelling . . . as another creature might, but in the same direct way that God knows the crea-ture's present. . . . Terms like "plan" and "purpose" obviously shift meaning when the element of time is absent. For God to plan is for the outcome to occur. There is no in-terval between decision and completion. (pp. 105–106)

In such a perspective, the concepts of chance and necessity also "shift their meanings." They are but two aspects of the same atemporal and totally global activity. God knows the outcomes of laws and chance not by calculating from the initial conditions, but in the same direct way as God knows everything. What for us is a chance, for God is a detail of the picture that is simply present.

Such an approach solves so many theological questions that it ought not to be hastily dismissed (and, as we have seen, it is in consonance with contempo-rary trends in theoretical physics). Its unpopularity among some theologians may well stem from the fact that this approach strongly emphasizes the tran-scendence of God, whereas nowadays we prefer speaking about God's imma-nence. However, we should not forget that in St. Augustine's teaching, God "is also immanent in every existent at every moment, sustaining it in being" (p. 105). Here again the noncommutative model of the atemporal Planck's era might be of some help to our imagination: macroscopic physics is only the re-sult of some "averaging" of what happens on the noncommutative, funda-mental level. Time is but an epiphenomenon of timeless existence.

43. Quoted after McMullin, art. cit., 105.

IO GENERALIZATIONS: FROM QUANTUM MECHANICS TO GOD

INTRODUCTION: EVOLUTION WITHIN THE CONCEPTUAL FRAMEWORK

The evolution of concepts is a driving force of scientific progress. A new concept contains in itself the heritage of its predecessors and, at the same time, is open to future generalizations. However, concepts never evolve "by themselves"; they participate in the struggle of solving problems. There is always a problem that has to be solved, a challenge to the concept currently in use. If an attempt to put a new content into an old concept produces paradoxes and inconsistencies, one is confronted with a crisis. Many such "critical situations" make the concept less resistant to change, and in this way a "conceptual revolution" is initiated.

In fact, there are no isolated concepts in science. Every change in the content of one concept results in shifts of meaning in many other concepts. It is, therefore, more correct to speak about evolution within the conceptual framework than about the evolution of particular concepts. There are various mechanisms of this evolution—from gradual modifications to sudden jumps. To describe them in particular cases, in as detailed a way as possible, is a task for historians of science, and to reconstruct different patterns of this evolution is a challenge for philosophers of science.

The evolution of concepts is reflected in the evolution of language. Some philosophers are inclined to reduce the evolution of science to the evolution of scientific language. It is usually easier to analyze terms as they appear in various linguistic contexts than to explore the meanings of concepts as they unfold in the historical process of the development of science. However, people engaged in creating science think rather than speak, or first think and then speak to each other; and thinking is in terms of concepts, whereas speaking is in terms of terms. This is why, in the following, I prefer to focus on concepts rather than on terms. The point is, however, that for the analyst the only way to concepts is through their linguistic counterparts, that is, through terms.

Evolution "within the conceptual framework" is especially clearly seen at the extremities of the history of science, that is, in its beginnings and in the current frontier of research. Let us consider an example.

The "great miracle," the origin of rational discourse concerning the world, happened around the sixth century B.C. in the Greek colonies on the coast of Asia Minor. Central to this process was the formation of the concept of necessity. This concept gradually replaced the former idea of the world as a stage of passion and a "free game" between gods or primitive elements. It is necessity that produces the natural order by linking different phenomena into chains of causes and effects. To express this idea the Greek thinkers used the term *ananke*, which in everyday language "literally meant the various means, from persuasion to torture, by which a criminal was made to confess."[1] In this way, the everyday concept changed its meaning to become a predecessor of such important concepts as law of nature, determinism, and causality. In the subsequent history of science these concepts were never static; they underwent many changes and transformations.

Now, let us go to the other extremity of history, to current research in quantum mechanics. The very same concepts—determinism, causality, law, and chance—are at the focus of the contemporary debate. Although all these concepts are outcomes of a long evolutionary chain of various adaptations and mutations, their contemporary meanings are shaped by problems in which they are involved and which remain to be solved. Such problems as "decoherence," "entanglement," "nonlocality" (to name only the most widely discussed) permeate the above-mentioned concepts and change their meanings from inside.

There are many patterns according to which concepts evolve, but in all these "adventures of ideas" one can quite easily discern a certain common feature: as concepts evolve, they become more and more general. The history of physics clearly shows that although the tendency to generalization has seldom been a leading motive for change, the new concepts were usually more general than the old ones. This process is by no means a linear one. It has many side-branches and ramifications. In particular, it may well happen that as time passes some concepts become more refined and more specific. After all, the goal of science is to explain each specific phenomenon, but to explain such a phenomenon means always to place it in a more general pattern. This seems to be consonant with the fact that in the generalization process old concepts are not eliminated but are limited in their validity to a smaller domain than originally

1. O. Pedersen, *The Book of Nature*, Vatican City State: Vatican Observatory Publications, 1992, 8.

envisaged. The point is that it is precisely the tendency toward more and more general horizons that makes the mainstream current in the evolution of science. One could risk the statement that the generalization of concepts and theories determines an "arrow of time" within the process of scientific transformation.

The history of science could be looked upon as a great attempt by humanity to catch reality in the net of concepts and theories. And every time we think the endeavor has succeeded, it turns out that reality is richer than the concepts and theories elaborated so far. The situation is not unlike the one in theology where one speaks about God even if one believes that God is infinite and, consequently, transcends all human conceptual and linguistic possibilities. Some theologians go so far as to say that everything we can assert about God is by negation *(via negativa)*. For instance, if we say that God is infinite, we in fact deny to God the property of being finite—the property which we know from our own experience, and about which we are able to speak sensibly. In the view of many theologians, some other concepts (whose origin is not so manifestly by negation as the concept of infinity), when referred to God, "though partly true, [are] ultimately false and must be transcended."[2] The concept of Being itself would belong to this class, although it was Duns Scotus who claimed that if we say "God exists," there is more falsehood than truth in this statement.

Does this mean that we should remain silent about God? Traditional theology never surrendered to this temptation. It is better to say something about God rather than nothing, even if it is at the cost of transcending the syntactic and semantic rules of ordinary language. Syntactic and semantic rules are indeed at the center of interest in modern analytic philosophy. After the first period of enthusiasm, it soon turned out that the purely formal approach to language was not enough. No language can fulfill its role without an interpretation, that is, without a world of "objects" or "states of affairs" to which it *refers*. The problem of *reference* became the central problem of the philosophy of language. Ludwig Wittgenstein in his *Tractatus Logico-philosophicus* went so far as to ask the question: What structure should be ascribed to the world to ensure the meaningfulness of language? He tried to answer this question in a purely formal way. However, he soon realized that the purely formalistic standpoint is not enough. In his *Philosophical Investigations* he claims that the meaning of a term is determined by the rules of its usage in a given context within a certain "linguistic game." If so, can we meaningfully speak about what goes beyond the domain of our "linguistic games," that is, beyond the domain of our everyday activity? And what about the language of science and philosophy? In both

2. R. C. Neville, *A Theology Primer,* New York: State University of New York Press, 1991, 179.

of these fields we try not only to describe what we see, but also (or even first of all) to understand what cannot be seen (e.g., the subatomic world). Ladrière regards this as a challenge for the "Great European Rationalism."[3]

In contemporary physics we are faced with insistent interpretative problems, focusing on the question of how to correlate our language with what we have been lucky to decipher regarding the quantum world. And this issue of interpretation is even more insistent in theology. It is true that we can speak about God only "on the ruins of our semantics," but I think that from the very fact that our language breaks down, and from trying to see how it does break down, we could be able to say more about God than by simply adding a negation functor to our utterances. In modern physics, the breakdown of language is an unmistakable sign that underlying concepts should be generalized. The assumption underlying the present study is that theology can learn something, in this respect (by analogy rather than in detail), from physics.

Of course, there is one great difference between physics and theology that should constantly be kept in mind. A generalized concept always transcends the concept of which it is a generalization. In physics, we can compare the two concepts with each other, and clearly see the semantic mechanisms that are at work in the generalization process. If this strategy is applied to language about God, we know that our everyday concepts must be transcended; but we can only speculate how this should be, and we will never know to what extent the newly elaborated concepts are adequate. In contemporary physical theories the degree of generalization is immense. Concepts that are now standard in physical theories are very distant from those we use in our everyday life. In theology the degree of transcendence goes much further.

The goal of this chapter is to look, in this respect, at contemporary quantum theory and try to derive from it a lesson for theology. To do so more effectively, in analyzing quantum physics I will use not quite standard (but perfectly legitimate) tools. My starting point is the fact that the main distinguishing feature of quantum mechanics is its noncommutativity (this is, of course, very well known); and to show the degree of generalization already present in this physical theory, I will use the recently discovered noncommutative geometry. It not only clearly shows the generalization mechanisms underlying the present theory; it also points toward its possible further generalizations.

ALGEBRAIC FORMULATION OF QUANTUM MECHANICS

How can we gain access to the quantum world, which, in itself, is closed to our sensory perceptions? We can only hope that some quantum phenomena,

3. J. Ladrière, *L'articulation du sens*, vol. 2, Paris: Éd. CERF, 1984, 109.

after being magnified to the classical level (spontaneously or through our artful inventions), could be detected by some of our measuring devices. Perhaps the fact that this sometimes does happen is not entirely surprising. After all, our macroscopic world has somehow emerged from the more fundamental quantum level. These properties of the quantum world, which can, at least in principle, be measured by our macroscopic devices, are called *observables*. The question that arises is, Can we construct a full theory of the quantum world based only on observables? The question itself and the positive answer to it, favored by some adherents of the so-called Copenhagen interpretation, are evidently philosophical in character. They were prompted by an empiricist presupposition that, in the circumstances, seemed to be entirely reasonable. Historically, of course, this presupposition owed much to the philosophy of logical positivism.

Today we think that the physics of quantum theory can be expressed not only in terms of observables alone (or operators, see below) or of the states of a quantum system alone (or vectors of a Hilbert space), but in ingenious combinations of the two (such as expectation values or transition matrix elements). We can choose as primitive elements of the theory either states or observables. In fact, the empiricist formulation of quantum mechanics based on observables came later, when the formulation in terms of unobservable states (represented as vectors in a Hilbert space) was already well known and thoroughly explored. Of course, what one needs is a certain mathematical representation of observables, but once one has it, the entire range of quantum mechanics can be expressed in terms of this representation. From the works of P. Jordan, J. von Neumann, and E. Wigner,[4] I. E. Segal,[5] and R. Haag and D. Kastler,[6] the formulation of quantum mechanics emerged that is now known as its *algebraic formulation*. One first defines an abstract C*-algebra (read: "C-star-algebra"), and it turns out that its elements can be regarded as mathematical representatives of observables (if there is no danger of misunderstanding, elements of the C*-algebra are also called *observables*). It can be proved that from the C*-algebraic formulation of quantum mechanics, one can recover its original formulation in terms of Hilbert spaces.[7] In fact, the C*-algebraic formulation of quantum mechanics is more general than its Hilbert space formulation, just to the extent needed. Quantum statistical mechanics and quantum systems with

4. P. Jordan, J. von Neumann, and E. Wigner, "On the Algebraic Generalization of the Quantum Mechanical Formalism," *Ann. Math.* 35 (1934) 29.

5. I. E. Segal, "Postulates for General Quantum Mechanics," *Ann. Math.* 48 (1947) 930–948; "Irreducible Representations of Operator Algebras," *Bull. Am. Math. Sic.* 53 (1947) 73–88.

6. R. Haag and D. Kastler, "An Algebraic Approach to Quantum Field Theory," *J. Math. Phys.* 5 (1964) 848–861.

7. See, for instance: W. Thirring, *Lehrbuch der Mathematischen Physik*, Wien: Springer, 1979.

an infinite number of degrees of freedom (field theories) are somewhat beyond the reach of the Hilbert space formulation, whereas the C*-algebraic formulation works in these areas very well. And it came as a nice surprise that, for some time, C*-algebras had been well known to mathematicians. Such algebras naturally appear in the theory of so-called Banach spaces, an important mathematical theory.

Physicists invented the C*-algebraic formulation of quantum mechanics by isolating some properties connected with measuring procedures from the usual Hilbert space formulation of this physical theory. This statement should be understood in the following way. As already mentioned, in the standard formulation vectors in a Hilbert space represent states of the quantum system under consideration. When a measurement is carried out of a quantum system in a given state, the measuring device interacts with this system, changing its state. Therefore, the measurement consists of a transition from one state to another, and the act of measurement is what causes this transition. Because states are vectors in the Hilbert space, formally the measurement should be described as something that, by acting on a vector in the Hilbert space, changes this vector into another vector in the same Hilbert space. Something that does this is known in mathematics as an operator (acting on a given Hilbert space). We can depict this in the following way:

$$\text{operator: vector } 1 \Rightarrow \text{vector } 2$$

Because various devices measure various physical properties (one measures position, another momentum, etc.), various operators can be identified with various physical properties of quantum systems. This is why operators on a Hilbert space are also called simply *observables,* and, if there is no danger of misunderstanding, the name is used interchangeably for physical properties and operators corresponding to them.

Once we are in the kingdom of mathematics, we can profit from its rich possibilities. For instance, we can use the mathematical concept of representation to understand the connection between the theory of C*-algebras and the theory of Hilbert spaces. To say that an abstract mathematical structure has a representation in a concrete mathematical structure means that the concrete mathematical structure has all the formal properties of the abstract structure—that it is its concrete incarnation. And it is exactly what happens in our case: every C*-algebra has a representation in a subset of (bounded) operators in a Hilbert space. The fact that the set of observables in quantum mechanics has formal properties of a C is not just a happy coincidence; it is rooted in deep mathematical results.

Now, we come to our main topic. C*-algebras that find their application in quantum mechanics, in particular in algebras of (bounded) operators on a Hilbert space, are *noncommutative* algebras. We say that a certain operation, for example, multiplication, is commutative if the order of factors does not affect the result. For instance, $3 \cdot 7 = 7 \cdot 3$, which means that the multiplication of numbers is commutative. If this property does not hold, we say that the operation is *noncommutative,* and in fact the multiplication of operators in a Hilbert space is noncommutative. As we can see, the concept of commutativity is a very simple concept, but it has far-reaching consequences. I would risk the statement that (besides linearity) it is precisely the noncommutativity of observables in quantum mechanics that is responsible for all the peculiarities of this physical theory. Let us consider an example.

For a newcomer into the field of quantum mechanics, the Heisenberg relations are always a great surprise. It turns out that they are the direct consequence of noncommutativity. Let, for instance, x be the position of a particle and p its momentum. If they multiply in the commutative way (as it is the case in classical physics), we would have

$$xp = px$$

or

$$xp - px = 0.$$

But in quantum mechanics we have

$$xp - px \neq 0,$$

and indeed this difference cannot be less than the Planck constant h, that is,

$$xp - px \geq h.$$

This is exactly the Heisenberg relation for the position and momentum. It can be interpreted in the following way. If we first measure the momentum of a particle and then its position (first p then x, we write it in the reverse order as xp), the measurement of momentum perturbs the position of the particle, and consequently the result is different from when we first measure the position of a particle and then its momentum (px) because in the latter case the measurement of the position disturbs the momentum of the particle (consequently, $xp \neq px$). And it is the Planck constant h that determines the lower bound of this perturbation.

It is a custom in mathematics to abbreviate the expression $xp - px$ to $[x, p]$ and to call it the *commutator* of x and p. Therefore, if x and p are the position and momentum of a classical particle, for example, of a billiard ball, we can write

$$[x, p] = 0;$$

and if x and p are the position and momentum of a quantum particle, we have

$$[x, p\,] \geq h.$$

Let A be a C*-algebra. If it is a commutative algebra, the commutators of all its elements vanish, that is,

$$[a, b] = 0,$$

where a and b are any elements of A. If A is a noncommutative algebra, the commutators of at least some of its elements, for instance, of a and b, do not vanish, that is,

$$[a, b] \geq k,$$

where k is a deformation parameter. Every commutative algebra can be made noncommutative by suitably perturbing it (with a certain perturbation parameter). In the light of the above we can say that, from the mathematical point of view, quantum mechanics is but a noncommutative C*-algebra, with the Planck constant playing the role of a deformation parameter. In fact, it must be assumed that the deformation parameter is only related to the Planck constant.

In the next section we will explore some important consequences of noncommutativity more deeply.

ONE STEP FURTHER

One of the main trends in modern physics is the tendency to geometrization. It can be traced back to Descartes, who claimed that extension (which is a purely geometric property) is the fundamental property of material bodies and, consequently, that physics should be carried on *more geometrico*. This tendency reached its peak with Einstein's general relativity, which is par excellence a geometric theory; its main idea is to present gravity as the curvature of space-time. On the other hand, quantum mechanics could hardly be called a geometric theory. Its strongly probabilistic features make it rather far away from anything we would be inclined to associate with geometry. This is certainly one of the reasons why it is so difficult to unify quantum mechanics with general relativity. However, we could at least try to look at quantum mechanics with a "geometric eye" and to geometrize at least some of its aspects.

It is rather evident that in this process the very concept of geometry would have to be generalized. It often happens that if a mathematical or physical theory admits more than one formulation, only one of these formulations can serve as a suitable starting point for the chain of subsequent generalizations. It turns out that in the case of quantum mechanics this role is fulfilled by its algebraic formulation (briefly presented in the preceding section) rather than by its usual formulation in terms of Hilbert space. To show this we must first turn to the very concept of geometric space.

In modern differential geometry, the concept of geometric space has been rigorously elaborated and is known under the technical term of "differential manifold" or simply "manifold." The standard way of defining this concept is in terms of coordinate systems with which this "space" can be equipped. This way of defining a manifold closely follows the practice of geometers who usually do their calculations in terms of coordinates of various geometric objects (points, vectors, curves) in a given manifold. It turns out, however, that this approach is rather rigid, not suitable for further generalizations. Happily enough, there is another equivalent method of defining a manifold that proves to be more flexible in this respect. Instead of considering coordinate systems on a given manifold, we can consider a family of all smooth functions on this manifold, and it can be shown that all relevant information about the manifold is contained in this family of functions. The essential point is that it forms an algebra. In principle, one can forget about coordinates and construct the geometry of the manifold entirely in terms of the algebra of smooth functions. To deal with functions is usually more difficult than to compute with the help of coordinates, but, as we have remarked above, the "functional" approach turns out to be more suitable for further generalization.

First, we can take any algebra of functions and treat it—*ex definitione*—as consisting of smooth functions on a certain space. Spaces that are introduced in this way are called *differential spaces* (or *structured spaces*), and they are more general than differential manifolds: each manifold is a differential space, but not every differential space is a manifold.[8]

Because functions are multiplied in a commutative way, all functional algebras (i.e., algebras the elements of which are functions) are commutative algebras, but we can go even further and claim that any algebra, not necessarily a commutative one, defines a certain space. In such a case, we speak about a *non-*

---

8. See M. Heller and W. Sasin, "Structured Spaces and Their Application to Relativistic Physics," *J. Math. Phys.* 36 (1995) 3644–3662. Structured spaces are somewhat more general than differential spaces.

commutative space. This is the main idea of the new branch of mathematics that is nowadays known under the name of *noncommutative geometry.* It has recently been elaborated, in great detail, by many mathematicians and theoretical physicists.[9]

POINTLESS SPACES

Noncommutative geometry is indeed a vast generalization of the standard geometry. Some "sets" or "objects," which did not surrender so far to the usual geometric methods and were regarded as pathologies rather than mathematically described "sets" or "objects," are now perfectly workable noncommutative spaces. One of the main peculiarities of noncommutative spaces is their totally global character. In principle, no local concept can be given any meaning in the context of noncommutative geometry. Typical examples of local concepts are those of point and neighborhood, and it turns out that, in general, we cannot say that a noncommutative space consists of points. Noncommutative spaces are indeed pointless spaces. Let us look more deeply into this matter.

As we know, noncommutative geometry is based on algebraic concepts, and if we want to reach the very roots of the point concept we should think in algebraic terms. In the standard approach, points of any differential manifold (which is a commutative space) are identified with the help of their coordinates, but how can one identify a point when one works with the algebra of smooth functions on a given manifold rather than with coordinate systems on it? The answer is quite straightforward. It is clear that every point is uniquely determined by all smooth functions that vanish at it. The family of such functions has certain properties that—in mathematical jargon—qualify them as *maximal ideals* of the algebra of smooth functions on the manifold under consideration. We can say that in the algebraic approach, the role of points is played by maximal ideals of a given algebra. In other words, in the standard (commutative) geometry, a point can be equivalently described either by specifying its coordinates (in a given coordinate system) or as a maximal ideal of the algebra of smooth functions on the manifold (space) under consideration. And here we touch on an important property of noncommutative algebras: in general, they have no maximal ideals, and consequently it is impossible to define points in noncommutative spaces. Similar reasoning shows also

---

9. See, for instance: A. Connes, *Noncommutative Geometry,* New York and London: Academic Press, 1994; G. Landi, *An Introduction to Noncommutative Spaces and Their Geometries,* Berlin, Heidelberg, and New York: Springer, 1997; J. Madore, *An Introduction to Noncommutative Differential Geometry and Its Physical Applications,* 2nd ed., Cambridge: Cambridge University Press, 1999.

that the concept of a neighborhood (of a given point) is meaningless in them.

To see the vastness of the generalization encountered here, let us look at this problem from yet another point of view. It is sometimes claimed that set theory can serve as a logical basis for all other mathematical theories. Of course, the crucial concept in set theory is that of "belonging to a set." For this concept to have a meaning, one must be able to identify elements of the collection under consideration by means of an at most denumerable family of properties. In noncommutative spaces, in general, there is no such possibility; one cannot distinguish the elements of such a collection from each other by means of a denumerable family of properties. (Each such property would define a measurable subset of the collection being considered.[10]) Alain Connes concludes: "The noncommutative sets are thus characterized by the effective indiscernability of their elements."[11]

The concept that is closest in this context to the concept of point is that of state. It is well known in both classical and quantum physics. Let us note, however, that it is a global concept. For instance, in classical mechanics the state of a system composed of n particles, where n can be as large a number as one wishes, is characterized by providing information about the positions and momenta of *all* particles. In quantum mechanics, states are represented by vectors in a Hilbert space and play the crucial role in the structure of this theory. The nonlocal character of this concept can be clearly seen, for instance, in the Einstein-Podolsky-Rosen-type experiments, in which two particles (e.g., electrons) that once interacted are described by the same state (or by a vector in a Hilbert space), even if they are now at opposite edges of the Galaxy.

We can now quite clearly see that there is a certain affinity between the main characteristic of quantum mechanics and that of noncommutative geometry. It looks as if a noncommutative space were underlying quantum phenomena. The Heisenberg relations, nonlocal effects, and the importance of the state concept are doubtlessly results of some underlying noncommutativity. As we remember from section 2, quantum mechanics can be expressed in terms of a noncommutative $C^{\star}$-algebra, and it is a straightforward thing to associate with such an algebra a noncommutative space. However, we will not pursue this line of research. Ambitions of physicists go much further than to obtain yet another formulation of that well-known theory. The main goal of current research in theoretical physics is to unify quantum mechanics with general relativity, and it seems that noncommutative geometry can offer new possibilities

10. This is valid provided one decides to use only measurable maps between spaces; see A. Connes, *Noncommutative Geometry*, 74.

11. Ibid.

here. In fact, there have been many attempts to formulate a noncommutative version of general relativity with the clear intention of making it later a quantum gravity theory.[12] In a series of papers, I have presented, together with my coworkers, a working model of how this could be done.[13] This is certainly not yet a full physical theory, but rather an attempt to find a new pathway that would possibly lead to the main goal of current investigations in physics. The first results are encouraging, but there is still a long way to go. In this study, I will not go into details of this approach but rather will sketch the philosophy underlying the project. In this chapter, I am interested not so much in physical results as in the "adventures of concepts" and in what can be learned from physical models about the limits of language and imagination.

NONCOMMUTATIVE REGIME

The main idea of the new approach is to suppose that the physics ruling the Universe on the fundamental level is based on a noncommutative geometry, and that on this level there is no distinction between physical processes and the (spatio-temporal) stage on which they develop. There is instead a nonlocal (noncommutative) "pregeometry" that encompasses everything. Only when we go from the fundamental level to the upper layers of the world's structure does the distinction between the spatio-temporal arena (governed by the ordinary, commutative geometry) and physical processes emerge. By the fundamental level we mean everything that happens below the Planck threshold. This threshold is encountered in two directions: first, if one goes *backward in time* until one reaches the moment at which the typical dimension of the Universe was of the order of 10^{-33} cm (the so-called *Planck length*); second, if one goes *now* to smaller and smaller distances until one reaches the distance 10^{-33} cm. Because below the Planck threshold there is no space and time, in the usual meaning of these terms, these two directions coincide in fact.[14]

12. See, for instance: A. H. Chamseddine, G. Felder, and J. Frölich, "Gravity in Non-Commutative Geometry," *Commun. Math. Phys.* 155 (1993) 205–217; A. H. Chamseddine and A. Connes, "Universal Formula for Noncommutative Geometry Actions: Unification of Gravity and the Standard Model," *Phys. Rev. Lett.* 24 (1996) 4868–4871; J. Madore and J. Mourad, "Quantum Space-Time and Classical Gravity," *J. Math. Phys.* 39 (1998) 4423–4442.

13. M. Heller, W. Sasin, and D. Lambert, "Groupoid Approach to Noncommutative Quantization of Gravity," *J. Math. Phys.* 38 (1997) 5840–5853; M. Heller and W. Sasin, "Emergence of Time," *Phys. Lett.* A250 (1998) 48–54; M. Heller and W. Sasin, "Noncommutative Unification of General Relativity and Quantum Mechanics," *Int. J. Theor. Phys.* 38 (1999) 1619–1642; M. Heller, W. Sasin, and Z. Odrzygóźdź, "State Vector Reduction as a Shadow of Noncommutative Dynamics," *J. Math. Phys.* 41 (2000) 5168–5179.

14. The Planck threshold is also characterized by other magnitudes: the *Planck time* equals 10^{-44} seconds, and the *Planck density* equals 10^{95} g/cm^3.

This idea did not appear from nothing; it was suggested by our work on classical singularities.[15] Roughly speaking, the (initial) singularity is a geometric counterpart of the Big Bang, and "classical" means that when investigating it we do not take into account quantum effects. To decipher the geometric structure of the Big Bang, we have used the methods of noncommutative geometry that turn out to be very effective in this respect. Our result was that at the level described by noncommutative geometry there is no space-time and no distinction between singular and nonsingular states. Both space-time and singularities appear as soon as we change to the usual, commutative description. Moreover, some mathematical techniques (operators on a Hilbert space) typical for quantum mechanics appear almost automatically. It was quite natural to take one further step and to speculate that these features are not just interesting coincidences. Rather, they indicate that the fundamental level is indeed noncommutative.

Let us describe, in a more detailed way, what the noncommutative regime of the fundamental level might look like. The most striking feature of this regime is its entirely nonlocal character. This creates also the main difficulty we encounter in thinking about it, because all our thinking takes place in local terms (I am a localized individual at a concrete place and in a concrete instant of time). Happily enough, the language of mathematics transcends the reach of imagination and gives us some insights into the realms of noncommutativity.

In the noncommutative regime, there is no time and no space with their accompanying concepts of point and time-instant. Does this mean that there is no motion and dynamics? Certainly! Without the usual concepts of space and time one cannot have the usual concept of motion. But this does not mean that there can be no dynamics in an admittedly generalized sense. Usually, dynamical magnitudes (such as velocity and momentum) are described by vectors that, as local concepts, do not appear in a noncommutative setting. But the idea of a vector field evidently has a global aspect (e.g., a vector field can be defined on an entire space), and as such it has its counterpart in noncommutative geometry. This counterpart is constituted by the so-called *derivation* of a given algebra. Such a derivation transforms one element of the algebra into another element of the same algebra (it therefore models a certain change in the system) and satisfies axioms typical for a vector field.[16] It turns out that it is possible to write down dynamical equations in terms of derivations. Although there is no

---

15. M. Heller and W. Sasin, "Noncommutative Structure of Singularities in General Relativity," *J. Math. Phys.* 37 (1996) 5665–5671; "Origin of Classical Singularities," *Gen. Relat. Grav.* 31 (1999) 555–570.

16. Linearity and the Leibniz rule.

space and no time, there can be an authentic (albeit generalized) dynamics (see below, subsection 7.2). This falsifies the claim of some philosophers and theologians that in the absence of time one is of necessity confronted with a purely inactive, static situation.[17]

As was mentioned above, one can meaningfully speak about states of the noncommutative Universe. And, as our model shows, all such states are on an equal footing; there is no distinction between singular and nonsingular states. Therefore, the very idea of the beginning of the Universe has to change its meaning radically. If there is no time, one cannot speak about a temporal beginning. This does not necessarily mean, however, that the idea of a "quantum tunneling out of nothing" could not be adapted to the noncommutative conceptual framework.

One of the central concepts of Western philosophy is that of the individual. This concept preserves its importance in classical physics; but already in quantum mechanics, and especially in quantum field theories, very serious difficulties connected with this concept appear.[18] If our hypothetical model is at least approximately true, these difficulties are but the remnants of the totally global character of the noncommutative stage.

We should mention yet another concept that in the noncommutative regime is highly generalized—the concept of probability. Standard probabilistic concepts come into play only when there are many individuals of a certain type. It seems that in quantum mechanics one can apply certain probabilistic concepts even to a single particle. In the noncommutative setting there are no individuals, but nevertheless the probability concept (in a generalized sense) survives.[19] This concept has very little in common with the idea of "counting the ratio of the frequency of favorable events to all possible events," although it reproduces this idea in the correct (commutative) limit. It preserves more abstract properties of the probability concept (such as that the outcome of probabilistic calculations must be always positive and not greater than one). The probabilistic character of quantum mechanics, together with all its probabilistic peculiarities, seems to be but the consequence of the deeper and more general concept of probability permeating the entire noncommutative regime. We will come back to this issue in subsection 7.2.

17. See, for instance, P. Tillich, *Systematic Theology,* London: SCM: 1978, 305; K. Barth, *Dogmatica ecclesiale,* Bologna: Il Mulino, 1968.

18. See, for instance, P. Teller, *An Interpretative Introduction to Quantum Field Theory,* Princeton: Princeton University Press, 1995, chs. 2 and 3.

19. The noncommutative counterparts of the concept of probability are the so-called von Neumann algebras.

EMERGENCE OF STANDARD PHYSICS

Of course, every scientifically valuable model of the pre-Planck era must reproduce the standard physics of the post-Planck Universe. This can be achieved quite naturally in our approach. A center of a noncommutative algebra is the set of all its elements that commute with all other elements of this algebra (i.e., the set of all elements of the algebra that multiply with all other of its elements in a commutative way). If we restrict the original noncommutative algebra to its center (or to a subset of the center), we recover an ordinary commutative algebra. This happens in our model.[20] In this way, we recover the usual physics with general relativity presenting gravity as the space-time curvature, and quantum mechanics as a probabilistic theory. This restriction of the original algebra to its subset can be interpreted as the first "phase transition" in the history of the Universe that gave birth to space, time, and multiplicity.

It is interesting that the detailed analysis of this "phase transition" shows that, together with space-time, classical singularities are born.[21] The situation is the following. From the point of view of an observer situated on the fundamental level (if there could be any), the Universe has no temporal beginning (all its states are on an equal footing), but a macroscopic observer can truly say that the Universe had a temporal beginning in its finite past (the initial singularity) and will possibly have an end in its finite future (the final singularity, if the Universe is spatially closed). This is a new possibility, one that has so far never been considered in cosmology. Until now people have envisaged two mutually exclusive possibilities: either the future quantum gravity theory will remove singularities from our picture of the world, or not. Now, a third possibility appears: singularities are but a part of our macroscopic perspective; regarded from the fundamental level, the question of the existence or nonexistence of singularities is meaningless.

By restricting the original noncommutative algebra to its center, we obtain ordinary physics, but not only that—we obtain something more. In "ordinary physics" there are certain phenomena of typically nonlocal character that either remain unexplained or require some additional (and very often artificial) hypotheses to explain them. Let us mention the Einstein-Podolsky-Rosen (EPR) type of experiments in quantum mechanics in which spacelike separated particles that once interacted "know about" each other, although there is no physical signal with the help of which they could communicate. To explain such phenomena, some exotic interpretations of quantum mechanics have

---

20. See footnote 13.
21. See our work "Origin of Classical Singularities" quoted in footnote 15.

been proposed. Another typically nonlocal phenomenon appears in cosmology as the so-called horizon problem—how parts of the Universe now far distant from one another that have never been in causal contact with one another can be characterized by exactly the same values of certain parameters (e.g., temperature corresponding to the microwave background radiation). This phenomenon is usually explained by the so-called inflationary model, which is an extracosmological hypothesis (one, by the way, to which some cosmologists strongly object).

All these nonlocal phenomena find their natural explanation within the noncommutative approach. Because the fundamental level is totally nonlocal, it is no wonder that some quantum phenomena (such as the EPR type of experiment) that are rooted in that level exhibit some nonlocal effects; they are but the tip of the iceberg of the "fundamental noncommutativity" that somehow survived the "phase transition" to the usual physics.[22] To explain the horizon problem, we should adopt another perspective and regard the "fundamental noncommutativity" as situated "in the beginning," in the pre-Planck epoch. According to our hypothesis, this epoch was totally global; no wonder, therefore, that when the Universe was passing through the Planck threshold, it preserved some global characteristics also at those places that never (after the Planck threshold) causally interacted with each other.

As I have mentioned, in spite of the fact that the noncommutative regime is timeless, it admits a generalized "global dynamics." In one of our works,[23] the equation describing such a dynamics has been proposed. Our model has (as it should) two "limiting cases": to general relativity and to quantum mechanics. It turns out that, when one goes to quantum mechanics, the noncommutative dynamics leads to the (unitary) evolution described by the Schrödinger equation. If one goes to general relativity, the noncommutative dynamics "projects down" to a process occurring in space-time that can be interpreted as the act of quantum measurement in which the so-called reduction of the state vector takes place.[24] This confirms the opinion, long defended by

22. To see why certain nonlocal effects survive the Planck threshold and can be observed, one should look at some mathematical properties of the noncommutative regime. Generally speaking, the transition from the noncommutative level to the ordinary physics in our model has the character of a projection. Such a projection, being always "onto," switches off all possible "short-distance correlations," but can leave "long-distance correlations." See, for instance, M. Heller and W. Sasin, "Einstein-Podolski-Rosen Experiment from Noncommutative Quantum Gravity," in *Particles, Fields and Gravitation,* ed. Jakub Rembieliński, Woodbury, New York: American Institute of Physics, 1998, 234–241; or M. Heller and W. Sasin, "Noncommutative Unification of General Relativity and Quantum Mechanics," sections 7 and 8.

23. See M. Heller and W. Sasin, "Emergence of Time."

24. M. Heller, W. Sasin, and Z. Odrzygóźdź, "State Vector Reduction as a Shadow of a Noncommutative Dynamics."

Roger Penrose,[25] that it is quantum gravity that is responsible for the phenomenon of the vector state reduction.

Although all the above effects seem to corroborate the idea of a "noncommutative fundamental level," I should stress once more that in this present chapter I am not so much interested in developing a noncommutative "final theory," but rather in treating this possibility as illustrating the "adventures of concepts" in modern physics.

ADVENTURES OF CONCEPTS

Quite independent of whether the hypothesis proposed by us about a noncommutative origin of the Universe is true or not, we can learn a lesson from it. Many important concepts involved in current scientific (and philosophical) research appear in the noncommutative context in a strongly generalized form. I do not claim that when we refer our everyday concepts to God, we should generalize them in a similar manner. My intention is to learn the way in which a concept can be generalized and to treat this as a warning for our theological discourse. Roughly speaking, if such drastic generalization of meanings is possible in physics, how much (infinitely!) more can this occur when we are speaking or thinking about God!

In the following, I will analyze a few concepts that are of great importance for philosophy and theology (such as causality, probability, and dynamics), when they are transferred from their usual context to the environment of the "noncommutative world." This world is powerfully shaped by its two principal (and mutually interconnected) properties: timelessness and nonlocality. Therefore, if we want to obtain "noncommutative counterparts" of the above-mentioned concepts, we must, first of all, strip them of their usual involvement with time and locality. Happily enough, in doing so we are not condemned to work only with the help of our intuition; we can also be guided by strict mathematical methods that securely lead from our well-behaved commutative world into the regions of noncommutativity.

Causality

The problem of causality is difficult even in the commutative world. I do not intend to go into all its subtleties; I will confine myself rather to its most common sense aspects. It seems obvious that causation presupposes distinct events.

25. See, for instance, R. Penrose, *The Emperor's New Mind*, New York and Oxford: Oxford University Press, 1989.

If *a* causes *b*, then *a* and *b* are distinct—that is, they are not identical and neither is a part of the other. The lightning and the thunder are distinct, and this is why it is possible for the lightning to cause the thunder.[26]

How is one to imagine causation in a totally global setting where no well-localized entities can exist?

It seems that causality presupposes a temporal order: causes usually precede their effects. As is well known, there were attempts to reduce causality to temporal sequences. According to Hume (and many of his followers), we cannot know that *"b propter a,"* but only that *"b post a."* What does remain of causality if we strip it from all temporal aspects?

We can, at least partially, answer these questions if we remain in the domain of mathematical models. Space-time in general relativity is equipped with what is called its *causal structure.* This structure is defined by the so-called *Lorentz metric,* which at each point of space-time introduces a light-cone determining how physical signals (or causal influences) can propagate throughout space-time. Every such cone is generated by light-rays emanating from a given point in space-time. No physical signal can propagate outside the light-cone which is equivalent to the fact that the velocity of light is the maximal physical velocity in nature. In this sense, the light-cone structure in space-time determines a "net of channels" through which causal influences can propagate.

When we change to a noncommutative setting, the causal structure drastically alters. First, space-time, as a set of well-localized points and their neighborhoods, disappears, and we are left with a "global" entity that can be in various states. In Connes' approach,[27] so far one has been unable to define a Lorentz metric, only a *Riemann metric.* The latter opens up light-cones in such a way that there is no limiting velocity imposed on physical signal propagation; everything in space-time can be causally connected with everything. However, by using the Riemann metric, one can define the distance between various states. It seems, therefore, that there are states that can be causally connected. In our approach,[28] one can define a Lorentz metric that, however, is totally nonlocal, in the sense that it does not define local light-cones but specifies which vector fields (regarded as global objects) can influence each other. Let us remember that derivations of a given algebra are noncommutative counterparts of vector fields, and, in our model, they are responsible for the dynamics

26. J-M. Kuczynski, "A Solution of the Paradox of Causation," *Philosophy in Science* 8 (1999) 81.
27. A. Connes, *Noncommutative Geometry,* chapter 6.
28. See our works quoted in footnote 13.

of the system. Therefore, we are entitled to say that, in this model, causality is incorporated into its noncommutative dynamics.

The general conclusion of this subsection is that it is possible to generalize the concept of causality so as to free it from the involvement in time and locality. What remains still deserves the name of (generalized) causality because it gives rise to the dynamics of the system. It seems that the essence of causality is a dynamical nexus rather than the distinctness of the cause and its effect, and their temporal order.[29]

Probability and Dynamics

The standard concept of probability also requires well-defined individual events, the probability of whose occurrence is to be computed. On the set of all such events, the so-called *distribution function* is defined, which to every event ascribes a real number from the interval [0, 1]. The *probability* of a given event is the value of the distribution function at this event. Additionally, one assumes that the sum of the probabilities of all events is equal to one (one of the events must occur). The latter assumption is often expressed by saying that probability is "normed to one." In the standard example of throwing dice we have six (elementary) events, and the distribution function for each of them ascribes the real number one-sixth. The sum of these numbers, for all events, is evidently one. The concept of probability in the above sense is a special instance of a more general concept, namely, that of measure, and the theory of probability is but a subchapter of mathematical measure theory. Measure in a generalized sense is a function on a family of subsets *(measurable subsets)* of a certain space *(measure space);* one assumes that values of this function must be positive numbers (including zero and plus infinity) without necessarily assuming that this function is "normed to one."

How can the idea of probability be transferred to the noncommutative environment where all concepts presupposing locality and individuality are in principle meaningless? It cannot be simply transferred but can be generalized, and a hint of how to do this is contained in the fact that the concept of probability is strictly connected with the concept of function (the distribution function). We cannot go into details here; let us mention only that the concept of measure finds its generalized counterpart in the so-called *von Neumann algebras*. Von Neumann algebra is, roughly speaking, a C*-algebra (see section 2) with a certain positive functional that is "normed to one" (such a functional is called a

29. This conclusion is consonant with the traditional pre-Humean notion of causality as linked primarily to agency and not to time-order.

state).[30] The concept of functional generalizes the concept of function,[31] and the fact that it is positive and "normed to one" is a trace of an affinity of this concept with the usual concept of probability.

Happily enough, the concept of generalized probability in the noncommutative regime is strictly connected with another important property: von Neumann algebras are "dynamical objects." In section 5, we said that in the noncommutative regime, a generalized dynamics can be constructed in terms of derivations of a given algebra, but if the algebra in question is a von Neumann algebra the dynamics significantly improves. On the strength of the famous Tomita-Takesaki theorem,[32] von Neumann algebras guarantee the existence of a certain parameter[33] which "imitates time" and in terms of which we can write generalized dynamical equations.[34] It is not yet the "true time," because it depends on the state of a physical system. In each state we have an essentially different "flow of time" with no possibility of synchronizing them! But we can write truly dynamical equations with the above parameter playing the role of the independent variable.

It is a remarkable fact that in von Neumann algebras the concepts of generalized probability and generalized dynamics are unified. We know from quantum mechanics that quantum systems evolve in a probabilistic manner. The dynamical equation, which in the case of quantum mechanics is the Schrödinger equation, does not describe the evolution of an elementary particle (e.g., of an electron), but rather the evolution of probabilities with which we ascribe certain properties (e.g., position or spin) to something we call an elementary particle. Let us notice that these evolving probabilities have a nonlocal character. It is just because of this nonlocal character that the act of measurement of a certain quantum property (e.g., of spin) performed at a particular location can affect an act of measurement separated from that location by a spacelike interval, that is, an interval that could be covered only by a superluminal signal. We could regard this peculiarity as a trace or a remnant of the noncommutative, totally nonlocal, fundamental level.

Probability, as we know it from standard mathematical measure theory or

---

30. For a precise definition, see, for instance: V. S. Sunder, *An Invitation to von Neumann Algebras*, New York and Berlin: Springer, 1986.

31. Roughly speaking, functional is a "function on functions."

32. The Tomita-Takesaki theorem essentially says that if A is a von Neumann algebra, then there exist mappings $a_t : A \rightarrow A$ forming one-parameter groups, called *modular groups*, which are dependent on the state of the algebra A (see V. S. Sunder, op. cit., ch. 2). These one-parameter groups can be used to parametrize the dynamics.

33. Strictly speaking, the existence of one-parameter groups.

34. See M. Heller and W. Sasin, "Emergence of Time."

from its quantum mechanical version, could be but a shadow of the noncommutative properties of the fundamental level encoded in a von Neumann algebra.

Finally, let us go back to the issue of time. With our von Neumann algebra A there is associated a group, called a *unitary group*. In terms of this group we can define a certain condition (called *inner equivalence*), and if the algebra A satisfies this condition (which glues together some elements of the algebra A, making it "coarser"), all state-dependent times can be synchronized to obtain the single "unitary" flow of time. We recognize in it the same time that measures the unitary evolution of observables in the usual quantum mechanics. However, only if the algebra A is restricted to its center does one recover the familiar macroscopic time. It seems, therefore, that the "emergence of time" is a gradual process that can be mathematically modeled.[35]

THEOLOGICAL CONSEQUENCES

The Primary Cause

As is well known, traditional philosophy and theology identified God with the Primary Cause. Although philosophical and theological texts were full of declarations that in this context causality should be understood in an analogous manner, it seems that in practice this concept was treated much more univocally than other concepts referred to God. The very distinction between the Primary Cause and secondary causes is based on everyday experience that teaches us "that individual things have their own operations, through which they are proximate causes of things, not of all things but only of some,"[36] and our own operations are so overwhelmingly causality-laden that we subconsciously attribute the same to God.

With the advent of modern science, the tendency arose to narrow the concept of causality only to efficient causality, and the great influence of Cartesian philosophy added to this concept an intuition of a direct contact between the cause and its effect. These ideas concerning causality were strengthened and consolidated by the progress brought about by Newtonian mechanics, although this branch of physics, with its *actio in distans* and its principle of extremal action (discovered soon after), was rather far from such simplistic

---

35. Details can be found in: M. Heller and W. Sasin, "Emergence of Time"; see also A. Connes and C. Rovelli, "Von Neumann Algebra Automorphisms and Time-Thermodynamics Relation in Generally Covariant Quantum Theories," *Class. Quantum Grav.* 11 (1994) 2899–2917.

36. St. Thomas Aquinas, *Scriptum super libros Sententiarum Petri Lombardi*, Book 2, Distinction 1. Question 1, Article. 4; English translation: *Aquinas on Creation*, trans. S. E. Baldner and W. E. Carroll, Toronto: Pontifical Institute of Medieval Studies, 1997, 83.

ideas.[37] In our time, quantum mechanics has virtually put an end to mechanistic and deterministic interpretations of the causal nexus, but some other forms of causality are in circulation.[38] So-called "bottom-up" causation exhibits a strong reductionist flavor, at least if the reductionism is understood in Steven Weinberg's sense of "petty reductionism," when a whole system, its structure and functioning, is regarded as arising from the sum of its constituent units, their properties, and their behavior.[39] This type of causation is often correlated with (not necessarily opposed to) "top-down" causation. The latter was first recognized in nonlinear dissipative systems in which

the changes at the microlevel, that of the constituent units, are what they are because of their incorporation into the system as a whole, which is exerting specific constraints on its units, making them behave otherwise than they would in isolation.[40]

It was soon extended beyond its original domain to denote something "more open and more non-local than that."[41]

It might seem that the causality encountered in noncommutative models (as it was discussed in subsection 7.1) is a kind of "top-down" causality. However, if we take into account the fact that, according to these models, this type of causality operates at the most fundamental level, it could almost equally well be called "bottom-up" causality. I think that its distinctive feature is not its "vertical" operation mode, but rather its atemporal and nonlocal behavior. And if we could learn from it something about God's possible ways of acting in the world, it would reveal first of all the drastic difference between this type

37. Newton himself was much subtler in his understanding of causality than many of his followers. At the end of his *Principia,* in the General Scholium, he wrote: "Hitherto we have explained the phenomena of the heavens and of our sea by the power of gravity, but have not yet assigned the cause of this power. This is certain, that it must proceed from a cause that penetrates to the very centres of the sun and planets, without suffering the least diminution of its force; that operates not according to the quantity of the surfaces of the particles upon which it acts (as mechanical causes used to do), but according to the quantity of the solid matter which they contain, and propagates its virtue on all sides to immense distances, decreasing always as the inverse square of the distances" (*Principia,* vol. II, trans. F. Cajori, Berkeley: University of California Press, 1962, 546).

38. In these forms of causality "the same cause is always followed by the same effect" does not necessarily hold.

39. S. Weinberg, "Reductionist Redux," *The New York Review,* (5 October 1995) 39–42.

40. A. Peacocke, "God's Interaction with the World—The Implications of Deterministic 'Chaos' and of Interconnected and Interdependent Complexity," in *Chaos and Complexity,* R. J. Russell and A. Peacocke, eds., Vatican City State: Vatican Observatory Publications; Berkeley: The Center for Theology and the Natural Sciences, 1995, 273.

41. J. Polkinghorne, "The Metaphysics of Divine Action," in *Chaos and Complexity,* 151. The problem of the "top-down" causation, referred to God's action in the world, was extensively discussed in the volume *Chaos and Complexity* in the present series of the Vatican–CTNS conferences; see papers by Arthur Peacocke, John Polkinghorne, Willem Drees, and William Stoeger.

of causality and what we would traditionally qualify as causality. I think, however, that in spite of this difference, the former deserves the name "causality." This terminological decision is justified by the fact that noncommutative causal structure (in the mathematical sense) is a legitimate generalization of the usual causal structure of space-time studied in general relativity. I by no means want to say that when speaking about God's causality we must regard it as a sort of noncommutative causality; I want only to emphasize that we must treat the doctrine of the analogous or metaphoric character of theological language more seriously.

We think about God as the Primary Cause because we regard the world (both in its entirety and in its details) as an effect of God's action. This causal nexus between God and the world is called *creation*. And it is precisely at this point that we must revise our theological concepts. In the light of the above analysis, we should take into account the possibility that the concept of causality does not necessarily presuppose a local interaction between the cause and its effect *(global aspect of causality)*, and that it does not necessarily include a temporal order *(atemporal aspect of causality)*. Let us notice that the time-honored metaphysical question (so persistently asked by Leibniz) "Why is there something rather than nothing?" has a strong globally causal flavor. By asking this question we do not restrict the world's existence (which we want to justify) to any particular place or time-instant. And the possibility, very seriously considered by St. Thomas Aquinas, that the world could exist from eternity and nevertheless be created by God, emphasizes an atemporal aspect of God's causality. It is truly worthwhile to read old masters from the perspective of the most recent scientific theories! The point is, however, that one should not repeat their doctrines blindly but look at them with an eye sharpened by the enlargements of imagination prompted by the achievements of modern science.[42]

Ernan McMullin in his recent study[43] takes over the traditional doctrine of creation. Alluding to St. Augustine's view, he contemplates the "Creator in the fullest sense," a "Being from whom the existence of all things derives" (p. 104). Such a Being cannot be subject to any constraints, and temporality is certainly a severe constraint.

Time is a condition of the creature, a sign of dependence. . . . The act of creation is a single one, in which what is past, present or future from the perspective of the creature issues as a single whole from the Creator. (p. 105)

42. See Chapter 9.
43. E. McMullin, "Evolutionary Contingency and Cosmic Purpose," *Studies in Science and Theology* 5 (1997) 91–112. In the following, numbers in parentheses refer to the pagination of this paper.

In this sense, the Creator is "outside" the transient passage of time. Of course, it is only a metaphor but an important one. If we enrich it with Boethius' famous definition of eternity as "the whole, simultaneous and perfect possession of boundless life,"[44] it conveys not so much an image of timelessness, as of fullness of time.

The concept of existence is crucial for the traditional creation doctrine. However, it is notoriously vague and fuzzy.[45] In contrast with the concept of atemporality, one can hardly find in contemporary physics anything that would help one to understand better the meaning of "existence." Perhaps the only hint that the process of physicalization can one day embrace the idea of existence is the dispute in the conceptual foundations of quantum field theories concerning the identity of elementary particles.[46] The discovery that they are lacking what could be termed "primitive thisness"[47] is at least a signal that the problem of *modus existendi* could have a physical component.

Chance and Purpose

We usually think about chance and purpose in terms of probabilities. For instance, if an event of very small probability happens, we say that it has either happened by chance or has been purposefully chosen by an intelligent agent. We claim that, given a long enough span of time, even events of the slightest probability will be realized. If this type of argument is applied to the Universe as a whole, it often assumes the form of various teleological or antiteleological disputes. All of them tacitly assume that the "classical concept of probability" is valid on all levels of reality. As we have seen above (see subsection 7.2), such a view is simply naïve. There are strong reasons to believe that "the classical concept of probability" is—as are many other concepts—valid only within the "classical domain" (i.e., within the domain the linear dimensions of which are comparable to those of our body). Such a possibility has a powerful impact on the philosophical and theological polemics in this context.

To claim that God uses a noncommutative probabilistic measure in designing the Universe would display an equally enormous naïveté. But the very exis-

---

44. Boethius, *The Consolation of Philosophy,* 5.6.

45. This does not refer to the term "existence" as it is analyzed, for instance, by Frege, Tarski, Leśniewski, and others. However, their analyses are valid only in the context of a given formal logic, and it is by no means clear which kind of logic one would have to use with regard to the sought-after fundamental theory of physics.

46. See, for instance, P. Teller, *An Interpretative Introduction to Quantum Field Theory,* Princeton: Princeton University Press, 1995.

47. This term has been used by P. Teller (op. cit., 17) as a modern counterpart of the medieval *heacceitas.*

tence of noncommutative dynamical models shows that the idea of an atemporal existence is not contradictory in itself (as has been claimed by many thinkers, especially those belonging to the Whiteheadian school of process philosophy). It would be interesting, then, to look at processes that happen by chance (in the macroworld) from the perspective of the hypothetical Creator who exists "outside" the macrocosmic temporal order and creates the world in an atemporal manner (see subsection 8.1).

Such a Creator knows the cosmic past, present and future in a single unmediated grasp. God knows the past and the future of each creature, not by memory or by foretelling, then, as another creature might, but in the same direct way that God knows the creature's present. (p. 105)

Our concepts of design or teleology are heavily laden with the all-pervading idea of temporality: pursuing a purpose is a temporal process, and knowledge of its outcome is possible only if the process is strictly deterministic and if its unfolding does not too sensitively depend on the initial conditions. However, the atemporal Creator's knowledge "is not discursive" (p. 106): God does not infer or compute future states of the Universe from knowledge of its previous states. God knows what we call the past and the future by inspection, and consequently in his planning outcomes there is no aspect of expectation. "For God to plan is for the outcome to occur. There is no [time] interval between decision and completion" (p. 106).

The shift of meanings of such interconnected concepts as probability, chance, and purpose has obvious consequences as far as philosophical and theological disputes on the "design argument" are concerned. Let us once more hear what McMullin has to say on this topic:

It makes no difference, therefore, whether the appearance of Homo sapiens is the inevitable result of a steady process of complexification stretching over billions of years, or whether on the contrary it comes about through a series of coincidences that would have made it entirely unpredictable from the (causal) human standpoint. Either way, the outcome is of God's making, and from the Biblical standpoint may appear as part of God's plan. (p. 106)

There still remains the problem of creaturely freedom in such an atemporally created temporal world. Let us notice only that if God does not compute the future but rather sees it from his atemporal perspective, it is immaterial whether the process itself is strictly deterministic or not. For God the outcome is just present.

CONCLUDING STORY

In his commentary on the *Sentences* of Peter Lombard,[48] St. Thomas Aquinas deals with the following problems:

1. whether there is only one principle; 2. whether from that principle things come forth by way of creation; 3. whether things are created only by that one principle, or whether they are also created by secondary principles; 4. whether one thing is able to be the cause of another in some way other than by way of creation; 5. whether things have been created from eternity; 6. on the supposition that things have not been created from eternity, in what way God is said to have created the heavens and the earth "in the beginning."[49]

It is interesting to notice that in the first four questions there is no direct mention of time. The temporal aspect of the creation problem appears only in Article 5, "Whether things have been created from eternity," in which St. Thomas presents his famous, and for many surprising,[50] doctrine that the concept of the world existing from eternity but nevertheless created by God is not contradictory. In his view, we know by revelation that the world had a temporal beginning, but this cannot be demonstrated by reason alone. After pondering all arguments for and against the temporal beginning of the world and finding that neither side can convince the other, St. Thomas anticipates the disappointment of his readers and switches to a more rhetorical style (unusual in his writings):

If someone should argue on the basis of the full-grown man what must be true of the man in an incomplete state in the womb of his mother, he would be deceived. Accordingly, Rabbi Moses, *The Guide of the Perplexed*, tells the story of a certain boy whose mother died in his infancy, who was raised on a solitary island, and who, at the age of reason, asked someone whether and how men were made. When the facts of human generation were explained to him, he objected that such was impossible, because a man could not live without breathing, eating, and expelling wastes, so that it would be impossible for a man to live for even one day in his mother's womb, let alone nine months. Like this boy are those who, from the way that things happen in the world in its complete state, wish to show either the necessity or the impossibility of the beginning of the world.[51]

48. St. Thomas Aquinas, *Scriptum super libros Sententiarum Petri Lombardi*, Book 2, Distinction 1, Question 1.

49. *Aquinas on Creation*, 63.

50. To another of St. Thomas's works on this topic, the posterity gave a telling title: *De aeternitate mundi contra murmurantes* (*On the Eternity of the World against Those Who Murmur*), see *Aquinas on Creation*, 114–122.

51. *Aquinas on Creation*, 97.

Today we ask such questions as: How old is the Universe? Did it initiate in a "Big Bang"? Will the future theory of quantum gravity remove the initial singularity appearing in the standard cosmological model? Is the fundamental level of the world atemporal and nonlocal? There are many other like queries. All these questions are purely scientific, and we hope that, with the continuous progress in developing our theoretical and empirical tools, we will sooner or later find answers to some of them. I do believe that this will greatly contribute to our better posing of philosophical and theological questions, and more cautiously formulating tentative answers to them. The main lesson we should learn from science in this respect is that we must always be open to broader and broader horizons. St. Thomas drew a similar conclusion from Rabbi Moses' story:

What now begins to be begins through motion; hence what causes motion must always precede [the motion] in duration and in nature, and there must be contraries; but none of these are necessary in the making of the universe by God.[52]

52. Ibid.

II CHAOS, PROBABILITY, AND THE COMPREHENSIBILITY OF THE WORLD

INTRODUCTION: COMPRESSIBILITY AND COMPREHENSIBILITY

There are quotations that mark important steps in the history of human thought. One of them is certainly this passage from Einstein:

> The very fact that the totality of our sense experiences is such that by means of thinking (operations with concepts, and the creation and use of definite functional relations between them, and the coordination of sense experiences to these concepts) it can be put in order, this fact is one which we shall never understand. One may say "the eternal mystery of the world is its comprehensibility."[1]

This mystery is seminally present in our prescientific cognition, but it reveals itself in full light only when one contemplates, as it has been expressed by Wigner, "the unreasonable effectiveness of mathematics in the natural sciences."[2]

What is meant here by the *effectiveness* of mathematics in the natural sciences is rather obvious (at least for those of us who are accustomed to the methods of modern physics). We model the world in terms of mathematical structures, and there exists an admirable resonance between these structures and the structure of the world. By means of experimental results the world responds to questions formulated in the language of mathematics. But why is this strategy *unreasonable*? In constructing mathematical theories of the world, we invest into them information we have gained with the help of the joint effort of former experiments and theories. However, our theoretical structures give us back more information than has been put into them. It looks as if our mathematical theories were not only information-processing machines, but also information-creating devices.

Let us consider an outstanding example. In 1915, after a long

1. A. Einstein, "Physics and Reality," chapter in *Ideas and Opinions,* New York: Dell, 1978, 283–315.
2. E. Wigner, "The Unreasonable Effectiveness of Mathematics in the Natural Sciences," *Communications in Pure and Applied Mathematics* 13 (1960) 1–14.

period of struggle and defeat, Einstein finally wrote down his gravitational field equations. He succeeded in deducing from them three, seemingly insignificant effects by which his general theory of relativity differed from the commonly accepted Newtonian theory of gravity. These effects were so small that the majority of physicists at that time could see no reason to accept a theory that required such a huge mathematical structure and yet explained so little. However, "the equations are wiser than those who invented them."[3] This is certainly true as far as Einstein's equations are concerned. In about half a century, physicists and mathematicians found a host of new solutions to these equations. Some represent neutron stars, gravitational waves, cosmic strings, stationary and rotating black holes, and so on. Fifty years ago nobody would even have suspected the existence of such objects. Now some of them have been discovered in the Universe,[4] and our confidence in Einstein's equations has grown so much that we are sure that the existence of at least some others will soon be experimentally verified. New information seems not only to be created by the mathematical equations, but surprisingly often it also corresponds well to what we observe if we focus our instruments on domains suggested by the equations themselves. It looks as if the structure of Einstein's equations somehow reflected the structure of the world: information about various strata of the world's structure seems to be encoded in the equations. By finding their correct solution and correlating it, through suitable initial or boundary conditions, with the given stratum of the structure of the world, we are able to decipher this information, and it often happens that the information was unavailable before we solved the equations.

We often read in philosophy of science textbooks that the mathematical description of the world is possible owing to *idealizations* made in the process of constructing our theories (we neglect the air resistance, the medium viscosity, or we invent nonexisting motions along straight lines, under the influence of no forces, and so on). This is a typical half-truth. At least in many instances, it seems that the idealization strategy does not consist in putting some information aside, but instead it is one of the most powerful mechanisms of the creation of information. For instance, the law of inertia (uniform motion under the influence of no forces!) has led us into the heart of classical mechanics. We should also notice that there were not experimental results that suggested which "influences" should be neglected, but it was the form of the equations of motion that selected those aspects of the world upon which the experiments should focus. The quantum world would remain closed to us forever if not for

3. This saying is ascribed to Hertz.
4. In this chapter, "Universe" will be used to refer to the Universe in the maximal possible sense. Later we will see that the Universe may contain many universes.

our mathematical models and idealizations on which they are based. Here we had no possibility at all to choose what should be taken into account and what should be left aside. We were totally at the mercy of mathematical structures. Almost all of the more important concepts of our everyday experience—such as localization, motion, causality, trajectory in space and time, individuality— drastically change their meanings when we move from the macroscopic world to the quantum world of elementary interactions. The only way to visualize what happens in this world is to enforce our imagination to follow mathematical structures and surrender to their explicative power.

Mathematics, as employed to reconstruct physical situations, enjoys another "unreasonable" property—it has enormous unifying power. In an almost miraculous way it unifies facts, concepts, models, and theories far distant from each other. The huge field of phenomena, investigated by contemporary physics, has been divided into a few subdomains, with each subdomain governed by a single equation (or system of equations). The equations of Einstein, Schrödinger, and Dirac are the best known representatives of this aristocratic family of equations. One printed page would be enough to write down the entirety of physics in a compressed form. We prefer fat volumes because we want to explore the architecture of these mathematical structures. We gain understanding by analyzing, step by step, the system of inferences, and by interpreting the formal symbols, triggering this subtle resonance between the logical structure and the results of measurement. We feel entitled to believe that these subdomains of physics, which until now were separated from each other, are but different aspects of the same mathematical structure. Although still remaining to be discovered, it is often credited with the name "Theory of Everything."

To express a law of physics in the form of a differential equation means to collect a potentially infinite set of events into a single scheme, in the framework of which every event, by being related to all other events, acquires significance and is explained. This is an example of what is called the *algorithmic compressibility*. However, what is really important is that it is always possible to disentangle what has been compressed. In the case of need, each event can be extracted from the entirety (but already in its reprocessed, significant form) by finding a suitable solution and choosing the corresponding boundary conditions. Today Einstein's question "Why is the world so comprehensible?" is very often formulated: "Why is the world algorithmically compressible?"[5] Indeed,

5. I will not discuss here the question of whether the statements "The world is comprehensible," and "The world is algorithmically compressible" are equivalent, or whether the latter is but a part of the former.

without the development of algorithmic compressions of data all science would be replaced by mindless stamp collecting—the indiscriminate accumulation of every available fact. . . . Science is predicated upon the belief that the Universe is algorithmically compressible and the modern search for a Theory of Everything is the ultimate expression of that belief, a belief that there is an abbreviated representation of the logic behind the Universe's properties that can be written down in finite form by human beings.[6]

All these properties of mathematics, when applied to physical theories, often evoke in scientists the feeling of encountering something that is extremely beautiful. One could ask: Is mathematics beautiful because it is effective? This would be a utilitarian theory of beauty. In the more Platonic vein, one could ask: Do only beautiful mathematical structures prove to be effective in physics? Probably, these questions have no straightforward answers, but the fact that they are so often asked points toward the significant (albeit not yet sufficiently acknowledged) role of esthetics in the philosophy of science.

Was Einstein right when he was expressing his belief that the comprehensibility of the world will remain its "eternal mystery"? There is an attempt to neutralize Einstein's puzzlement over the question of why the world is so comprehensible by reducing all regularities present in the Universe to the blind game of chance and probability.

It is just possible that complete anarchy may be the only real law of nature. People have even debated that the presence of symmetry in Nature is an illusion, that the rules, governing which symmetries nature displays, may have a purely random origin. Some preliminary investigations suggest that even if the choice is random among all the allowable ways nature could behave, orderly physics can still result with all the appearances of symmetry.[7]

Two essentially different implementations of this philosophy have been envisaged. The first, less radical, is an attempt that seeks to explain all regularities observed in the present Universe by reducing them to the chaotic (i.e., "most probable") initial conditions. The second, maximalistic one claims that the only fundamental law is the "game of probabilities," and all the so-called natural laws are but averages that won in this game. Although only partial results have been so far obtained in both of these approaches, the philosophical ideas lying behind them seem to be an interesting counterproposal with respect to Ein-

6. J. D. Barrow, *Theories of Everything: The Quest for Ultimate Explanation,* Oxford: Clarendon Press, 1991, 11. See also Joseph Ford's essay, "What is chaos, that we should be mindful of it?," in *The New Physics,* ed. P. Davies, New York: Cambridge University Press, 1989, 348–372, for clarification regarding the belief that the Universe is algorithmically compressible.

7. J. D. Barrow and J. Silk, *The Left Hand of Creation: The Origin and Evolution of the Expanding Universe,* London: Unwin, 1983, 213.

stein's philosophy, and certainly are worthwhile to discuss. This is the goal of this chapter.

The problem is of key importance for the topic of this chapter. In its most fundamental sense, God's action in the world consists in giving to the world its existence and giving it in such a way that everything that participates in existence also participates in its rationality, that is, is subject to mathematically expressible laws of nature. If Einstein's "mystery of comprehensibility" is indeed neutralized by the "pure game of chance and probability," then the central meaning of God's action in the world seems to be in jeopardy; anarchy takes over, and the world at its foundations is not rational. Because rationality and existence are very close to each other, the existence of the world, in turn, no longer seems to be the most profound locus of God's action but a random outcome of a degraded mystery.

Hence, I will show that such an attempt to neutralize Einstein's fascination with the comprehensibility of the world leads us even deeper into the mystery. Probability calculus is as good as any other mathematical theory; and even if chance and probability lie at the core of everything, the important philosophical and theological problem remains of why the world is *probabilistically comprehensible*. Why has God chosen probability as God's main strategy? In fact, the theory of probability permeates all aspects of our present understanding of the world. In particular, deterministic chaos theory and the theories of complexity and self-organization work because the world enjoys certain probabilistic properties.

We begin by presenting in more detail those approaches that attempt to explain the present world's regularities probabilistically. In section 2, we turn to the question of whether the chaotic initial conditions for the Universe are able to explain its actual structure. In section 3, we discuss the program of reducing all physical laws and symmetries to pure chance and randomness. To deal responsibly with the problems posed in the two preceding sections we must undertake a thorough discussion of the foundations of the probability calculus. This is the aim of section 4. The conclusions are drawn, and their theological implications are discussed in section 5.

"THE SHARPEST NEEDLE STANDING UPRIGHT ON ITS POINT"

Although the need to justify some large-scale properties of the observed Universe (such as its spatial homogeneity and isotropy) was noticed rather early by many authors, it was the paradigm of the anthropic principle that stressed the fact that the initial conditions for the Universe had to be extremely "fine tuned" to produce a world that could be subject for exploration by a living observer. There is no need to repeat here all arguments that have been quoted on behalf of this thesis.[8] All these arguments point to the fact that the present state of the Universe is as hard to produce from random initial conditions as it is hard to make "the sharpest Needle stand Upright on its Point upon a Looking-Glass" (this is Newton's expression ushered, essentially, in the same context).[9]

The additional difficulty is that each mechanism proposed to explain the large-scale properties of the Universe must first be able to overcome the barriers created by the existence of the limiting velocity of the propagation of physical interactions (the so-called horizon problem). Within the standard world model, to answer the question why a certain property of the Universe (e.g., the temperature of the microwave background radiation) is the same in regions that were never able to communicate with each other, one essentially needs to postulate the fine tuning of the initial conditions responsible for this fact.

An early proposal to overcome these difficulties goes back to C. W. Misner's classical works[10] on the so-called Mixmaster program in cosmology, nowadays more often known under the name of the chaotic cosmology. The idea is that it was the "mixing" character of physical processes in the very young Universe that led its large-scale properties to their present shape, independent of any initial conditions. To put it briefly, the "mixing" processes end up always producing identical universes regardless of their initial state. Various processes were tried as mixing candidates—hadron collisions, particle creation, neutrino viscosity—but all these mechanisms are strongly constrained by the horizon problem. This means that they can work efficiently only in those cosmological models that enjoy a very special geometric property: the expansion rate of the Universe must be related to the velocity of propagation of the mixing process such that the mixing should be able to reach distant regions of the Universe before they are too distant to be affected by them (the goalpost cannot recede faster than the runner can run). This means that there must exist a large-scale property of the Universe that controls the mixing process by synchronizing it with the global expansion rate and does this without exchanging physical signals between distant parts of the Universe. But this is exactly what we wanted

8. See J. D. Barrow and F. J. Tipler, *The Anthropic Cosmological Principle,* Oxford: Clarendon Press, 1986.

9. See the quotation in Chapter 9.2.

10. C. W. Misner, "The Isotropy of the Universe," *Astrophysical Journal* 151 (1968) 431–457; "Mixmaster Universe," *Physical Review Letters* 22 (1969) 1071–1074.

to avoid.[11] Let us note that this problem is strictly connected with the phenomenon of deterministic chaos. In fact, the Misner program does not work because—as deterministic chaos theory predicts—the relaxation time in the Mixmaster model is reached after an infinite lapse of time (the so-called Omega time appearing in Misner's equations).

The newer attempt to solve these difficulties, proposed by A. Guth[12] and A. D. Linde,[13] is known as the "inflationary scenario." In its standard version, at the epoch when the Universe was 10^{-35} seconds old, the splitting of the strong nuclear force from the electroweak force made the factor driving the world's evolution negative, and caused a rapid (exponential) expansion of the Universe, to be superimposed on its ordinary expansion. In the fraction of a second the radius of the Universe increased from about 10^{-23} cm to 10 cm (22 orders of magnitude!); that is, from something that was 10 billion times smaller than the size of a proton to something about the size of an orange. After this dramatic inflation phase, the Universe came back to its standard, much slower expansion. Such a rapid inflation erased from the Universe all vestiges of its pre-inflationary state; in this way, the initial conditions are unimportant. On the other hand, regions of the Universe, now very distant from each other, remember information from the epoch when they were in mutual contact. In this way the horizon problem can be overcome.[14]

However, one should notice that the inflationary strategy is able to explain probabilistically the present large-scale properties of the Universe only if the set of initial conditions leading to the inflationary phase is "large enough" in the space of all initial conditions. There are strong suspicions that this is not the case.[15] If this is true, we again face the problem of fine tuning to explain the inflation itself. And so, difficult questions return through the back door.

LAWS FROM NO-LAWS

The standard view today, underlying all efforts to achieve the final unification of physics, is that at extremely high energies, somewhere beyond the

11. See Z. Golda, M. Szydlowski, and M. Heller, "Generic and Nongeneric World Models," *General Relativity and Gravitation* 19 (1987) 707–718; A. Woszczyna and M. Heller, "Is a Horizon-free Cosmology Possible?" *General Relativity and Gravitation* 22 (1990) 1367–1386.

12. A. Guth, "Inflationary Universe: A Possible Solution to the Horizon and Flatness Problems," *Physical Review* D23 (1981) 347–356.

13. A. D. Linde, "A New Inflationary Scenario: A Possible Solution of the Horizon, Flatness, Homogeneity, Isotropy and Primordial Monopole Problems," *Physical Letters* 108B (1982) 389–393.

14. See *Inflationary Cosmology*, ed. L. F. Abbot and So-Young Pi, Singapore: World Scientific, 1986.

15. See G. F. R. Ellis and W. Stoeger, "Horizons in Inflationary Universes," *Classical and Quantum Gravity* 5 (1988) 207–220.

Planck threshold, everything had been maximally symmetric, and that subsequent breaking of this primordial symmetry led the Universe to its present diversified richness of forms. There is, however, another possibility: there could be no symmetry at high energies at all, or, equivalently, all possible symmetries could coexist on an equal footing, with order and law emerging only later from the primordial chaos. Barrow and Tipler, considering this possibility, ask: "Are there any laws of Nature at all? Perhaps complete microscopic anarchy is the only law of Nature."[16] What we now call the laws of nature would be the result of purely statistical effects, a sort of asymptotic state after a long period of averaging and selecting processes.

It is possible that the rules we now perceive governing the behavior of matter and radiation have a purely random origin, and even gauge invariance may be an "illusion": a selection effect of the low-energy world we necessarily inhabit.[17]

There are several attempts to implement this philosophy in working physical models. I will mention two of them.

Within the so-called *chaotic gauge* program only preliminary results have been obtained so far. The idea is to show that physical laws and symmetries should arise, by some averaging processes, from a fundamental, essentially lawless and nonsymmetric level. In this approach, at low energies (i.e., on our macroscopic scale) one sees maximum symmetry, but this gradually disappears if we penetrate into more fundamental levels of high energies.[18] In particular, this approach should refer to gauge symmetries, which seem to play an ever-increasing role in contemporary physics. The proponents of this program write: "It would be nice to show that gauge invariance has a high chance of arising spontaneously even if nature is not gauge invariant at the fundamental scale."[19] Or more technically, "it would be nice" to show that if the Lagrangian, from which physical laws are to be derived, is chosen at random, then at low energies local gauge invariance will emerge, and it will be a stable property in the space of all possible Lagrangian-based theories. However, the same authors were able to show that only a gauge theory arises at low energies from a theory that at high energies differs from the exactly gauge invariant theory by no more than a specified amount of noninvariant interactions; that is, that it is enough to assume an approximately gauge invariant theory at high energies to obtain the usual gauge theory on our scale. Advocates of this program express

16. J. D. Barrow and F. Tipler, *The Anthropic Cosmological Principle*, 256.

17. Ibid.

18. See J. Iliopoulos, D. V. Nanopoulos, and T. N. Tomaras, "Infrared Stability or Anti-Grandunification," *Physics Letters* 94B (1980) 141–144.

19. D. Foerster, H. B. Nielsen, and M. Ninomiya, "Dynamical Stability of Local Gauge Symmetry," *Physics Letters* 94B (1980) 135–140.

their hope that, by using this strategy, it would be possible to estimate the order of magnitude of at least some fundamental constants and to demonstrate their quasi-statistical origin.

Another possibility is Linde's *chaotic inflationary cosmology*.[20] The dynamics of the Linde universe is dominated by a nonequilibrium initial distribution of a noninteracting scalar field φ with the mass m much less than the Planck mass $M_p \sim 10^{19}$ GeV. If the Universe contains at least one domain of the size $l \geq H^{-1}(\varphi)$ with $\varphi \geq M_p(M_p/m)^{\frac{1}{2}}$, where $H = R'/R$, R being the scale factor of the locally Friedman universe, it endlessly reproduces itself in the form of inflationary mini-universes. In fact, this reproduction process leads to an exponentially growing number of causally noninteracting universes. Because the birth of each new mini-universe is independent of the history of the mother universe, "the whole process can be considered as an infinite chain reaction of creation and self-reproduction which has no end and which may have no beginning."[21] When, during such a birth process, the Universe splits into many causally disconnected mini-universes of exponentially growing sizes, "all possible types of compactification and all possible vacuum states are realized."[22] This leads to various physics in various daughter-universes. Linde writes:

When several years ago the dimensionality of spacetime, the vacuum energy density, the value of electric charge, the Yukawa couplings, etc., were regarded as true constants, it now becomes clear that these "constants" actually depend on the type of compactification and on the mechanism of symmetry breaking, which may be different in different domains of the universe.[23]

In this way, a "chaos"[24] is realized not within the one Universe but within the ensemble of many universes, and some sort of the anthropic principle is necessary if our "local Universe" is to have the physical laws we now discover and the structure we now observe.[25]

20. See A. D. Linde, *Fizika Elementarnykh Chasitis I Inflatsonnaia Kosmologiia* [Physics of Elementary Particles and Inflationary Cosmology], Moscow: Nauka, 1990, and by the same author, "Inflation and Quantum Cosmology," in *300 Years of Gravitation,* ed. S. W. Hawking and W. Israel, Cambridge: Cambridge University Press, 1987, 604–630.

21. A. D. Linde, "Inflation and Quantum Cosmology," 618.

22. Ibid., 627. Roughly speaking, by compactification Linde understands the process by which the number of space-time dimensions is established inside the newly-born mini-universe; this number may be different from that in the mother universe.

23. Ibid.

24. In this case, as in the case of a chaotic gauge program, the term "chaos" is not used in the technical sense of deterministic chaos, although one could expect that in both cases deterministically chaotic phenomena (in the technical sense) are involved.

25. See J. D. Barrow, *The Worlds Within the World,* Oxford: Clarendon Press, 1988, 281–289. Later on, Linde's hypothesis was modified and developed by Lee Smolin; see his book *The Life of the Cosmos,* Oxford: Oxford University Press, 1997. Critical remarks in the following sections refer to his ideas as well.

PROBABILISTIC COMPRESSIBILITY
OF THE WORLD

The strategies presented in the two preceding sections were aimed at understanding the Universe by reducing its laws and structure to a pure game of probabilities. Our first reaction to such strategies is that if one of them succeeds (especially one of their stronger versions presented in section 4), then the "eternal mystery of the world's comprehensibility" that Einstein stressed would disappear: comprehensibility would give place to probability, and mystery would change into averaging mechanisms. However, to go beyond "first reactions" and to assess critically such an approach to the "rationality of the world," we must turn to the foundations of the probability calculus. This is the aim of this section.

Many branches of modern mathematics have their origin in an interplay of theory and application. This is also true as far as the probability calculus is concerned. Moreover, one would be inclined to say that in this case more depends on application than on theory. This is not only because the probability calculus originated from experience but mostly because it is very difficult to separate the very notion of probability from its empirical connotations. This fact gave rise to many philosophical discussions concerning the foundations of probability. In what follows I will try to avoid entering into these discussions; instead, I will trace the meaning of some fundamental concepts by placing them within the mathematical structure of the probability theory in its standard (Kolmogorov) formulation.[26]

In the contemporary standard approach, probability theory is a special instance of measure theory. *Measure,* in the mathematical sense, is a function defined on subsets of a certain space called the *measure space.* These subsets, called *measurable subsets,* can be thought of as objects to be measured. The function defined on these objects ascribes to each of them the result of a measurement (i.e., its measure, a number). For instance, the objects in question could be subsets of the Euclidean space, and the measure a function ascribing to each subset its volume. From the mathematical point of view, the essential circumstance is that outside the measure space the concept of measuring is meaningless.

Some cases are known in which not every subset of a given space is measurable. In such a space there are "things" (subsets) that cannot be measured, that

26. Regarding different views and philosophies of probability, see D. Home and M. A. B. Whitaker, "Ensemble Interpretations of Quantum Mechanics: A Modern Perspective," *Physics Reports* 210 (1992) 233–317.

is, no measurement result can be meaningfully ascribed to them. This runs counter to the common view that "what cannot be measured does not exist." Such subsets might indeed seem rather unusual, but one can find them even in the open interval (0,1) of real numbers.[27]

Probability is just a measure satisfying one additional condition: the measure of the entire space should be equal to one. Consequently, the measure of any of its subsets is either zero or a fraction between zero and one. If this axiom is satisfied the measure space with its measurable subsets is called *probability space,* and the measure defined on it the *probability distribution.*

Let us notice that so far there is nothing in our theory that would suggest an uncertainty or indeterminacy we intuitively connect with the idea of probability. All consequences follow from their axioms in a strictly apodictic manner, exactly the same as in mathematical theories. Intuitions that we connect with the concept of probability enter our theory via its reference to reality, that is, via its interpretation. The standard method of referring mathematics to reality is by the intermediary of physics. Some mathematical structures are used as building blocks of a physical theory, and the task of this theory is to investigate the world. The mathematical theory of probability, however, seems to relax this rule. It often makes references to reality with no direct help of a physical theory. For instance, when making probabilistic predictions of the outcome of throwing dice or of the price increase in an approaching fiscal year, a certain physical-like interpretation of a mathematical structure must intervene; but it is so natural and so closely linked to the mathematical structure itself that we prefer not to call it a physical theory but rather a *probabilistic model* of a given situation (with no reference to physics).

To be more precise, physical intuition enters the probabilistic model through the definition of the probability distribution. For instance, if we want to model playing with ideal dice mathematically, we define the probability distribution as a function that ascribes to each *elementary event*—that is, to each of six possible outcomes—the value of the probability measure equal to $1/6$. This particular value is taken from experience, namely, from a long series of throwing dice, but once put into the definition of the probability distribution, it becomes a structural part of the mathematical theory itself.

The feeling of a "probabilistic uncertainty" is connected with the *frequency*

27. For example, let a and b be real numbers in the open interval (0,1). If $a–b$ is a rational number we write $a \# b$. This is clearly an equivalence relation. We define A to be a subset of real numbers consisting of exactly one number of each equivalence class. It can be shown that A is not measurable. See R. Geroch, *Mathematical Physics,* Chicago: University of Chicago Press, 1985, 254–255.

interpretation of the distribution function defined in the above way. The value 1/6 of the distribution function at a given (elementary) event—for instance at the event "outcome three"—is interpreted as giving the relative frequency of the "outcome three" (i.e., the ratio of the number of the fortuitous events, in our case "outcome three," to all possible events) in a long series of throwing dice. Indeed, such experiments show that, in this circumstance, relative frequencies are approximately equal to 1/6. The longer the series of throws, the closer the relative frequency approximates this value. This property of the world is known as its *frequency stability*. It is a property of the world and not the property of the mathematical theory, because it is taken from experience and has no justification in the theory itself.

The frequency stability of the world is of fundamental importance for our analysis. In both everyday life and physics, we often meet random events or random experimental results. The result of an experiment is said to be random if it is not uniquely determined by the conditions under which the experiment is carried out and which remain under the control of the experimenter. Subsequent results of such an experiment are unpredictable. If in a series of n such experiments, n_A experiments give the result A, and $n-n_A$ give some other results, the number $f(A) = n_A/n$ is called the *frequency* of A. It turns out that as n is larger and larger, $f(A)$ approaches a certain number more and more closely. This tendency to certain numerical results reflects the world's frequency stability.

This is indeed an astonishing property. One cannot see any a priori reason why the world should be stable in this respect. But the world is frequency stable, and it is clear that without this property the probability calculus could not be applied to analyze the occurrence of events in the world. We can say that owing to its frequency stability the world is *probabilistically compressible*. A priori we could expect that truly chaotic or random phenomena would evade any mathematical description, but in fact the description of phenomena we call random or chaotic is not only possible but can be compressed into the formulae of the probability theory. The probabilistic compressibility of the world turns out to be a special instance of its algorithmic compressibility, and one would dare to say that it is the most astonishing (or the most unreasonable) instance of it.

This is even more the case if we remember that the applicability of probabilistic ideas to the real world underlies much of the foundations of statistical physics, and also the derivation of the classical limit of quantum theory, as well as the analysis of observations. All these aspects of probability applications are closely related to the problem of the arrow of time. Because the laws of fundamental physics are time reversible they must be involved in a subtle game of probabilities in order to produce irreversible phenomena on a macroscopic scale. There are strong reasons to suspect that the answer to the question of why the cosmic process evolves in time, rather than being reduced to an instant, is but another aspect of the probabilistic compressibility of the world.

We should not forget that probability theory is as good as any other mathematical theory. The distribution function is defined by idealizing some experimental results, but the probabilistic model, once constructed, produces uniquely determined results. The frequency interpretation of the probabilistic axioms does not influence formal inferences or the manipulation of formulae; it only allows us to look at the Universe in a special way—in a way in which events are not just given but seem to have a certain potentiality to happen, and the cosmic process does not just unfold but seems to have the possibility of choosing various branches in this unfolding.

The above considerations have shown that even if we were able to reduce the comprehensibility of the world to its probabilistic compressibility (as it was presupposed by the strategies and philosophies presented in sections 2 and 3), the questions would remain: Why does the probability theory apply to our world? Why has our world the property of being frequency stable?

When we ask the question, "Why is the world mathematical?" we should also wonder why is it subject to the "game of probabilities." Clearly, the riddle of probability does not eliminate the mystery of comprehensibility.

GOD OF PROBABILITIES

The ideas presented in sections 2 and 3 have their origin in an interesting property of the human mind, for which the high probability of an event is a kind of sufficient reason for its occurrence, but low probabilities always call for some special justification. One could guess that this property of our mind has evolved through an intricate agglomeration of selection effects in the world, the structure of which is predominantly shaped by frequency stable processes.

In classical natural theology, the justification of low probability events was often sought in the direct action of God. The low probability itself was considered to be a gap in the natural course of events, a gap that had to be filled in by the "hypothesis of God." In this way, high probability becomes a rival of God. We hear the echo of such views in metaphors contemporary scientists sometimes evoke to impress the reader with how finely the initial conditions should be tuned to produce the Universe in which the reader-like being could be born and evolve. For instance, in the famous book by Roger Penrose, the caption under the picture of God pointing with the pin to the initial conditions (or equivalently to the point in the phase space) from which God intends to create the world, reads:

In order to produce a universe resembling the one in which we live, the Creator would have to aim for an absurdly tiny volume of the phase space of possible universes—about the entire volume.[28]

On the contrary, the attempt to reduce phenomena to random events hiding behind them (e.g., to random initial conditions) is often thought of as supporting an atheistic explanation. For instance, the main argument of Leslie's book on the anthropic principles[29] is that the principal competitor of the God hypothesis is the idea of multiple worlds in which all possibilities are realized, along with some observational selection effects that would justify our existence as observers of the world. The God hypothesis relies on the argument from design, which is "based on the fact that our universe looks much as if designed." However, there might be immensely many universes.

And their properties are thought of as very varied. Sooner or later, somewhere, one or more of them will have life-permitting properties. Our universe can indeed look as if designed. In reality, though, it may be merely the sort of thing to be expected sooner or later. Given sufficiently many years with a typewriter even a monkey would produce a sonnet.[30]

A different view on probability came with the advent of quantum mechanics. The Hilbert space, an arena (in fact, the phase space) on which quantum processes occur, is a very beautiful and very solid mathematical structure, but when interpreted in a standard probabilistic way it reveals the unexpected image of the microworld. Wave functions, containing all information about a quantum object, are essentially nonlocal entities; they are defined "everywhere": for instance, from the wave function you can compute the probability of finding an electron at any place in the Universe. Wave functions evolve in time in a strictly deterministic way, but when a measurement is performed, deterministic evolution breaks down, all available information reduces to the unique measurement result, an infinite number of possibilities collapse to the

---

28. R. Penrose, *The Emperor's New Mind: Concerning Computers, Minds, and the Laws of Physics*, New York: Oxford University Press, 1989, 343.

29. J. Leslie, *Universes*, London and New York: Routledge, 1990. See also, J. D. Barrow and F. J. Tipler, *The Anthropic Cosmological Principle*.

30. J. Leslie, *Universes*, 1. Leslie clearly expresses his own opinion: "While the Multiple Worlds (or World Ensemble) hypothesis is impressively strong, the God hypothesis is a viable alternative" (p. 1).

single eigenvalue of the measurement operator.[31] Less informed philosophers speak about the free will of electrons; better informed ones begin to see that the time-honored antinomy between lawfulness and probability should be reconsidered *ab initio*.

Recent developments in deterministic chaos theory have shown that this is also true as far as the macroscopic world is concerned. An instability of the initial conditions leads to unpredictable behavior at later times, and there are strong reasons to believe that a certain amount of such a randomness is indispensable for the emergence and evolution of organized structures.

The shift we have sketched in our views on the significance of probability has had its impact on modern natural theology. Randomness is no longer perceived as a competitor of God, but rather as a powerful tool in God's strategy of creating the world. For instance:

God is responsible for ordering the world, not through direct action, but by providing various potentialities which the physical universe is then free to actualize. In this way, God does not compromise the essential openness and indeterminism of the universe, but is nevertheless in a position to encourage a trend toward good. Traces of this subtle and indirect influence may be discerned in the progressive nature of biological evolution, for example, and the tendency for the universe to self-organize into a richer variety of ever more complex forms.[32]

Or:

On this view God acts to create the world through what we call "chance" operating within the created order, each stage of which constitutes the launching pad for the next. However, the actual course of this unfolding of the hidden potentialities of the world is not a once-for-all pre-determined path, for there are unpredictabilities in the actual systems and processes of the world (micro-events at the "Heisenberg" level and possibly non-linear dynamical complex systems). There is an open-endedness in the course of the world's "natural" history. We now have to conceive of God as involved in explorations of the many kinds of unfulfilled potentialities of the universe(s) he has created.[33]

Still, either a God with a sharply pointed pin in hand choosing the improbable initial conditions for the Universe, or a God exploring the field of possibil-

31. In quantum theory, any measurement is represented by an operator acting on the corresponding wave function. Eigenvalues of this operator represent possible results of the measurement.

32. P. Davies, *The Mind of God: The Scientific Basis for a Rational World*, New York: Simon and Schuster, 1992, 183. Davies refers here to Whitehead's philosophy of God.

33. A. R. Peacocke, "God as the Creator of the World of Science," in *Interpreting the Universe as Creation: A Dialogue of Science and Religion*, ed. V. Brümmer, Kampen, The Netherlands: Kok Pharos, 1991, 110–111.

ities by playing with chance and randomness, seems to be but a Demiurge constrained by both a chaotic primordial stuff and the mathematical laws of probability (just as Plato's Demiurge was bound by the preexisting matter and the unchanging world of ideas). Of course, we could simply identify the laws of probability with God (or with the ideas present in God's mind), but this would bring us back to all traditional disputes surrounding the Platonic interpretation of God and mathematics.

Instead of immersing ourselves in risky disputes, I believe we should once more ask Einstein's question: Why is the world so comprehensible? As we have seen, there is no escape from this question via the "game of probabilities," for if we reduce comprehensibility to probability, new questions will emerge: Why should the theory of probability be privileged among all other mathematical theories?[34] Why is the world probabilistically compressible? And if the answer to the last question is: The world is probabilistically compressible because it enjoys the property of being frequency stable, we will then ask: Why is it frequency stable?

Any natural theology is sentenced to the "God-of-the-gaps" strategy. But if there are no gaps in the natural order of things, if the world is a self-enclosed entity, then there is no way from the world to its maker. The essential point is to distinguish between spurious gaps and genuine ones. Spurious gaps are temporary holes in our knowledge usually referring to an incomplete scientific theory or hypothesis and to a restricted domain of phenomena. Genuine gaps are truly disastrous; they overwhelm everything. I think that all gaps are spurious except for the following two or three.

First is the *ontological gap*. Its meaning is encapsulated in the question: Why is there something rather than nothing? The problem at stake is sheer existence. Even if we had a unique theory of everything (and some physicists promise us we will have it in the not too distant future), the question would remain of who or what "has breathed fire into the equations" to change what is merely a formally consistent theory into one modeling the real universe.

Second is the *epistemological gap:* Why is the world comprehensible? I have dealt with this question in the present chapter. It is truly a gap. Science presupposes the intelligibility of the world but does not explain it. Philosophy of science can at most demonstrate the nontrivial character of this question, but remains helpless if one further asks, "Why?"

From the theological perspective, both gaps, the ontological gap and the epistemological one, coincide: everything that exists is rational, and only the

---

34. To see that this question is not trivial, see section 4.

rational is open for existence. The source of existence is the same as the source of rationality.

I strongly suspect that there is a third genuine gap; I would call it the *axiological gap*—it is connected with the meaning and value of everything that exists. If the Universe is somehow permeated with meaning and value, they are invisible to the scientific method, and in this sense they constitute the real gap as far as science and its philosophy are concerned. Here again, by adopting the theological perspective, I would guess that the axiological gap does not differ from the remaining two: the source of existence, rationality, and value is the same.

Modern developments in science have discovered two kinds of elements (in the Greek sense of this word) shaping the structure of the Universe—the *cosmic elements* (integrability, analycity, calculability, predictability) and the *chaotic elements* (probability, randomness, unpredictability, and various stochastic properties). I think I have convincingly argued in this chapter for a thesis that the chaotic elements are in fact as "mathematical" as the cosmic ones, and if the cosmic elements provoke the question of why the world is mathematical, the same is true as far as the chaotic elements are concerned. On this view, *cosmos* and *chaos* are not antagonistic forces but rather two components of the same Logos immanent in the structure of the Universe.[35] Einstein's question, "Why is the world so comprehensible?", is a deeply and still not fully understood theological question.

35. For examples of such a cooperation between "cosmic" and "chaotic" elements, see my paper: "The Non-Linear Universe: Creative Processes in the Universe" (especially section 5), in *The Emergence of Complexity in Mathematics, Physics, Chemistry, and Biology*, ed. B. Pullman, Pontificiae Academiae Scripta Varia, vol. 89, Vatican City, 1996, 191–209.

PART FOUR

TRANSCENDING SCIENCE

In every encounter of science and religion the limits of science are involved. We usually think of limits as border lines separating two territories: here ends one territory, and there another begins. In this case, it is a misleading metaphor. There is not something like a vast domain or realm of scientific investigations beyond which the power of science expires. The domain of science is potentially infinite. Nevertheless, the limits in question do exist. However, they are not far away, beyond the horizon. On the contrary, they are within any scientific research, whatever its object is, be it a distant cluster of galaxies or a minuscule virus. Each time science tries to understand itself, it touches its limits. Why does the world exist? Why is it comprehensible? One could leave these questions with no answer or admit a kind of metaphysical wonder as the only response to them. I think, however, that such an attitude would be against the spirit of science that enforces on the scientist the duty never to cease looking for further explanations. It is here that science meets theology. This does not mean that theology is a "continuation" of science. It means only that theology provides a creative environment to think about science, its achievements, its methods, and its value.

One of the greatest mysteries of the scientific method—if not simply the greatest mystery of all—is how purely formal mathematical structures can so faithfully correspond to the structure of the real world. In spite of the fact that the role of mathematics in the natural sciences cannot be reduced to its function as a language of science, the tools of logical linguistics prove to be useful in expressing some fundamental problems in the philosophy of science. For instance, the above-mentioned "greatest mystery of the scientific method" can assume the form of the question: How does one change from syntaxis, that is, from purely linguistic relations, to semantics, that is, to relations between the language and to what this language refers? "Illicit jumps" from syntaxis to semantics usually lead to logical antinomies. It seems, however, that exactly to this procedure science owes its very existence. In Chapter 12, we trace the vestiges of this strategy in three great "languages" of science: the DNA code, the neuronal language of the brain, and the laws of nature in general.

The problem of limits makes its direct entry in Chapters 13 and 14. Do the limits of science coincide with the limits of rationality *tout court*? In Chapter 13 it is argued that the "field of rationality" embraces the "domain of science," and that—as history teaches us—science and theology always interacted, and continue doing so, within this field. Moreover, the choice of rationality, on which every scientific endeavor is based, is a choice of value, therefore a moral choice. This fact opens new horizons for theological reflection on the meaning of science.

The same issue can be considered from the point of view of "theological interests." This aspect of the problem assumes the form of Schrödinger's question: What has the progress of science given to the religious outlook of the world? My answer to this question is: The sense of Mystery. What, on the side of science, is the problem of limits, from the side of theology can be interpreted as an envoy of Transcendence. In this view, the existence of the world, its rationality, and the moral choice that underlies all science are but intimations of a horizon that seems to be far away, yet it permeates everything.

12 "ILLICIT JUMPS"—THE LOGIC OF CREATION

LOGICAL STRUCTURE OF LANGUAGE

In spite of the many breathtaking achievements in neuroscience, we still do not know the most important thing of all: how do neural signals become transformed into consciousness? The following remarks are aimed at expressing this ignorance in a quasi-logical way. It is essential to know clearly what (and how) we do not know. This seems to be a precondition to even starting to move in the correct direction.

The logic of language is traditionally divided into three parts: (1) *syntaxis,* which investigates the relations between the expressions of a given language; (2) *semantics,* which investigates the relations between a language and what that language refers to; (3) *pragmatics,* which investigates the relations between the expressions of a language and its users. Syntactic investigations remain inside the language, whereas semantical and pragmatic investigations go from the language to the world it describes and to the people who speak it, respectively. In the following, I will base my considerations on the interplay between syntaxis and semantics, putting aside, for the time being, their pragmatic aspect. After all, pragmatics is certainly a less developed branch of the logic of language.

There exist languages that completely lack a semantic aspect. They are purely formal languages and are often called artificial languages. In all other languages, syntaxis and semantics are in a constant interplay with each other. The terms "meaning," "reference," and "denotation" are semantical terms, or better, "semantical operators." They "act" on the language and have their "values" in the world the language describes. Owing to such operators, a given language can be a language about something.[1]

---

1. Sometimes one speaks about a meaning in relation to purely formal languages, but in such a case the meaning of a given expression is to be inferred from the rules of how this expression is used within the language.

It can happen that a language refers to itself. If we treat a reference as a semantical operator then this language operates on itself. Strictly speaking, we should distinguish here two languages: the language that operates—which is called "metalanguage" (or the language of the second order)—and the language that is operated on, which is just called "language" (or the language of the first order). There can be languages of many orders.

Here we must be on our guard against sophisticated traps. On the one hand, jumping from a language to the metalanguage (or vice versa) can create antinomies (the so-called semantical antinomies) such as, for example, the famous antinomy of the liar ("What I am saying now is a lie"—is this statement true or false?). On the other hand, however, a skillful manipulating of the languages of various orders can be a very efficient method by which to prove subtle theorems related to the foundations of logic and mathematics. For instance, Kurt Gödel proved his outstanding incompleteness theorem by, first, translating utterances about arithmetics into numbers, then by performing arithmetical calculations on these numbers, and finally by translating the obtained results back into the language about arithmetic. This strategy is called the "self-reference method" and nowadays is more and more appreciated. In general, however, jumping from one linguistic level to another linguistic level, if done without a rigorous logical control, is dangerous and trouble-generating.

In fact, this rigorous logical control is possible only as far as purely formal languages are concerned. Although, in principle, such languages have no semantics at all, semantics can be "artificially" attached to them, and precisely because it is "artificial" we obtain full control of the process. This is done by creating an *interpretation* of a given purely formal language. The truly ingenious idea is to create a purely formal linguistic substitute of the reality the language has to describe. This substitute is called a *(semantical) model* of a given language (I will not go into technical details here). When such a model is created we say that the considered formal language has acquired its *(semantic) interpretation*. Having at our disposal a formal language and its model, the rules of going from the language to its model, and vice versa, can be fully codified. To do this is the principal goal of semantics. Tarski's famous definition of truth says that an utterance (belonging to a given formal language) is true if and only if it asserts something about its model and this really occurs in the model.

However, if we go beyond the realm of formal languages a mess dominates the scene. Almost every transition from syntax to semantics (and vice versa) is, from the point of view of strict logic, an "illicit jump." In spite of this, we all speak natural languages and surprisingly often we understand each other (with a degree of accuracy sufficient to act together and communicate with each other). But this is a pragmatic side of the story that we have decided to put to one side.

LINGUISTIC TRAPS AND GOD'S EXISTENCE

In the traditional philosophy, going back to medieval scholasticism, there was a fundamental distinction between the epistemological (or logical) order (or level) and the ontological order (or level). It roughly corresponded to the modern distinction between syntax and semantics, with a shift of emphasis from the relationship between language and what it describes (the modern distinction) to the relationship between "what is in the intellect" and "what is in reality" (traditional distinction). The latter distinction appeared, for example, in the criticism by St. Thomas Aquinus of the famous "ontological argument" for the existence of God proposed by St. Anselm of Canterbury. "God is something the superior of which cannot be thought of *(aliquid quo nihil majus cogitari possit)*. And what does exist is superior than what does not exist. Thus God does exist"—claimed St. Anselm. St. Thomas did not agree. The statement "God is something the superior of which cannot be thought of" belongs to the epistemological order, whereas "God does exist" belongs to the ontological order, and the "proof" consists of the "illicit jump" between the two orders. This distinction became one of the cornerstones of the Thomist system and was strictly connected with its epistemological realism. Discussions like the one between St. Anselm and St. Thomas (and its continuation by Descartes, Leibniz, and Kant) paved the way for the modern logical analysis of language.

Strangely enough, modern tools of linguistic analysis can be used to understand more effectively the functioning of the universe, or, more strictly, to see more clearly where the gaps in our knowledge of it are located. The point is that nature seems often to employ linguistic methods in solving some of its fundamental problems. I will briefly touch upon three domains in which this "linguistic strategy" of nature can be seen quite transparently. All these domains are in fact fundamental as far as our understanding of the world is concerned.

LINGUISTIC PROBLEMS WITH
THE GENETIC CODE

The first of these domains is the genetic code. In fact, "code" is here a synonym for the "language." As is well known, it consists of linear strings of only four bases playing the role of letters in the "alphabet of life."

The linear sequence of these four letters in the DNA of each species contains the information for a bee or a sunflower or an elephant or an Albert Einstein.[2]

This is clearly the syntactic aspect of the genetic code. The point is, however, that the "syntactic information" must be implemented within the biological machinery. Syntaxis must generate semantics—and even more than this. After all, living beings are not purely linguistic concepts, but things that are real. For this reason, the old philosophical vocabulary about the epistemological and ontological orders seems to be more adequate in this context. The vocabulary is more adequate but not the rules of traditional philosophy! The phenomenon of life testifies to the fact that, contrary to these rules, the "illicit jump" from the epistemological order to the ontological order has been made. The genetic code does not only describe certain modes of acting but also implements the action within the concrete biological material.

Jacques Monod sees this "semantic antinomy" in the following way. The biological code would be pointless without the possibility of being able to decode it or to translate it into action. The structure of the machine which does that is itself encoded into the DNA. The code cannot be decoded unless the products of the code are involved. This is the modern version of the old *omne vivum ex ovo*. We do not know when and how this logical loop has been closed.[3]

LANGUAGE AND CONSCIOUSNESS

Another domain in which nature uses linguistic tricks to solve its problems is the functioning of the brain. In this case, the language consists of electric signals propagating along nerve fibers from neuron to neuron across the synaptic clefts. In this case the "illicit jump" does not consist of changing from a purely linguistic level to something external it describes, but rather in creating something real that did not exist previously, namely, consciousness. The problem at stake is much more complex here, and our knowledge about it is less adequate. Let us notice that it is consciousness that has produced human languages, and, in this way, the linguistic property, the starting point of our analysis, is not the beginning but rather the final product of the whole evolutionary process.

FROM MATHEMATICS TO EXISTENCE

The third domain in which a "linguistic approach" seems to be essential is the Universe itself or, to be more precise, the laws of nature that constitute it or structure it. It is a commonplace to say that the laws of nature are expressed

2. J. V. Nossal, *Reshaping Life: Key Issues in Genetic Engineering*, Cambridge: Cambridge University Press, 1985, 14.

3. J. Monod, *Le hasard and nécessité*, Paris: Éd. du Seuil, 1970, 182.

in the language of mathematics. Our textbooks of physics are full of mathematical formulae that are nothing but a certain formal language (although rather seldom a purely formal language, i.e., the one put into the form of an axiomatic system). Physicists claim that some of the formulae of this language express the laws of nature. This means that the language has its "semantic reference," that it is an interpreted language. Very roughly speaking, the Universe is its "model." I put the word "model" in quotation marks because the Universe is not a set of utterances, and consequently it is not a model in the technical, semantic sense. In fact, logicians and philosophers of science construct such semantic models. The strategy they adopt is the following. They try to express all experimental results, relevant for a given physical theory, in the form of a catalogue of sentences reporting these results (they are called *empirical sentences*). They then compare the two languages—the theoretical language consisting essentially of mathematical formulae with the catalogue of empirical sentences. Physicists are usually not impressed by this procedure and prefer to stick to their own method of approaching the "language of nature."

Here we also encounter an "illicit jump" from the epistemological order to the ontological order. After all, no mathematical formula, even if it is semantically interpreted in the most rigorous way, is a law of nature operating in the Universe.

In the case of the genetic code and of the neural code, the language in question could be regarded as a language of nature (the sequences of bases in DNA and electrical signals in neural fibers are products of natural evolution), and in this context how to change from syntax to semantics seems to be a nontrivial problem. However, as far as the laws of nature are concerned, the mathematical language in which they are expressed is the language created by us. By using this language we *only describe* certain regularities occurring in the real Universe, and we could claim that the problem of the mutual interaction between syntax and semantics is no more complicated than in our human languages.

I do think, however, that there is a subtle and deep problem here. Every property of the world can be deduced from a suitable set of laws of nature, that is, from a suitable set of suitably interpreted mathematical formulae—all with the exception of one, the most important one, namely, the existence. Nowadays physicists are able to produce models of the quantum origin of the Universe out of nothingness, but in doing so, they must assume (most often they do so tacitly) that the laws of quantum physics exist a priori with respect to the Universe (a priori in the logical sense, not necessarily in the temporal sense). Without this assumption physicists would be unable even to start constructing their models. But somehow the Universe does exist. Is there here a similar illicit jump as in the case of the genetic and neural codes? If so, this illicit jump would be no more and no less than the mystery of creation itself.

A FACILE TEMPTATION

We would fall victim to a facile temptation if we treated the above considered illicit jumps as gaps in the structure of the Universe that could be (or even should be) filled in with the "hypothesis of God." The true duty of science is never to stop asking questions and never to abandon looking for purely scientific answers to them. In my view, what seems to be an illicit jump from the point of view of our present logic is in fact nature's fundamental strategy in solving its most important problems (such as the origin of life and consciousness). Limitations of our logic are too well known to be repeated here (Gödel's theorems, problems with applications of the standard logic to quantum theory, etc.). My hypothesis is that our "Aristotelian logic" is too simplistic to cope with the problems considered in this chapter. What we need is not another "nonstandard" logical system that is constructed by changing or rejecting this or that axiom or this or that inference rule. What we need is something radically new, a far-reaching revolution comparable to changing from linear physics to nonlinear physics.

I do not think that we would have any chance of inventing such a logic by experimenting with purely symbolic operations and having it at our disposal only to apply it successfully to solve the problem of life and consciousness. On the contrary, such a logic will probably emerge from the analysis of concrete empirical investigations and will constitute only one component of the solution of the problem.

13

SCIENCE AND FAITH
IN INTERACTION

THE FIRST ENCOUNTER

Each theology derives from the encounter of human thought with something that, concerning itself, asserts it is a revealed truth.[1] I do not claim it is *religion* that derives from this encounter, but theology. Whatever definition of theology one might accept, one always agrees that it is an attempt at reflection, some sort of attitude, an effort to determine one's own relation to the encounter of human thought with revelation. This can be an encounter "under various aspects": axiological, anthropological, ethical, and so forth. This depends on the theology in question and on the position one takes; but one way or another, there are always two sides: human thought and something it encounters. This encounter, or confrontation, more often assumes the form of a conflict. A conflict is unavoidable if human thought encounters something that is given to it "from above."

Thought penetrates all areas of human activity, but certainly science is the most conspicuous product of human thought. The twentieth century was more than ever before shaped by the language, methods, and many achievements of various sciences. For this reason the scientific component of human thought should play an ever greater role in contemporary theology.

The conflict of science and theology is not unique to modern times. Before true sciences appeared, human thought in this conflict was represented by various "presciences": philosophy, common sense, ancient wisdom, and so forth. Even before Christian theology crystallized in the writings of the Church Fathers, the conflict was present "in the heads" of early Christians. On the one hand, Christianity had to express itself through the language of the Judeo-Greco-Roman culture that was for it a natural environment; and, on the other hand, this culture could not remain indifferent to

1. This chapter is partially based on passages from my books: *The World and the Word: Between Science and Religion,* Tucson: Pachart, 1986, and *The New Physics and a New Theology,* Vatican City State: Vatican Observatory Publications, 1996.

the new Christian contents. Today, after unquestionable achievements of analytical and hermeneutic philosophy, we understand better than ever before how much content depends on the language through which it is expressed. The essence of the conflict consisted in a tension between the deepest content of the Christian doctrine and the conceptual and linguistic tools through which this doctrine had to express itself.

One can easily find some external appearances of this deep conflict in the New Testament writings. For instance, the word "salvation" *(soteria),* which soon became a technical term in early Christian theology, originally belonged to the medical vocabulary.

It meant that the "crisis" was over and the patient on the way to recovery. In a more extended sense it could denote the safe return of a traveller from the dangerous voyage; this usage explains why there were temples for Zeus Soter in many Mediterranean ports.[2]

Another example of this type is the term "redemption" taken from the vocabulary of legal institutions. The original meaning referring to a legal action "by which a slave was made a free citizen" was given a new significance of "the fundamental change of the human condition."[3] The Pauline letters are full of such "truly linguistic experiments in which ordinary words of the ordinary Greek language were forced to serve this purpose."[4]

The flagrant polemics that soon took place between representatives of pagan philosophy and Christian apologists, or debates among Church writers concerning the proper attitude toward "Greek wisdom," were but a consequence and an outward sign of the basic conflict between the transcendental content and the available means of its expression.

Toward the end of Antiquity, Greek wisdom gave up its place in the historical arena to Christian wisdom, but it passed to Christian theology its conceptual framework, or in any case the philosophical substance from which such a framework could further be elaborated. In this way, human thought penetrated into the very heart of Revelation, and that is how it remained. This form of conflict cannot be avoided. In whatever language, through whatever conceptual tools we might want to apprehend Revelation, there will always be an abysmal lack of proportion between the content and the means of expression at our disposal. The conflict did not end in 313 with the Edict of Milan.

2. O. Pedersen, *Interaction between Science and Theology,* Seven Lectures delivered in Cambridge, 1988, manuscript, 2:17.

3. Ibid.   4. Ibid.

THE ADVENT OF SCIENCE

With the rise of the natural sciences, a qualitatively new element has appeared in the conflict between faith and reason. The imposing authority of the sciences consists in the relative independence of their methods and their results from the minds of those who create them. This is a phenomenon with no precedent in human thought. In philosophy one can hardly distinguish the philosopher from his doctrine, and the study of philosophy is, to a large extent, the study of its history. In the sciences, on the other hand, from the very moment of its origin a theory is distinct from the person of its inventors. At most their names appear, so to speak, on a label of a scientific theory or model.

The method of the natural sciences is extremely ascetical. The reality under examination is often simplified even to the limit where it would be totally deformed. An example would be the motion that goes on to infinity under the influence of no forces, or models of the sun and the planets as a system of moving points. The fact that more and more extensive regions of reality were conquered by this highly idealizing method gave rise to the ever more frequent accusation of the "totalitarianism" of the scientific method. This aggressive character of the sciences is a significant factor in their frequent conflicts with other areas of human culture, with theology in particular.

Almost from the very beginning, mathematics was regarded as the language of the natural sciences. Empirical results were incorporated into scientific knowledge only after they had been related to symbols present in a mathematical formalism. As time went on mathematics became not only the language of the sciences but also their content. First, the simplest geometrical and mechanical properties, which were traditionally regarded as "quantities" (velocity, acceleration, forces, etc.), surrendered to mathematical modeling. Then the so-called "qualities" (heat, sound, colors, etc.) were mathematized. Finally, in modern quantum field theories, matter has been totally decomposed into mathematical structures. Although we continue to think of the scientific image of the world in terms of a material substrate that comes to fill the formal structure, there is, in fact, absolutely nothing in modern physics that would force one to presuppose such a substrate. To use Aristotelian terminology, we might say that for modern physics "matter" is "form without matter," and mathematics is a "science of form."

This extraordinary efficacy of mathematics in the natural sciences often assumes a totalitarian guise when it gives rise to the statements that there is nothing that will not, sooner or later, succumb to the empirical-mathematical method. In the first half of the twentieth century, the totalitarian tendencies in science took on extreme forms. The following strategy was often used. If empiricism is not efficacious in some area of reality, that area of reality should be eliminated from the field of human knowledge. Those questions to which the empirical sciences have no response are to be considered meaningless. On the strength of this criterion, there is no place in rational thinking for philosophy, theology, or religion.

Logical positivism was an imposing, but fleeting, phenomenon. There were two main factors that contributed to the fall of this school of thinking in the 1960s. First, beginning with the paper by Quine on "The Two Dogmas of Empiricism,"[5] there was a growing awareness that "positivistic philosophy" was involved in many simplifications and even self-contradictions. Second, recent physical theories developed beyond all expectation and broke all the rules set by positivistic methodology. These factors (and some others as well) worked together, but it seems that the second has played a more important role in compromising the narrow empiricism of the logical positivists. It is certainly true that positivism, as a major current of thought, has exited the stage of contemporary philosophy, but still we should not harbor illusions: basic tenets of the positivist-like empiricism still preserve their tempting power. The essence of the problem assumes, in my opinion, the following form.

Science—whatever it might be, more or less empirical, objectivistic, or anthropological—is solely a work of man. It is man himself, with the methods he invented himself and the tools he himself constructed, who discloses a hidden information and interprets and tests it. Science is the product of man's brain. On the other hand, faith, in the religious sense, is by definition an acceptance of a "voice from beyond." The rational activity of man in this domain consists only in applying certain criteria to this "voice" on evaluating its credibility. The rest is either rejection or acceptance, and a reflection *ex post* on what has been accepted. This is how theologies are born (both theologies of Great Schools and private theologies of men and women).

There is an unavoidable strangeness between the "attitude of science" and the "attitude of faith," and the essence of this strangeness consists in the fact that the former comes "from the Earth," and the latter comes "from Heaven." This is the source of both methodological distinctions that are to be made and psychological tensions that are to be overcome. We have here another unavoidable conflict; this time it comes from deep strata of the human psychology. It stems from the fact that a mind trained in scientific methods, and thus in inde-

---

5. W. Van Omran Quine, "The Two Dogmas of Empiricism," in *From a Logical Point of View,* Cambridge, Mass.: Harvard University Press, 1971.

pendent and autonomous investigation of reality, hesitates to accept "information from the outside."

Recent theological formulations have tried to mitigate this strangeness, presenting Revelation not so much as "information from above," but rather as a personal dialogue of man with the Revealing One. This style of doing theology is certainly valuable, but in no ways does it alter the strangeness we are discussing. In every dialogue there is that Other One who speaks. This feeling of strangeness is fundamental and, in my view, cannot be eliminated by any measure. I would even say that authentic faith requires its continual sharpening. Faith, after all, is trust in the Other One.

THE LIMITS OF SCIENCE AND THE LIMITS OF RATIONALITY

Let us, therefore, leave for the time being this feeling of strangeness as it is, and let us pass to another temptation of empiricism. It consists in identifying rationality with the mathematical-empirical method of the natural sciences or, equivalently, in identifying the limits of the mathematical method with the limits of the Universe. What is beyond the limits of this method is beyond the limits of the Universe. It simply does not exist.

Are we facing here the problem of the definition? For if one defines rationality to be the same as the mathematical-empirical method, then indeed the limits of this method coincide with the limits of the Universe. However, we must not kill the authentic problem with purely conventional meanings. The point is that, independent of any conventions, there are some ways of knowing that merit the name of *rational* knowledge, and some other ways of knowing that do not, although it could be extremely difficult to force these "ways of knowing" into the form of strict definitions. This is so because one cannot analyze rationality without using some rational methods. Every discourse, if it is to be of any value, presupposes some sort of rationality.

This self-referential character of rationality is the first thing one must take into account when dealing with the problem of the limits of science and the limits of the Universe. Let us consider the statement: "The mathematical-empirical method is rational." The adherent of the belief that the limits of rationality coincide with the limits of the Universe would certainly qualify it as a rational statement. It is obvious, however, that it can be neither verified nor falsified with the help of the mathematical-empirical method. Therefore, rationality goes beyond the scientific method.

I think that an important *diagnostic property* of rationality can be expressed in the form of the postulate that statements, aspiring to constitute rational knowledge, should be *critically argued for.* An argumentation is *critical* (1) if one does not cease to look for argumentation as long as there remains something to be argued for; (2) if one is ready to consider impartially all possible counterarguments, that is, if it is open for criticism. Karl Popper and his followers have amply discussed the second of these conditions. Let us focus on the first one.

I think many people so easily identify rationality with the scientific method because the scientific method constitutes the easiest type of rationality. Within this method we have at our disposal the most efficient tools to distinguish scientifically valuable information from that which is of no value. Beyond the domain controlled by the scientific method, valuable and valueless ideas have much greater chances to coexist. Many people dissatisfied with this fact surrender to the temptation of narrowing the field of rationality to the field of the scientific method. However, such an approach is against the first of the above-formulated conditions of critical knowledge. As we have seen, whenever a question is addressed to the scientific method itself, one goes immediately beyond the limit of this method, but to cease asking such questions would be a sin against rationality. Moreover, there are some particular questions having their origin in science that cannot be answered with the help of scientific methods. To dismiss these questions as pointless would mean to stop pursuing the main goal of all sciences—to understand the Universe. Here is the typical example.

WHERE DO THE LAWS OF PHYSICS COME FROM?

The goal of science is to explain the functioning of the Universe with the help of physical laws, but the question concerning the nature and the origin of these laws goes beyond the scientific method. This does not prevent many physicists from asking this question again and again. After all, to understand the functioning of the world ultimately comes down to the question, Where do the laws of physics come from? It seems that the only way to settle this question without going beyond the scientific method is to eliminate the question itself, that is, to demonstrate that "on the fundamental level" no physical laws exist.

Roughly speaking, there are two strategies to reach this goal. The first consists in showing that on the fundamental level everything is allowed, there reigns the "complete anarchy," and what we now call laws of physics are but purely statistical results, the effects of probabilistic averaging processes.[6] The second strategy accepts the "complete chaos" not on the fundamental level, but rather in the set of all possible universes: there are infinitely many univers-

6. See Chapter 11.

es and in each of them different physical laws with different values of physical constants are in power. We are living in the Universe, highly ordered by what we call physical laws, because in all other universes the life like ours is excluded. The laws of physics are, in a sense, a selection effect. There were some attempts to implement the first strategy,[7] but their successes are moderate.[8] The second strategy was propagated by Andriej Linde[9] and has recently been expanded by Lee Smolin.[10]

Both these strategies are based on the probability calculus and its derivative—statistics. The averaging processes, which constitute the core of the first strategy, make direct reference to probability, and the selection principle that is supposed to explain the Universe and its laws, in the second approach, reduces, in fact, to the probability calculus. If there is a suitably large set of elements competing with each other in some respect, an interplay of probabilities automatically puts into action selection mechanisms. In both these approaches, probability is the ultimate limit of rationality. Doubtlessly, the calculus of probability is a very effective, and indeed very beautiful, chapter of mathematics. Einstein's question (in Wigner's wording), "Why is mathematics so effective in the natural sciences?", certainly refers also to this chapter. Let us look at this problem more carefully.

The axioms of the probability calculus express some abstract properties of a family of functions that are defined on subsets of a certain bigger space. These properties are purely formal properties and have nothing in common with a feeling of uncertainty or indeterminacy that we usually associate with the concept of probability. In fact, we do associate this "uncertainty feeling" with the probability concept by suitably interpreting the probability axioms. The most common interpretation consists in treating the functions appearing in the axioms (called distribution functions) as describing the relative frequency of events, that is, as the ratio of the number of successful events to the number of all possible events. This interpretation is based on a strong additional assumption. It asserts that in a long series of experiments of the same type (for instance, throwing dice) relative frequencies will only slightly differ from the relative frequency really observed. The longer the series of experiments is, the smaller this difference. For instance, in a long series of throwing

7. See, for instance, D. Foerster, H. B. Nielsen, and M. Ninomiya, "Dynamical Stability of Local Gauge Symmetry," *Physics Letters* 94B (1980) 135–140.

8. See also J. D. Barrow and F. J. Tipler, *The Anthropic Cosmological Principle,* Oxford: Clarendon Press, 1986, 255–258.

9. Andriej Linde modified his idea several times; see, for instance, his book *Physics of Elementary Particles and the Inflationary Cosmology,* Moscow: Nauka, 1990 (in Russian).

10. L. Smolin, *The Life of the Cosmos,* New York and Oxford: Oxford University Press, 1997.

dice, the number of events the outcome of which is "6" will be only slightly different from 1/6. This property is called the *frequency stability of random events*. We should emphasize this strongly: it is the property of the world and not the property of our formal model. Were the world deprived of this property, there could be no question about any reduction of physical laws to the probability calculus.

Why does the Universe have this property? And consequently, why can it be so effectively investigated with the help of probability and statistics? In both strategies discussed above, these questions have no answers. It is interesting to note that Smolin when considering Leibniz's question, "Why does there exist something rather than nothing?" plainly admits:

I do not see, really, how science, however much it progresses, could lead us to an understanding of these questions. In the end, perhaps there must remain a place for mysticism. But mysticism is not metaphysics, and it is only that I seek to eliminate.[11]

The question concerning the effectiveness of probabilities is of similar weight. It does not matter whether we call these questions mysticism or metaphysics. The problem remains open. At the very foundations of our efforts "to explain the Universe in terms of the Universe itself" there is something unexplained that points out beyond the Universe.

A MORAL CHOICE

Rationality demands that we base our convictions on rational arguments or demonstrations. The question immediately arises, How do we rationally demonstrate the necessity to base our convictions on rational arguments or demonstrations? It is obvious that it is impossible to answer this question without presupposing the answer that has to be given. To break this vicious circle, one must make the choice—the choice between rationality and irrationality. Because rationality, as confronted with irrationality, is clearly a value, it is the *moral choice*. This moral choice has deep consequences in many areas of human life. In his *The Open Society* Popper wrote

The choice before us is not simply an intellectual affair or a matter of taste. It is a moral choice. For the question whether we adopt some more or less radical form of irrationalism, or whether we adopt that minimum concession to irrationalism which I have termed "critical rationalism," will deeply affect our whole attitude towards other men, and towards the problem of social life.[12]

11. Ibid, 198.
12. K. Popper, *The Open Society and Its Enemies*, vol. 2, London: Routledge and Kegan Paul, 1974, 232.

This moral choice was done at the very beginning of European history, when the Greeks discovered that it is worthwhile to search for answers to the questions concerning the world and ourselves in terms of arguments and demonstrations, without looking for help "from outside." It gradually matured into the history of philosophy and science. The invention of the mathematical-empirical method of investigating the world is, in a sense, the culminating point of this process. Each scientific success, each bit of information decoded from the structure of the Universe, should be regarded as the corroboration of the correctness of this choice.

However, this choice is not only, so to speak, a social problem; it has to be made by each man and woman who should decide whether to remain within the vicious circle of nonsense or to face the challenge of rationality. Faith in reason (this is another name of this choice) lies at the very basis of every conscious human activity, and especially at the foundations of all attempts to understand the world and oneself. Faith in logic is the "driving force" of science, but faith in reason is indispensable for logic not to sink to the level of schematic conventions of thinking. We believe in reason because it is a value. Faith in reason is but a specific case of faith in values. If we believe in anything at all, we believe because it represents a value for us.

The faith of which we speak is a priori with respect to any organized rational thinking, although sometimes very advanced rational thought is required in order to detect the existence of this faith. Just as existence is a priori to thinking ("I exist, therefore I think"), thinking can be proof of existence ("I think, therefore I am"). This is more than an analogy. Faith is very close to existence—at least in the sense that without faith rational existence is impossible.

I offer here my personal confession. For me, religious faith is a natural extension of this fundamental "faith in reason." A logic that would be only a by-product of gray cells, and would die along with them, would ultimately be an illusion rather than logic. Only living in a world of Value and Meaning is it truly worth taking up science.

14 SCIENCE AND TRANSCENDENCE

LIMITS OF LANGUAGE AND COMMON SENSE

We all are realists. If we were not, the surrounding world would soon destroy us. We must take seriously information given us by our senses. If, when crossing the street, we looked for extrasensory inspiration instead of watching the traffic lights, we would have been very quickly eliminated from this game. Poets and philosophers seem odd and impractical to others because abstract worlds of ideas divert their sight from earthly things. From our everyday contacts with the surrounding world (but also from many slips and bruises) our common sense is born—that is, the set of practical rules that tell us how to behave in order to minimize the damage the world could inflict upon us.

We like to quote science to justify our common sense. The scientific method is but a sharpening of our common sense. Experience constitutes the base of every science, and measuring instruments we use in our laboratories are "prolongations" of our senses. The world of technology, from the computer on my desk to artificial satellites, testifies to the ability of our common sense, which has so efficiently conquered the world of matter.

Such views, although flattering to our ears, are totally false. Widely spread imaginings concerning science do not match what science really is. Contemporary physics, this most advanced of all sciences, provides us an example fatally destroying these imaginings.

What could be more in agreement with our common sense than the fact that we cannot go back to our childhood? Time is irreversible. It flows irrevocably from the past to the future. However, this is not that obvious in physics. We know that to every elementary particle there corresponds an antiparticle. Such an antiparticle has the same mass as the corresponding particle but the opposite electric charge. When a particle collides with its antiparticle, they both change into energy. These are the experimental facts, but the first information about the existence of antiparticles came from theory. Since 1926 it has been known that the motion of an electron is described by the Schrödinger equation. The discovery of this equation by Schrödinger was a major breakthrough. Together with the works of Heisenberg, it has created the foundations of modern quantum mechanics. However, the Schrödinger equation had a serious drawback: it did not take into account the laws of special relativity discovered by Einstein two decades earlier. Einstein's theory is a physical theory of space and time. Although we can ignore it when dealing with the first approximation to the real world, if we want to be more precise in our investigation of the world we cannot avoid using a relativistic approach. The relativistic counterpart of Schrödinger's equation was discovered by Dirac in 1928. It turned out that Dirac's equation admitted two types of solutions. One of these types described well the elementary particles known at the time. The remaining solutions referred to similar particles but going back in time. How should this be understood? Dirac was audacious enough to claim that such particles really existed and coined the name "antiparticles." This step was not an easy one. Our common sense had to be put upside down. To make this step easier, Dirac helped his imagination with the picture of the void with holes in it, and he interpreted these holes as antiparticles. It does not matter whether we would prefer holes in the void or time flowing backward; our common sense is jeopardized.

Let us consider another example. An atom emits two photons (quanta of light). They travel in two different directions, and, after a certain lapse of time, they are far away from each other (it does not matter how far; they can even be at two opposite edges of the Galaxy). Photons have the property called spin by physicists. It can be measured, and quantum mechanics teaches us that the results of the measurements can assume only two values. Let us denote them symbolically by +1 and −1. However, the situation is much more delicate than our inert language allows us to express. Strictly speaking, we cannot claim that an electron possesses the spin in such a manner as we say that Mr. Smith is tall or has twenty dollars in his pocket. When we are measuring the photon's spin, it behaves as if it were always there. In fact, before the act of measurement, the photon had no spin. Before the act of measurement, a probability existed that the act of measurement would yield, if performed, a given result with a given probability. Let us assume that we have performed the measurement obtaining the result +1. In such a case, on the strength of the laws of quantum mechanics, another photon acquires spin −1, even if it is at the other edge of the Galaxy. How does this photon *instantaneously* know about our measurement on the first photon and the result it yields?

This experiment was invented as a purely *Gedanken* experiment by Einstein, Podolsky, and Rosen in 1935 in order to show that the laws of quantum mechanics lead to nonsensical conclusions. However, the physicists—against the opinion of Einstein and his two collaborators—were not much surprised when Allain Aspect, together with his team, performed Einstein's *Gedanken* experiment in reality, and it has turned out that quantum mechanics was right. Aspect was able to perform this experiment owing to enormous progress in experimental methods, but also owing to a theoretical idea of John Bell that enabled him to express Einstein's intuitions in the form of precise formulae (the so-called Bell inequalities), which could be compared with the results of measurements.

What happens to photons in Aspect's experiments? When our intuition fails, we must look for help from the mathematical structure of the theory. In quantum mechanics, two photons that once interacted with each other are described by the same vector of state. Strictly speaking, positions of elementary particles behave like spin; an elementary particle is nowhere in space until its position is measured. The state vector of a given quantum object contains information only about probabilities of outcomes of various measurements.

We are met here not only with particles that live "backward in time" but also with particles for which space distances are no obstacles. It looks as if elementary particles did not exist in space and time—as if space and time were only our macroscopic concepts, the usual meaning of which breaks down as soon as we try to apply them to the quantum world. Moreover, can one speak about the individuality of a particle (before its properties are measured) that exists neither in space nor in time? If we agree to consider as a single object something that is described by a single vector of state, could we treat two photons (which previously interacted with each other) situated at two different edges of the Galaxy as the single object?

Contemporary physics has questioned the very applicability to the quantum world of such fundamental concepts as space, time, and individuality. Is not our common sense put upside down?

Some philosophers claim that what cannot be said clearly is meaningless. The intention of this claim is praiseworthy; its aim is to eliminate verbosity, which does not contain any substance. However, modern physics has taught us that the possibilities of our language are limited. There are domains of reality—such as the quantum world—at the borders of which our language breaks down. This does not mean that within such domains anything goes—far from it. It turns out that mathematics constitutes a much more powerful language than our everyday means of communication. Moreover, mathematics is not only a language that describes what is seen by our senses. Mathematics is also a tool that discloses those regions of reality that without its help would forever remain inaccessible for us. All interpretational problems of modern physics can be reduced to the following question: How can all these things that are disclosed by the mathematical method be translated into our ordinary language?

I think that the greatest discovery of modern physics is that our common sense is limited to the narrow domain of our everyday experience. Beyond this domain a region extends to which our senses have no access.

SCHRÖDINGER'S QUESTION

The world of classical mechanics seemed simple and obvious, but in fact it never was simple or obvious. The method discovered by Galileo and Newton did not consist in performing many experiments with pendulums and freely falling bodies, the result of which would later be described with the help of mathematical formulae. Newton, led by his genius, posed a few hazardous hypotheses that suggested to him the mathematical shape of the laws of motion and those of universal gravity. His formulae did not describe the results of experiments. Nobody ever saw a particle uniformly moving to infinity because it was not acted upon by any forces. Moreover, there is no such particle in the entire Universe. And it is exactly this statement that is at the very foundations of modern mechanics.

The world of classical mechanics is doubtlessly richer than the world we penetrate with our senses. The most fundamental principle of physics was discovered within the domain of classical mechanics—a principle that could be reached only by mathematical analysis. It is called the principle of the least action, and its claim is indeed extraordinary. It asserts that every physical theory—from classical mechanics to the most modern quantum field theory—can be constructed in the same way. First, one must correctly guess a function called Lagrangian (which is different for different theories). Then, one computes an integral of this function, called action. And finally, one obtains the laws of this theory by postulating that the action assumes the extreme value (usually the least one, but sometimes the greatest one). Physicists often speak about a superunification of physics, that is, about such a theory that would contain everything in itself. We do not yet have such a theory, but its chances that we will are becoming greater and greater. In fact, we already have, in a sense, the unification of the method; all major physical theories are obtainable from the principle of the least action.

With our senses we cannot grasp the fact that all bodies around us move in such a way that a certain simple mathematical expression (the action) assumes the minimal value. But the bodies move in this way. We live surrounded by things that cannot be seen, or heard, or touched. It was Schrödinger who once asked himself: Which achievements of science have best helped the religious outlook of the world? In his answer to this question he pointed to the results of Boltzmann and Einstein concerning the nature of time. Time, which can change its direction depending on the fluctuations of entropy, which can flow differently in different systems of reference, is no longer a tyrant Chronos, whose absolute regime destroys all our hopes for nontemporal existence, but a physical quantity with a limited region of applicability. If Schrödinger lived today, he could add many new items to his list of achievements that teach us the sense of Mystery. Personally, I think, however, that particular scientific achievements do not do this work best, but rather the scientific method itself. Spectacular results of the most recent physical theories are but examples of what was present in the method of physics for a long time, although it was understood only by a very few.

TWO EXPERIENCES OF HUMANKIND

If we pause for a moment, in our competition for new achievements, to look backward on the progress of science during the last two centuries, we can see an interesting regularity. In the nineteenth century humankind went through the great experience of the efficiency of the scientific method. It was a deep experience. Today, we speak of the century of "vapor and electricity" with a touch of irony in our voice. We must know, however, that the road from a candle to the electric bulb, and from a horse-drawn carriage to the railroad train, was longer and more laborious than that from the propeller plane to the intercontinental jet. In the twentieth century technology made a great jump, but in the nineteenth century it had started almost from nothing. But even then it was obvious that it would change the shape of the civilized world. In the nineteenth century technology was treated, like never before or after, as a synonym of progress and of the approaching new era of overwhelming happiness. Positivistic philosophy, regarding science as the only valuable source of knowledge, and scientism, wanting to replace philosophy and religion with science, could be considered as a philosophical articulation of this great experience— the experience of the efficiency of the scientific method. In the nineteenth century, any suggestion that there could exist any limits beyond that the scientific method does not work, would have been regarded as a senseless heresy. Nobody would have taken it seriously.

The nineteenth century came together with its wars and revolutions. In my opinion, the revolution that took place in the foundations of physics, in the first decades of the twentieth century (and which, I think, is still taking place), had more permanent results for our culture than the political turmoil that shaped the profile of our times. First of all, it turned out that classical mechanics—once believed to be the theory of everything—in fact has but a limited field of applicability. It is limited on two sides: from below—in the domain of atoms and elementary particles the Newtonian laws must be replaced by the laws of quantum mechanics; and from above—for objects moving with a speed comparable to that of light, classical physics breaks down and should be replaced by Einstein's theory of relativity. Moreover, the new theories are also, in a sense, limited: the finite value of Planck's constant essentially limits the questions that can be asked in quantum physics, and the finite velocity of light determines horizons of the information transfer in the theory of relativity and cosmology.

The method physics used from the times of Galileo and Newton (and possibly even from the time of Archimedes) consists in applying mathematics to the investigation of the world. The certainty of mathematical deductions is transferred to physics, and it is one of the two sources of the efficiency of the physical method (the other one being controlled experiment). It came as a shock when, in the third decade of the twentieth century, Kurt Gödel proved his famous theorems which assert that limitations are inherent in mathematics itself: no system of axioms could be formulated from which entire mathematics could be deduced (or even a part of mathematics that is at least as rich as arithmetic). Such a system would be either incomplete or self-contradictory.

Today, there is no doubt that the twentieth century has confronted us with the new great experience—the experience of limitations inherent in the scientific method. Philosophers have understood this relatively late. In the first half of the twentieth century, positivism, in its radical form of the logical empiricism, dominated the scene. Only in the 1960s did it become evident that one cannot philosophically support an outdated vision of science. I do not here have in mind those anti-scientific and anti-intellectual currents that nowadays so often fanatically fight science in the name of supposed interests of humanity. I have in mind a philosophy of science that recognizes the epistemological beauty of science and its rational applications in the service of man, but does this based on the correct evaluation of both scientific method and the limitations inherent in it.

SCIENCE AND TRANSCENDENCE

Science could be compared to a great circle. The points in its interior denote all scientific achievements. What is outside the circle represents not-yet discovered regions. Consequently, the circumference of the circle should be interpreted as a place in which what we know today meets with what is still unknown, that is, as a set of scientific questions and unsolved problems. As science progresses, the set of achievements increases and the circle expands; but, together with the area inside the circle, the number of unanswered questions and unsolved problems becomes bigger and bigger. It is historical truth that each resolved problem poses new questions calling for new solutions.

If we agree to understand the term *transcendence*—as suggested by its etymology—as "something that goes beyond," then what is outside the circle of scientific achievements is transcendent with respect to what is inside it. We can see that transcendence admits a graduation: something may go beyond the limits of this particular theory, or beyond the limits of all scientific theories known till now, or beyond the limits of the scientific method as such. Do such ultimate limits exist?

Usually three domains are quoted as forever inaccessible to all attempts of the mathematico-empirical method: the domain of existence, the domain of ultimate rationality, and the domain of meaning and value.

How does one justify the existence of the world? Why does something exist rather than nothing? Some more optimistic physicists believe that in the foreseeable future one will be able to create the Unique Theory of Everything. Such a theory would not only explain everything, but it would also be the only possible theory of that type. In this way, the entire Universe would be understood; there would be no further questions. Let us suppose that we have such a theory—the set of equations fully describing (modeling) the Universe. One problem would remain: How can one change from the abstract equations to the real world? What is the origin of those existents that are described by the equations? Who or what ignited the mathematical formulae with existence?

Science investigates the world in a rational way. Knowledge is rational if it is rationally justified. Here new questions arise: Why should we rationally justify our convictions? Why is the strategy of rational justifications so efficient in investigating the world?

One cannot give a rationally justified answer to the first of these questions. Let us try doing this; that is, let us try to rationally justify the statement that everything should be rationally justified. However, our justification (our proof) cannot presuppose what it is supposed to justify (to prove). Therefore, we cannot assume that our convictions should be rationally justified. Consequently, when constructing our proof we cannot use rational means of proving (because they presuppose that we are to prove something); that is, the proof cannot be carried out.

There is no other way out of this dilemma but to assume that the postulate to rationally justify our convictions is but our *choice*. We have two options, and we must choose one of them: either, when doing science, we do it in a rational way or we admit an irrational way of doing science. Rationality is a *value*. This can be easily seen if rationality is confronted with irrationality. We evaluate rationality as something good and irrationality as something bad. When choosing rationality we choose something good. It is, therefore, a moral choice. The conclusion cannot be avoided; at the very basis of science there is a moral option.

This option was made by humankind when it first formulated questions addressed to the world and started to look for rationally justified answers to them. The entire subsequent history of science could be regarded as a confirmation of this option.

Now follows the second question: Why is the strategy of rational justifications so efficient in studying the world? One could risk the following answer: The fact that our rational methods of studying the world lead to such wonderful results suggests that our choice of rationality is somehow consonant with the structure of the world. The world is not a chaos but an ordered rationality. Or: the rational method of science turns out to be so efficient because the world is permeated with meaning. We should not understand this in an anthropomorphic manner. Meaning, in this context, is not something connected with the human consciousness; it is this property of the world because of which the world discloses its ordered structure, provided it is investigated with the help of rational methods.

SCHRÖDINGER'S QUESTION ONCE MORE

After all these considerations, it would be worthwhile to go back to Schrödinger's question: Which achievements of science have best helped the religious outlook of the world? I think that contemporary science teaches us, as never before, the sense of mystery. In science, we are confronted with mystery on every step. Only outsiders and mediocre scientists believe that in science everything is clear and obvious. Every good scientist knows that he is dancing on the edge of a precipice between what is known and what is only feebly felt in just-formulated questions. He also knows that the newly born questions open vistas that go beyond the possibilities of our present imagination—imagination that has learned its art in contact with these pieces that we had so painfully extracted from the mysteries of the world.

Let us imagine a very good scientist of the nineteenth century, for instance, Maxwell or Boltzmann, who is informed by his younger colleague coming to him from our twenty-first century about recent developments of general relativity or quantum mechanics. Maxwell or Boltzmann would never believe in such "nonsense." Now consider this question: How would we behave if a physicist from the twenty-second century told us about his textbook physics? Only a very shortsighted scientist can be unaware of the fact that he is surrounded by mysteries.

Of course, I have in mind relative mysteries, that is, such mysteries as now go beyond the limits of our knowledge but perhaps tomorrow will become well-digested truths. Do not such mysteries point toward the Mystery (with the capital M)? Does not what today transcends the limits of science suggest something that transcends the limits of all scientific methods?

I have expressed these ideas in the form of questions on purpose. Plain assertions are too rigid; they assert something that is expressed by its words and syntactic connection between them, but remain silent about what is outside the linguistic stuff. Therefore, let us stick to questions that open our intuition for regions not constrained by grammatical rules. Are these unimaginable achievements of science, which revolutionize our vision of the world (time flowing backward, cured space-time, particles losing their individuality but communicating with each other with no interaction of space and time), not clear suggestions that the reality is not exhausted in what can be seen, heard, touched, measured, and weighed?

• Does not the fact that there exists something rather than nothing excite our metaphysical anxiety?

• Does the fact that the world is not only an abstract structure—never a written formula, an equation solved by nobody, yet something that can be seen, heard, touched, measured, and weighed—direct our thought to the Ultimate Source of Existence?

• Does not the fact that the world can, after all, be put into abstract formulae and equations suggest to us that the abstract thought is more significant than concrete matter?

• Does the rationality that is presupposed but never explained by every scientific investigation not express a reflection of the rational plan hidden in every scientific question addressed to the Universe?

• Does not the moral choice of the rationality that underlies all science offer a sign of the Good that is in the background of every correct decision?

These questions are not situated far away, "beyond the limits." The concreteness of existence, the rationality of the laws of nature, the meaning touched by us when we make our decisions are present in every atom, in every quantum of energy, in every living cell, in every fiber of our brain.

It is true that the Mystery is not in the theorems of science but in its horizon. Yet this horizon permeates everything.

ACKNOWLEDGMENTS

Permission to reprint from the following sources is gratefully acknowledged:

CHAPTER 1   Astronomical Society of the Pacific: "The Abuse of Cosmology," *Mercury* 26 (no. 6), 1997, 19–21.

CHAPTER 2   Vatican Observatory, Vatican City State and The Center for Theology and the Natural Sciences, Berkeley: "On Theological Interpretations of Physical Theories," *Quantum Cosmology and the Laws of Nature,* Vatican Observatory–CTNS, 1993, 91–102.

CHAPTER 3   European Society for the Study of Science and Theology: "Scientific Image of the World," *Studies in Science and Theology* 6, 1998, 63–69.

CHAPTER 4   European Society for the Study of Science and Theology: "A Program for Theology of Science," *Studies in Science and Theology* 4, 1996, 41–44.

CHAPTER 5   Pontifical Academy of Sciences, Vatican City State: "From the Privileged Margin to an Average Centre," *Commentarii* 3 (no. 33), 1992, 1–18.

CHAPTER 6   Vatican Observatory, Vatican City State and The Center for Theology and the Natural Sciences, Berkeley: "Scientific Rationality and Christian Logos," *Physics, Philosophy, and Theology—A Common Quest for Understanding,* Vatican Observatory–CTNS, 1988, 141–150.

CHAPTER 7   Joint Publication Board of Zygon: "Teilhard's Vision of the World and Modern Cosmology," *Zygon* 30, 1995, 11–23.

CHAPTER 8   Journal Revue des Questions Scientifiques: "Lemaître—Priest and Scientist," *Revue des Questions Scientifiques* 165, 1994, 237–242.

CHAPTER 9   Joint Publication Board of Zygon: "Cosmological Singularity and the Creation of the Universe," *Zygon* 35, 2000, 665–685.

CHAPTER 10   Vatican Observatory, Vatican City State and The Center for Theology and the Natural Sciences, Berkeley: "Generalizations: From Quantum Mechanics to God," *Quantum Mechanics,* Vatican Observatory–CTNS, 2001, 191–210.

CHAPTER 11   Vatican Observatory, Vatican City State and The Center for Theology and the Natural Sciences, Berkeley: "Chaos, Probability, and the Comprehensibility of the World," *Chaos and Complexity,* Vatican Observatory–CTNS, 1995, 107–121.

CHAPTER 12   Pontifical Academy of Sciences, Vatican City State: "'Illicit Jumps'— The Logic of Creation," *Pontificae Academiae Scientiarum Scripta Varia 99: Science and the Future of Mankind,* Vatican City, 2001, 501–506.

CHAPTER 13   Saint Joseph's University Press, Philadelphia: "Science and Faith in Interaction," *The Human Search for Truth: Philosophy, Science, Theology,* Saint Joseph's University Press, Philadelphia, 2002, 98–107.

CHAPTER 14   European Society for the Study of Science and Theology: "Science and Transcendence," *Studies in Science and Theology* 4, 1996, 3–12.

APPENDIX
CENTER FOR INTERDISCIPLINARY
STUDIES AND ITS WORK FOR SCIENCE
AND RELIGION

This book is not an outcome of a solitary author isolated from the rest of the world. On the contrary, its writing would not be possible without manifold links with other people and strong involvement in the course of events creating recent history. The matters of science and religion are so intimately personal that they cannot be separated from real life, and real life is nothing else but a net of mutual relations between people and their histories.

In the mid-seventies, when Poland was still deep under the communist regime, a group of people gathered around Joseph Życiński (who later became the Archbishop of Lublin) and this author to study and discuss problems arising at the interface of science and philosophy, science and theology, and science and general culture. Cracow, the city in which this took place, is a wonderful city with a rich history. History is never closed but always alive. If something happens in Cracow twice it becomes a tradition. In this way, the group of people mentioned above soon started calling itself the Center for Interdisciplinary Studies (CIS). At that time, we—Joseph and myself—were connected with the Theological Faculty in Cracow, and this is why CIS began to be regarded as a part of it.

Here I must make a recourse to history. In 1364 Pope Urban V instituted the *Studium Generale* in Cracow. It could not be considered a full-fledged university because it did not have a theological faculty. Only later, in 1397, Queen Hedwig, the wife of King Ladislaus Jagiello, obtained from Pope Boniface IX the privilege of opening the Theological Faculty in Cracow, changing the *Studium Generale* into the Jagiellonian University.

During its history the University well fulfilled its scientific, educational, and cultural mission. Among its alumni were many outstanding scholars and scientists, Nicolaus Copernicus among them. It is worthwhile to mention that at the beginning of the Second World War, almost all professors of the Jagiellonian University were arrested, and many of them were killed in concentration camps. In spite of this, during the Nazi occupation the University, together with its Theological Faculty, continued its didactic role clandestinely. In those dark years, Karol Wojtyla, the future Archbishop of Cracow and Pope, was a student at the Faculty of Humanities and then at the Faculty of Theology.

In 1954 the Theological Faculty was expelled from the University by the government of the Stalinist regime in Poland, but also this time it did not cease its activities. The Sacred Congregation of Seminaries and Universities in Rome, in its decree of 16 December 1959, bestowed the title "Pontifical" on the Theological Faculty in Cracow. This was due in no small part to the personal intervention of Cardinal Wojtyla, at that time already Archbishop of Cracow. To be on the Pontifical Faculty served as protection against attempts of the communist regime in Poland.

In 1981 Pope John Paul II, by the *Motu Proprio* "Beata Hedvigis," created the Pontifical Academy of Theology in Cracow, with its three faculties: theological, philosophical, and historical. After the fall of the communist regime, the Pontifical Academy of Theology in Cracow was officially recognized by the Polish government as a Church University. It closely collaborates with the Jagiellonian University, and it forms with it a "Federation."

CIS is now affiliated with the Philosophical Faculty of the Pontifical Academy of Theology in Cracow. The activities of CIS are many. It conducts interdisciplinary research in the field of philosophy (including philosophy of science), history of science, and the interaction between science and theology; it popularizes these fields in broader circles of society; it organizes seminars, conferences, and international symposia; and it publishes books and two journals, namely:

- *Filozoficzne Zagadnienia w Nauce (Philosophical Problems in Science)*, in cooperation with Biblos, Tarnów, Poland; and
- *Philosophy in Science*, in cooperation with Pachart Publishing House, Tucson, Arizona.

In the following, I enumerate a selection of books, published by CIS or written by authors connected with CIS and published by other publishers, that are related to the field of "science and religion":

- *The Galileo Affair: A Meeting of Faith and Science*, edited by G. V. Coyne, M. Heller and J. Życiński, Specola Vaticana, Città del Vaticano, 1985. Proceedings of the Cracow Conference 24–27 May 1984.
- *Newton and the New Directions in Science*, edited by G. V. Coyne, M. Heller, and J. Życiński, Specola Vaticana, Città del Vaticano, 1988. Proceedings of the Cracow Conference 25–28 May 1987.
- M. Heller and J. Życiński, *The Roads of Thinkers*, PTT, Kraków, 1980, in Polish. A selection of readings on science and religion from works of various scientists and philosophers with ample comments.
- M. Heller and J. Życiński, *The Universe—A Machine or Thought?* PTT, Kraków, 1988, in Polish. A history of mechanical philosophy.

- J. Dembek, *Space and Infinity*, OBI*, Kraków, 1994, in Polish. Philosophical views of Hermann Weyl.
- M. Heller and J. Życiński, *Dilemmas of Evolution*, PTT, Kraków, 1990; second edition in 1996 by Biblos, Tarnów, in Polish.
- W. S. Stoeger, *The Laws of Nature: The Range of Human Knowledge and Divine Action*, OBI, Kraków and Biblos, Tarnów, 1996.
- J. Kloch, *Consciousness of Computers*, OBI, Kraków and Biblos, Tarnów, 1996, in Polish.
- Z. Liana, *The Idea of Logos and of Nature in the School of Chartres*, OBI, Kraków and Biblos, Tarnów, 1996, in Polish. Historical and philosophical study of heuristic functions of the Christian idea of Logos in forming the modern concept of nature.
- B. Wójcik, *Postmodern Consciousness and Its Criticism*, OBI, Kraków and Biblos, Tarnów, 1997, in Polish. Concerning philosophical views of D. C. Dennett.
- O. Pedersen, *Conflict or Symbiosis?* OBI, Kraków and Biblos, Tarnów, 1997, in Polish. Lectures delivered at Cambridge University by the eminent historian of science on some aspects of the history of science-religion dialogue, translated from English by W. Skoczny.
- T. Sierotowicz, *Science and Religion: The Space of a Dialogue*, OBI, Kraków and Biblos, Tarnów, 1997, in Polish. An enlarged version of *La casa nel mondo interpretato*, Specola Vaticana, Città del Vaticano, Centro di Studi Interdisciplinari, Cracovia, 1995.
- S. Wszołek, *Irremovability of Metaphysics*, OBI, Kraków and Biblos, Tarnów, 1998, in Polish. Some aspects of the debate of Rudolf Carnap with Ludwig Wittgenstein and Karl Popper.
- J. Mączka, *From Mathematics to Philosophy*, OBI, Kraków and Biblos, Tarnów, 1999, in Polish. The evolution of scientific and philosophical views of A. Whitehead.
- Z. Kępa, *Marxist Philosophy and Evolution*, OBI, Kraków and Biblos, Tarnów, 1999, in Polish. A history of Marxist antireligious propaganda in 1948–1956.
- *Reflections on the Crossroads*, edited by S. Wszołek, OBI, Kraków and Biblos, Tarnów, 2000, in Polish. A selection of classical texts on science and religion.
- M. Heller, Z. Liana, J. Mączka, and W. Skoczny, *Natural Sciences and Theology: Conflict and Coexistence*, OBI, Kraków and Biblos, Tarnów, 2001, in Polish. A history of mutual relations between science and theology from Antiquity to Galileo. A characteristic feature of this book is a combination of the historical account with the philosophical and methodological analysis.
- J. Dadaczyński, *Mathematics in the Eyes of the Philosopher*, OBI, Kraków and Biblos, Tarnów, 2002, in Polish. Eleven essays on the philosophy of mathematics; some of them are related to the science-religion dialogue, for instance, Cantor's view on infinity.

* OBI, abbreviation of *Ośrodek Badań Interdyscyplinarnych*, is a Polish counterpart of CIS.

- K. Wójtowicz, *Platonism in the Philosophy of Mathematics*, OBI, Kraków and Biblos, Tarnów, 2002, in Polish. Philosophical views of Kurt Gödel.
- J. Metallmann, *Determinism in Biology*, edited by J. Maczka, OBI, Kraków and Biblos, Tarnów, 2002, in Polish. Critically edited manuscript, discovered in Kraków archives, of the book by a famous Polish philosopher from the first half of the twentieth century.
- J. Mączka, *The Structural Universe*, OBI, Kraków and Biblos, Tarnów, 2002, in Polish. An extensive study comparing structuralist views of J. Metallmann with the structuralism of modern science.

Finally, I would like to mention the following of my books which, although written on different occasions, somehow present the evolution of my thinking of science and religion:

- *The World and the Word: Between Science and Religion*, Pachart, Tucson, 1986. Translated by A. C. Kisiel from Polish (Znak, Kraków, 1981; second enlarged edition in 1994).
- *The New Physics and a New Theology*, Vatican Observatory Publications, Città del Vaticano, 1996. Translated by G. V. Coyne, S. Giovannini, and T. Sierotowicz from Polish (Biblos, Tarnów, 1992).
- *Is Physics an Art?*, Biblos, Tarnów, 1998, in Polish.
- *The Meaning of Life and the Meaning of the Universe*, Biblos, Tarnów, 2002, in Polish.
- *Questions to the Universe: Ten Lectures on the Foundations of Physics and Cosmology*, Pachart, Tuscon, 1986.
- *Theoretical Foundations of Cosmology: Introduction to the Global Structure of Space-Time*, World Scientific, Singapore/London, 1992.
- *Lemaître, Big Bang, and the Quantum Universe: With His Original Manuscript*, Pachart, Tuscon, 1996.
- Derek J. Raine and Michael Heller, *The Science of Space-Time*, Pachart, Tuscon, 1981.

INDEX